# TEACHING AS
# COMMUNITY PROPERTY

# TEACHING AS COMMUNITY PROPERTY

*Essays on Higher Education*

Lee S. Shulman

○

*Edited by* Pat Hutchings

**JOSSEY-BASS**
A Wiley Imprint
www.josseybass.com

Published by Jossey-Bass

A Wiley Imprint

989 Market Street, San Francisco, CA 94103-1741   www.josseybass.com

Jossey-Bass books and products are available through most bookstores. To contact Jossey-Bass directly call our Customer Care Department within the U.S. at 800-956-7739, outside the U.S. at 317-572-3986 or fax 317-572-4002.

Jossey-Bass also publishes its books in a variety of electronic formats. Some content that appears in print may not be available in electronic books.

**Library of Congress Cataloging-in-Publication Data**

Shulman, Lee S.
    Teaching as community property : essays on higher education / Lee S. Shulman ; edited by Pat Hutchings.— 1st ed.
        p. cm. — (The Jossey-Bass higher and adult education series)
    Includes bibliographical references and index.
    ISBN 0-7879-7201-0 (alk. paper)
    1. Education, Higher. 2. College teaching.  I. Hutchings, Pat. II. Title. III. Series.
    LB2305.S58 2004
    378— ▓▓▓▓▓▓▓▓▓▓▓▓▓
                                                                    2003026853

Printed in the United States of America

FIRST EDITION

*HB Printing*        10 9 8 7 6 5 4 3 2 1

*To the memory of my parents,*
*Sonia and Albert Shulman,*
*for whom nothing was more precious*
*than a good education.*

# CONTENTS

Sources                                                                    xi
About the Author                                                          xiii
Acknowledgments                                                             xv
Foreword                                                                   xvii
    *Pat Hutchings*
Introduction                                                                 1
    *Russell Edgerton*

### PART ONE
### Learning

1. Professing the Liberal Arts                                             11
2. Taking Learning Seriously                                               33
3. Problem-Based Learning: The Pedagogies of Uncertainty                   49
4. Making Differences: A Table of Learning                                 63

### PART TWO
### The Profession of Teaching

5. Knowledge and Teaching: Foundations of the New Reform                   83
6. Learning to Teach                                                      115
7. Toward a Pedagogy of Substance                                        127
8. Teaching as Community Property: Putting an End
   to Pedagogical Solitude                                                139
9. The Scholarship of Teaching: New Elaborations,
   New Developments                                                       145
10. From Minsk to Pinsk: Why a Scholarship of Teaching
    and Learning?                                                         155
11. Lamarck's Revenge: Teaching Among the Scholarships                    163

## PART THREE
## Practices and Policies

12. From Idea to Prototype: Three Exercises
    in the Peer Review of Teaching                              175
13. The Pedagogical Colloquium: Three Models                    185
14. Course Anatomy: The Dissection and Analysis
    of Knowledge Through Teaching                               191
15. Visions of the Possible: Models for Campus Support
    of the Scholarship of Teaching and Learning                203
16. The Doctoral Imperative: Examining the Ends of Erudition    219

Index                                                           233

# SOURCES

CHAPTER ONE

"Professing the Liberal Arts." In R. Orrill (ed.), *Education and Democracy: Re-imagining Liberal Learning in America*. New York: The College Entrance Examination Board, 1997. Copyright © 1997 by the College Entrance Examination Board. Reproduced with permission. All rights reserved. www.collegeboard.com.

CHAPTER TWO

"Taking Learning Seriously." *Change*, 1999, *31*(4), 10–17. Reprinted with permission of the Helen Dwight Reid Educational Foundation. Published by Heldref Publications, 1319 18th St., NW, Washington, DC 20036–1802. www.heldref.org. Copyright © 1999.

CHAPTER FOUR

"Making Differences: A Table of Learning." *Change*, 2002, *34*(6), 36–44. Reprinted with permission of the Helen Dwight Reid Educational Foundation. Published by Heldref Publications, 1319 18th St., NW, Washington, DC 20036–1802. www.heldref.org. Copyright © 2002.

CHAPTER FIVE

"Knowledge and Teaching: Foundations of the New Reform." *Harvard Educational Review,* 1987, *57*(1), 1–22. Copyright © 1987 by the President and Fellows of Harvard College. All rights reserved.

CHAPTER SIX

"Learning to Teach." *AAHE Bulletin,* 1987, *40*(3), 5–9.

CHAPTER SEVEN

"Toward a Pedagogy of Substance." *AAHE Bulletin,* 1989, *41*(10), 8–13.

CHAPTER EIGHT

"Teaching as Community Property: Putting an End to Pedagogical Solitude."
  *Change*, 1993, *25*(6), 6–7. Reprinted with permission of the Helen Dwight
  Reid Educational Foundation. Published by Heldref Publications, 1319
  18th St., NW, Washington, DC 20036–1802. www.heldref.org.
  Copyright © 1993.

CHAPTER NINE

Hutchings, P., and Shulman, L. S. "The Scholarship of Teaching: New Elaborations, New Developments." *Change*, 1999, *31*(5), 10–15. Reprinted with
  permission of the Helen Dwight Reid Educational Foundation. Published
  by Heldref Publications, 1319 18th St., NW, Washington, DC
  20036–1802. www.heldref.org. Copyright © 1999.

CHAPTER TEN

"From Minsk to Pinsk: Why a Scholarship of Teaching and Learning?" *Journal
  of the Scholarship of Teaching and Learning*, 2000, *1*(1), 48–52.
  [http://www.iusb.edu/~josotl/search_archives.htm].

CHAPTER TWELVE

"From Idea to Prototype: Three Exercises in the Peer Review of Teaching."
  In P. Hutchings (ed.), *From Idea to Prototype: The Peer Review of Teach-
  ing: A Project Workbook*. Washington, D.C.: American Association for
  Higher Education, 1995.

CHAPTER THIRTEEN

"The Pedagogical Colloquium: Three Models." *AAHE Bulletin*, 1995, *47*(9),
  6–9.

CHAPTER FOURTEEN

"Course Anatomy: The Dissection and Analysis of Knowledge Through Teaching." In P. Hutchings (ed.), *The Course Portfolio: How Faculty Can Improve Their Teaching to Advance Practice and Improve Student Learning*.
  Washington, D.C.: American Association for Higher Education, 1998.

CHAPTER FIFTEEN

"Visions of the Possible: Models for Campus Support of the Scholarship of
  Teaching and Learning." In W. E. Becker and M. L. Andrews (eds.), *The
  Scholarship of Teaching and Learning: Contributions of Research Univer-
  sities*. Bloomington: Indiana University Press, 2004.

# ABOUT THE AUTHOR

LEE S. SHULMAN is a Chicagoan, despite his years at Michigan State University, Stanford University, and his current tenure as president of The Carnegie Foundation for the Advancement of Teaching. It was in the city of his birth that he received not only his elementary and secondary education but also all of his academic degrees. The reverence for classic texts, the familiarity with dissecting original sources, and the generalist and collegial philosophy of learning in the Chicago education institutions where Lee studied and learned were the perfect foundation for his lifelong scholarly inquiry and work.

Shulman's family owned a small delicatessen in the Logan Square neighborhood, and many of his perspectives on life were formed through interactions with customers and vendors. His formal education began at an Orthodox Jewish day school, where he studied Talmud in the morning and secular subjects in the afternoon. He went on to learn at the Hutchins College of the University of Chicago, where the generalist curriculum revered the Great Books, encouraged student engagement, and echoed the respect for classic texts that marked his Talmudic studies. The small seminar classes encouraged a collegial way of working that continues to shape his views on scholarship and teaching to this day.

Shulman entered the university's doctoral program in educational psychology because of a full-tuition fellowship, which included enough of a stipend to embolden him into proposing to a young Judy Horwitz, who has been his partner in the joys of family, community, and scholarship since 1960. From 1963 to 1982, Shulman was professor of educational psychology and medical education at Michigan State University, where with Judith Lanier he founded and codirected the Institute for Research on Teaching. From 1982 through 2000, he was on the faculty at Stanford University, first as a professor of educational psychology and then as the Charles E. Ducommun Professor of Education. He investigated and promulgated a way of studying teaching, and in his efforts to make teaching a profession, he helped found the National Board for Professional Teaching Standards.

Shulman's research and writings have dealt with the study of teaching and teacher education; the growth of knowledge among those learning to teach; the assessment of teaching; medical education; the psychology of instruction in science, mathematics, and medicine; the logic of educational research; and the quality of teaching in higher education. His most recent studies emphasize the importance of "teaching as community property" and the central role of a "scholarship of teaching" in supporting needed changes in the cultures of higher education.

In 1997, he was selected as the eighth president of The Carnegie Foundation for the Advancement of Teaching, a research and education policy center in Stanford, California, created by Andrew Carnegie in 1905. He continues to work to elevate teachers and the profession of teaching, as well as to deepen understanding of preparation for service in other professions such as medicine. Under his leadership, the Carnegie Foundation supports the study of moral and civic education; professions that include law, the clergy and engineering; liberal and doctoral education; and the preparation of teachers. Shulman continues to expand the notion of a scholarship of teaching and learning through the Carnegie Academy for the Scholarship of Teaching and Learning.

Shulman is past president of the American Educational Research Association (AERA) and received its highest honor, the career award for Distinguished Contributions to Educational Research. He is a member of the National Academy of Education, having served as both vice president and president. He is the recipient of the American Psychological Association's 1995 E. L. Thorndike Award for Distinguished Psychological Contributions to Education. Shulman has also been a Guggenheim Fellow and a Fellow of the Center for Advanced Study in the Behavioral Sciences. He was named an American Association for the Advancement of Science (AAAS) Fellow in 2002 for his "fundamental contributions that have deeply impacted educational research, policy, institutional practices, and teacher education in science and mathematics worldwide." He is a Fellow of the American Academy of Arts and Sciences.

In a profile written for his inclusion in *Fifty Modern Thinkers on Education,* the authors wrote

> Shulman has had enormous impact on the field of education, in large part because of the grand ideas and visions that have marked his work.
>
> His visions now permeate everyday discourse about teaching, in talk about teaching portfolios, pedagogical content knowledge, and the scholarship of teaching. Shulman's genius lies in his ability to unite the worlds of thought and action, to turn his creative energies not only to research but into building institutions and structures that transport his visions of the possible into the world of practice.

# ACKNOWLEDGMENTS

PUTTING TOGETHER THIS VOLUME and its companion, *The Wisdom of Practice,* was no easy task. For me it meant reflection on work over several decades, emotionally difficult choices about what to include, and visions and revisions of what it all means and what it adds up to. But many of the real challenges fell to others, and I'm more grateful than I can say for the assistance of a very considerable group of colleagues whose work made this project possible.

First, I want to thank Pat Hutchings for her good counsel about selections and arrangement; when she and I first began collecting the essays we agreed that *Teaching as Community Property* should be a relatively slim volume, limited to pieces that speak directly to a higher education audience. Pat served as editor of this volume, and her resolve kept things moving in that direction. I also want to thank Sherry Hecht and Ruba Ahmed, who formatted and compiled the manuscript, and Gay Clyburn, the Carnegie Foundation's director of information and communication, who worked closely with Jossey-Bass and its able editor David Brightman, all along the way, from initial conception to final production.

It was also Pat Hutchings who suggested Russ Edgerton as a commentator and author of the Introduction, and I join her in expressing my deep gratitude to Russ for his thoughtful comments about the themes that have run through my work over the years. Were it not for Russ Edgerton, I would never have considered treating higher education as a field of study. Russ discovered my work on K–12, the professions, and teacher education, and speculated that it could become useful in his own world of higher education. He pressed me to address those issues, and repeatedly offered me venues at American Association for Higher Education meetings to present those ideas. As he did for Ernest Boyer's ideas in *Scholarship Reconsidered,* Russ became an evangelist for conceptions of peer review, teaching as community property, and the scholarship of teaching. And no one was more instrumental in persuading the Carnegie Foundation board to offer me the foundation's presidency. Russ and Pat have been partners in several projects over the years that helped shape my thinking, so their involvement feels not only appropriate but necessary.

There is another reason to thank Pat Hutchings. Although only one of the articles in this collection is explicitly co-authored with her, she should more accurately be counted as a collaborator on many more of them. You see, most of these papers began as speeches to higher education audiences in a number of venues. I have the bad habit of working very hard on crafting a speech, delivering it from detailed notes and with an uncontrolled readiness to improvise on the spot, and then putting it all away for an unspecified rainy day. Pat attended most of those talks, and had the sense (or at least the discipline) to have them recorded and transcribed. Then Pat, with her doctorate in English and her experience as a teacher of writing, would edit the transcript with the combination of devotion, scholarship, and brutality that a gifted editor needs. She would then hand me the much-improved draft and dare me to ignore it. At least half the essays in this volume were prepared in that manner, and without Pat they would have been long forgotten. The more we have worked together, both prior to our Carnegie colleagueship and at present, the more difficult I find the challenge of distinguishing my ideas from Pat's.

Finally, I want to thank colleagues from the various contexts in which I've been lucky enough to do my work over the past several decades; my thinking has been consistently enriched by their generosity, creativity, and thoughtfulness. Andrew Carnegie's generosity made possible the invention of this remarkable institution I now serve. The leadership of a number of educators, from Henry Pritchett and Abraham Flexner, through John Gardner, Allan Pifer, and Clark Kerr, and my remarkable predecessor Ernest Boyer, shaped The Carnegie Foundation for the Advancement of Teaching into an internationally respected research and policy center. I hope that these collected essays help to move that work ahead, and to contribute to Carnegie's mission for the Foundation, "to do and perform all things necessary to encourage, uphold, and dignify the profession of the teacher."

*Lee S. Shulman*

# FOREWORD

SEVERAL YEARS AGO AT A CONFERENCE session where Lee Shulman was speaking, a woman sitting behind me, apparently having noticed my Carnegie Foundation name tag when I sat down, tapped me on the shoulder. "I have an idea," she whispered. "Why doesn't someone pull together Shulman's writing over the past couple of decades and publish a collection? I've read *some* of the important pieces," she continued, "but I'd love to see what I *haven't* read and to find it all in one place."

That suggestion stayed with me long after the conference, and I heard it affirmed by comments from others as well. Now, some three years later, this volume and its companion collection respond to my fellow conference-goer's excellent idea. *The Wisdom of Practice: Essays on Teaching, Learning, and Learning to Teach* is a collection of most of Lee Shulman's work on educational research, teacher education, and K–12 teaching. *Teaching as Community Property* provides a selection of his writing on higher education. Some of what you'll find in both volumes has been previously published, but a number of pieces are newly available, offering readers a chance to see the trajectory and significance of Shulman's work in ways that would otherwise not be possible.

It's important to say that this collection is not meant to stand for the work of the organization that Shulman now leads. Many of the pieces were written before he was appointed president of The Carnegie Foundation for the Advancement of Teaching in 1997, and, as he himself would insist on saying, the programs he directs in that role are shaped by the thinking of many colleagues on the staff and beyond, including our very thoughtful Board of Trustees. On the other hand, the ideas represented here are clearly evident in the Foundation's current efforts, and they are notable, as well, for their continuity with two features that have defined the organization's work since it was founded by Andrew Carnegie almost a century ago in 1905.

First, the Carnegie Foundation's animating interest and sustained commitment has always been the quality of the educational experience. For one hundred years, and in many different ways, the Foundation has been in the business of asking hard questions about good teaching: What knowledge, skills, and values are required? How are those best developed, and how can they be assured? How can teaching excellence be recognized, rewarded, and built upon?

A second hallmark of the Foundation's work has been a faith in the power of good ideas. As an advanced study center, Carnegie is committed, of course, to inquiry and to evidence, and it routinely puts its ideas to the test. But its most important products, I would argue, are fresh, vivid ideas about education and how to improve it. Carnegie is a think tank, an idea factory; ideas are the eggs we put in our baskets, the horses we place our bets on.

Shulman's work is completely in keeping with these two Carnegie hallmarks. What the essays collected here propose, and what they leave us with, are vivid, transformative ideas about educational quality. Central to these ideas is a view of teaching as intellectual work—not simply as a set of techniques for delivering content, that is, but as a set of practices that require preparation, documentation, inquiry, and improvement according to ambitious, professional standards. Moreover, it is a vision that implicates us all. The quality of teaching, as Shulman sees it, requires commitment and collaboration across the educational spectrum, not only in formal teacher education classrooms or professional development settings for K-12 teachers. Just as important are undergraduate classrooms where, for better or worse, many of us develop our ideas about what it means to teach, and in graduate education programs where the formation of future teachers and teachers of teachers—at all levels—succeeds or fails.

Editing this volume has, for me, been one of those proverbial labors of love that all of us hope to have in our professional portfolio—and all the more so, thanks to the work of the many good colleagues who assisted in its production. This is not the place to name them all but I want especially to thank Russell Edgerton (through whose good offices I originally met and got to know Lee Shulman); his opening essay provides a lively tour of Shulman's thinking and a synthesis of the key themes that have animated his work over several decades. And of course I cannot end without thanking, again, the woman in the row behind me at the conference where the idea for this project was first kindled.

*Pat Hutchings*
*Vice President*
*The Carnegie Foundation for the*
*Advancement of Teaching*
*Fall 2003*

# TEACHING AS
# COMMUNITY PROPERTY

# INTRODUCTION

IN 1987, LEE SHULMAN was at the top of his game as a scholar in the field of teacher education. Yet rather than stay within the confines of his field, Lee gradually began speaking and writing to wider audiences in higher education about issues of teaching and learning across the disciplines. By 1997, his work in both K–12 and higher education had become so widely admired that he was asked to become president of The Carnegie Foundation for the Advancement of Teaching, succeeding the distinguished educators who led the Foundation's programs in the past, including Clark Kerr, John Gardner, and Ernest Boyer.

This collection chronicles Lee's growing fascination with issues of teaching and learning in higher education.

As Lee roamed the country responding to invitations to present his ideas, he left wonderful speeches in his wake. Some remained fugitive documents; others were published in various magazines and journals. Were it not for this new book, much of the work might have drifted away. All of us who care about higher education owe a debt of thanks to members of the Carnegie Foundation staff who edited the materials and assembled them in this single volume. Now we can relive some of those marvelous occasions when we heard Lee speak, recover his wonderful metaphors, and—best of all—see and reflect on Lee's contributions as an evolving body of work.

Chronologically, the collection dates back to Lee's article "Knowledge and Teaching: Foundations of the New Reform," which was published in the February 1987 issue of the *Harvard Educational Review*. The product of years of research into the nature of medical and teaching expertise, the article opened up a new window on the world of teaching. It was as if the explorer had mapped a land that no one knew was there.

The new land was a domain of knowledge, a "missing paradigm" in the prevailing view of what expert teachers know and can do. Yes, Lee argued, expert teachers understand the subject matter they are teaching, and, yes, they have a grasp of general teaching techniques. But they also possess something more—a knowledge of how to transform the particular subject they are teaching into terms that their students can understand. In addition to *chemistry* (the subject) and *teaching* (generic methods) there is, Lee argued, a third domain of knowledge: the *teaching of chemistry.*

Lee's article was not only groundbreaking, it was also timely. In 1986, the Carnegie Forum on Education and the Economy issued *A Nation Prepared: Teachers for the 21st Century.* The report argued that schools had become the most Tayloristic of American organizations, that school reform would never succeed until schools stopped treating teachers like factory workers and started treating them as professionals. A consensus was emerging that the professionalization of teaching had to be a key strategy for school reform. Yet the claim that teaching deserves professional status assumed that there was indeed a knowledge base for teaching. Lee's gift was to identify what the character of that knowledge is.

I suspect that I was invited to write this introduction because I was partially responsible for enticing Lee to pursue the implication of his ideas for higher education at large. In 1987, as president of the American Association for Higher Education (AAHE), I was on the lookout for ways that AAHE could help put colleges and universities in the service of the schools. Deeply moved by *A Nation Prepared,* I let the Carnegie Corporation know that I wanted to help. In time, AAHE became part of a family of Carnegie Corporation initiatives. My initial assignment, working with Stanford University President Donald Kennedy, was to organize a retreat that would enlist the support of university presidents. Don suggested that, in developing the agenda for the retreat, I should go see his friend and colleague Lee Shulman.

I'll never forget that first meeting. Lee greeted me like a long-lost comrade, quickly assumed that my problem was our problem, and came up with an ingenious suggestion. "Presidents are busy people," he noted, "and we have only a small piece of their time. Instead of sending them a ton of reading, why don't we ask them to schedule a one-hour appointment with a member of their faculty who is outstanding at both research and teaching. Have them ask their faculty colleague to bring along a syllabus from a course they teach and walk through it, reflecting on the design of the course and how it works—-and then, at the retreat, have the presidents report out what they learned."

Well, the presidents arrived at the retreat brimming with ideas they wanted to share in discussions with their colleagues. Lee's creative "homework assignment" transformed the retreat into an engaging experience and also made the presidents receptive to Lee's second contribution to this work in higher education—a talk (see "Learning to Teach" in Section Two) that reframed the agenda. The presidents had come to the retreat believing that the problem was what to do to fix their schools and departments of education. They left realizing that the problem was not "teacher education" but "the education of teachers" by the entire university.

Lee returned to his "real work" at Stanford. I returned to AAHE marveling at what Lee had contributed. He had not only introduced a new perspective on the nature of the problem but had designed an ingenious task that engaged the presidents in inventing their own solutions. And he did so with zest, enthusiasm, and humor. The presidents left realizing that the topic of teaching could be intellectually interesting—and fun!

Over the next several years, my AAHE colleague Pat Hutchings (who would later join Lee at the Carnegie Foundation) and I conspired to lure Lee into a web of occasions. We convinced him to address AAHE's 1989 national conference, "Stand and Deliver," where he presented a talk entitled "Toward a Pedagogy of Substance." Pat launched a new AAHE program we called the Teaching Initiative, organized around Lee's ideas about the documentation and display of teaching. We used AAHE's national conference and annual special-purpose conferences as meeting grounds for Teaching Initiative projects, and Lee graciously attended and spoke at most of these meetings. We began a new annual national meeting—the Forum on Faculty Roles and Rewards—and enticed Lee to address that gathering on a regular basis.

By 1993, Lee's reputation and standing in higher education was approaching celebrity status. And he had begun to grapple seriously with a new set of intellectual challenges. It was clear that to improve the training of teachers, colleges and universities had to attend to the quality of teaching *throughout* the arts and sciences disciplines. But that imperative, in turn, introduced a larger, more ambitious agenda: improving the quality of teaching for *all* undergraduates. To do so meant tackling questions about how teaching could become a more respected dimension of all the disciplines and professional fields that make up the academic profession. This collection, then, traces Lee's evolving answers to this challenge.

○

Where does the collection lead us? What themes and patterns connect its various pieces? Let me suggest that it can be best appreciated if viewed from three perspectives: as *pedagogy,* as *prescription,* and as *philosophy.*

First, the pedagogical perspective. Most of these papers began as speeches. And if you know Lee, you'll know that he is a person who thrives on social interaction and is apt to give birth to his most creative ideas and metaphors on the eve of—or during—a major address. Thus, to think of these contributions simply as "papers" or "articles" is to miss seeing and appreciating something important: that these pieces arose out of, and brilliantly reflect, the very particular pedagogical circumstances of audience, setting, and purpose that Lee encountered in each rhetorical occasion.

Consider, for example, "Toward a Pedagogy of Substance," the speech Lee delivered to AAHE's 1989 National Conference on Higher Education. This is Lee's coming-out party, the first major occasion in which he explains his ideas about teacher knowledge to a large and heterogeneous audience. And look at what he does! The setting is Chicago, so he begins with an opening story about his cab ride to the hotel that beautifully sets up the larger point he wants to make. He builds his argument around an explanation of what makes Jaime Escalante—the amazing teacher who was the subject of the movie *Stand and Deliver,* who keynoted the conference the night before Lee's address—an excellent teacher. Escalante, Lee points out, did a lot more than stand and deliver; he was keenly aware of the prior knowledge that his students brought into the classroom, and he developed an extraordinary repertoire of physical representations, models, and stories to help represent the stuff of mathematics to Hispanic kids from Los Angeles.

"Toward a Pedagogy of Substance" offers a window on Lee as a master teacher, practicing what he preaches. But there's something else going on as well. Lee believes in the unity of the scholarly life; that acts of discovering, integrating, applying, and representing ideas are mutually reinforcing; that professing what one knows can lead to rich new discoveries. This process is on display throughout the collection. It's in the context of particular rhetorical occasions that Lee generates some of his best ideas and most creative metaphors.

This aspect of pedagogy is also very much evident in Lee's much-quoted piece, "Teaching as Community Property," originally a presentation to AAHE's 1993 Forum on Faculty Roles and Rewards, in San Antonio. This new series of forums was pitched to provost-level concerns about the faculty reward system and other issues about why teaching was undervalued. The occasion challenged Lee to view teaching from a perspective that was different from the one he had taken in his previous AAHE appearances. Characteristically, he refuses to buy into the familiar diagnosis of the conflict between teaching and research. Instead, he sets forth a fresh perspective, and out tumbles a new metaphor:

> I now believe that the reason teaching is not more valued in the academy is because the way we treat teaching removes it from the community of scholars. It is not that universities diminish the importance of teaching because they devalue the act of teaching itself. It is not that research is seen as having more intrinsic value than teaching. Rather, we celebrate those aspects of our lives and work that become, as we say in California, "community property." And if we wish to see greater recognition and reward attached to teaching, we must change the status of teaching from private to community property.

I don't know for sure whether the notion of community property popped into Lee's mind during the speech or the night before—but I'd bet the farm that it was the occasion of the speech that brought it forth.

This brings me to the second way we might look at this collection—as *prescription*. What is Lee's vision of how to go about improving teaching throughout the university?

It's important to remember that Lee engaged these issues a step at a time. Each new occasion challenged him to explore a new piece of the puzzle. So what we have here is a gradual unfolding and successive elaboration of Lee's core ideas. Conveniently, the essays are organized into families of topics. To whet your appetite, let me say just a word about each of these families.

The first section includes four essays in which Lee sets forth a vision of what it is that undergraduates need to learn. The most straightforward and revealing piece on this topic, and a good place to start, is the volume's opening essay, "Professing the Liberal Arts." Here Lee argues that the characteristics of a professional—which include not only learning a body of knowledge but coming to judgment, putting ideas into practice, and reflecting on this—are exactly what's needed to fix what's wrong with liberal learning, which is that students either forget or fail really to understand much of the material they encounter in their studies. The other essays in the section then elaborate on this core idea.

In the next section, we find several essays that deal with the importance of discipline-specific pedagogy and Lee's early interpretations of what this means. These then lead to additional later pieces that introduce, nurture, elaborate, and clarify an idea that is central to the work that Lee now directs as president of the Carnegie Foundation: that the key to improvement lies in a conception of teaching as a scholarly endeavor. "Teaching as Community Property" serves as a kind of trial balloon for this idea, arguing that teaching must be reconnected to scholarship. "The Scholarship of Teaching: New Elaborations, New Developments" then charts the progress of what was by the time of its writing in 1999 the beginning of a movement. In it, Lee and his colleague Pat Hutchings envision a world in which *all* faculty teach in a scholarly manner and *some* faculty in each discipline and professional field engage in serious investigations of issues of teaching and learning in their particular fields. As they candidly acknowledge, neither goal is easy. For serious investigations of teaching and learning to become legitimate areas of disciplinary scholarship, the disciplines themselves need to be open to a range of methods of inquiry, including case knowledge and other modes of reflection on the wisdom of practice. These are tall mountains. But the remarkable thing is that we can see them at all.

Finally we come to a section that deals with *enacting* the conception of teaching as scholarship in actual practice. Here, Lee "the generator of ideas" becomes Lee "the master architect," designing ways that people can move toward the larger vision.

How might faculty document their work and thinking as teachers in ways that can be reviewed by peers? "From Idea to Prototype: The Peer Review of Teaching" offers guidelines for faculty interested in exploring such a process.

What would a university do differently at the point of hire if it valued teaching as significant, scholarly work? See Lee's ingenious proposal for "The Pedagogical Colloquium," and the experience of several institutions that have experimented with it.

What would be different about promotion and tenure? For teaching to be regarded as scholarly work that merits peer review, faculty would need to learn how to think of their courses as scholarly projects that require thoughtful choices about how they should be designed and enacted, and how the results should be evaluated. Lee's essay on "Course Anatomy" models the kind of reasoning that might inform these choices.

What kind of support would the university provide to foster excellence in teaching? In "Visions of the Possible," Lee envisions sanctuaries and structures where faculty whose scholarly interests include teaching and learning can find safety, support, and colleagueship while working on the pedagogies of their fields.

The collection ends with a truly visionary essay that deals with what I believe Lee regards as the wellspring of the problem *and* the solution: the years of graduate training where faculty form their initial conceptions of professionalism. "The Doctoral Imperative: Examining the Ends of Erudition" includes Lee's description of the Carnegie Foundation's initiative aimed at tackling this central challenge. The doctorate, he reminds us, was originally a teaching degree. The medieval university believed that superior students were those who could teach what they understood—that, as Aristotle claimed, teaching was the highest form of understanding. It's time, he tells us, to reclaim this legacy and treat the Ph.D. as a *professional degree*. All those who earn a doctorate should learn how to profess their fields to others.

Characteristically, Lee doesn't just leave us with a big idea. He spells out a program of action that engages faculty in the act of reinvention: "The questions that are now in the air about graduate education are not questions that can be solved by rhetoric, or by speculation, or by enlightened policymaking. They are questions that will need experimentation, assessment, evaluation, and data-based deliberation. My hope is that our re-envisioning of the Ph.D. becomes, not a new set of unexamined orthodoxies to replace the old, not a new set of doctrines to supplant their predecessors, but a commitment to develop new models and possibilities and an accompanying body of evidence that suggests why some of those models and possibilities deserve greater warrant than others."

○

This brings me to the third and final perspective from which to view this volume: as *philosophy*, especially Lee's philosophy about how to go about the improvement of teaching. Lurking underneath Lee's prescriptions and creative designs I detect a cogent philosophy, partly implicit and partly explicit, about what is important to change and how this change can best be brought about. In addition to exemplary pedagogy and refreshing prescriptions, you will find an approach to change that challenges prevailing notions about the reform of higher education. Here I call your attention to four examples.

The first is Lee's worldview about *what* needs to change. Most of the scripts for improving higher education assume that the *unit* of change is the college or university; many further assume that the instruments of change lie in top-down efforts to change public policy, governance, and management. Lee's attention, in contrast, is focused on the faculty as members of *two* professional communities: the community represented by their scholarly discipline or professional field, and the community they become part of when they accept employment in a college or university—the academic profession writ large. In Lee's view, significant change means altering the conceptions that faculty hold about what it means to be a professional, and the norms that guide professional practice.

The essays also reflect a view of *how* to bring about change. Lee is no great believer in extrinsic rewards. He assumes that faculty change in lasting ways when they become intellectually excited about new ideas or are introduced to a better way to do something. The task of leaders is to envision new possibilities and to design tasks that will translate these possibilities into practice. As an envisioner and designer of ways to improve teaching, Lee has no peer.

Third, I'm struck by the number of times in these essays that Lee warns us not to let today's solution become tomorrow's orthodoxy. This warning clearly arises from deep convictions—convictions that were, I suspect, shaped during his undergraduate and graduate years at the University of Chicago. A liberal education, he once wrote, "is a combination of the passionate embrace and understanding of general simplifications of facts and ideas along with the development of critical, skeptical attitudes." In other words, trust—but verify.

Finally, this attitude leads to a further belief that there is no final resolution, no educational model that will work for everyone, or everywhere, or forever. There is only the perpetual, self-renewing experiment. Indeed, as I read through these pages, this seems to be Lee's ultimate message. Teaching across the university *should be* a perpetual experiment. That it is not regarded as such is the fundamental problem we need to address, and the way to address it is to go about teaching in a scholarly manner and to foster a scholarship of teaching within each academic profession.

Lee's arguments double-back, pick up steam, and become more powerful as they go. So start anywhere. Wherever you begin in the essays that follow here, you're in for a treat.

*Russell Edgerton*
*Fall 2003*

# LEARNING

# INTRODUCTION

# PROFESSING THE LIBERAL ARTS
# (1997)

IN FEBRUARY 1997, The College Board and Rollins College organized a small invitational colloquy entitled "Toward a Pragmatic Liberal Education: The Curriculum of the Twenty-First Century." The aim of the event was to revisit historical trends and tensions that have defined the liberal arts tradition, especially as reflected in the work of John Dewey. "Professing the Liberal Arts" is based on Lee Shulman's address to the group. One of his first public presentations after assuming the presidency of The Carnegie Foundation for the Advancement of Teaching, it sets out principles that subsequently shaped many of the Foundation's programs, bringing together two visions of education—the liberal and the professional—that have, in Shulman's view, been disconnected to the detriment of both. Thus, he argues that the problem facing liberal education is that it needs to be more, not less, professional. The essay was previously published in *Education and Democracy: Re-imagining Liberal Learning in America,* a collection of presentations from the colloquy.

# PROFESSING THE LIBERAL ARTS

ONE OF THE PREVAILING THEMES of this volume is the presumed tension between the *liberal* and the *pragmatic*. These strains are often associated with a distrust of "the vocational" or "the professional" among liberal arts faculty and administrators, who view these orientations as slippery slopes down which unsuspecting educators might slide into a horrific purgatory. Liberal learning, we are warned, is pursued for its own sake, and cannot be subordinated to the aims of application or vocation. I come to offer a shocking alternative view. I wish to argue that the problem with the liberal arts is not that they are endangered by the corruption of professionalism. Indeed, their problem is that they are not professional enough. If we are to preserve and sustain liberal education, we must make it more professional; we must learn to *profess the liberal arts*.

I offer this heresy as a peculiar hybrid of two ostensibly incompatible traditions. I am a graduate of the College of the University of Chicago, which ought to identify me as a devotee of the purest form of liberal education, the Hutchins orientation toward the great books, the traditional canon itself. And I view my education in the Hutchins College as the most precious gift I have ever received. However, I am also a student of Joseph Schwab, the Chicago biologist and philosopher who was one of John Dewey's strongest advocates and spokespersons in higher education, even though he was also seen as a protégé of Hutchins. Many educators whom I respect deeply, such as Tom Ehrlich, point out that the Hutchins and Dewey views of liberal education are inherently incompatible. Yet I would claim, without embarrassment, that I define myself as a legitimate offspring of that liaison between Dewey and Hutchins and I feel unusually blessed to be progeny of that unlikely coupling.

I am reminded of David Hume's clever characterization of abstract ideas such as "cause" or "external existence," which he claimed were illegitimate logical constructs because they lacked direct empirical sources. How was it possible that the human knower could be so confident that he could use concepts such as "cause" even though they were not adequately connected to experience? Hume dubbed such concepts "bastards of imagination impregnated by experience." These abstract ideas were the illegitimate offspring of a liaison between imagination and experience, but could claim no legitimate epistemological standing. In that spirit, I come to you as a bastard of Deweyan progressivism impregnated by the Hutchins College. I am the illegitimate issue of an illicit liaison between two incompatible philosophies. As with most other bastards, I not only insist that I can live my life without being crippled by an ancestry, I claim that this merger of perspectives offers an unusually fruitful perspective.

I am also, I must confess, someone who does not spend most of his time engaged with the liberal education of undergraduates. I've actually spent most of my career of more than 30 years actively engaged in the education of two distinct groups of professionals called school teachers and physicians. I have designed new programs for the education of these professionals. I have taught in these programs. I have conducted empirical research on the processes and outcomes of such professional education. I have attempted to develop theories of learning and of action that explain how such professionals learn and how they organize and use their knowledge and skill. I am, in both senses of that ambiguous phrase, a "professional educator." Education is my profession and the education of professionals is my area of inquiry.

I come to challenge you, therefore, with these questions. What if all those who fear the corruption of liberal education by professionalism and vocationalization have got it wrong? What if the problem of liberal education is that it isn't professional or vocational enough? If, indeed, we were to professionalize liberal education, might we not only give it an end, a purpose in practice and in application and in human service, and instead of thereby diluting and corrupting it, might we even make it more liberal? I hope you will find that a provocative conjecture.

## The Challenges of Professional Learning

### Features of a Profession

I am prepared to argue that the idea of a "profession" describes a special and unique set of circumstances for deep understanding, complex practice, ethical conduct, and higher-order learning, circumstances that define the complexity of the enterprise and explain the difficulties of prescribing both policies and curriculum in this area. What do we mean by a *profession* and what is so hard about preparing people for professions? Let us begin with a recent definition:

> As an ideology, professionalism had both a technical and a moral aspect. Technically, it promised competent performance of skilled work involving the application of broad and complex knowledge, the acquisition of which required formal academic study. Morally, it promised to be guided by an appreciation of the important social ends it served. In demanding high levels of self-governance, professionals claimed not only that others were not technically *equipped* to judge them, but that they also could not be *trusted* to judge them. The idea was expressed in classic form by R. H. Tawney: "[Professionals] may, as in the case of the successful doctor, grow rich; but the meaning of their profession, both for themselves and for the public, is not that they make money, but that they make health or safety or knowledge or good government or good law. . . . [Professions uphold] as the criterion of success the end for which the profession, whatever it may be, is carried on, and [subordinate] the inclination, appetites, and ambition of individuals to the rules of an organization which has as its object to promote performance of function." These functions for Tawney and for many other advocates of the professions, were activities that embodied and expressed the idea of larger social purposes.[1]

Steven Brint's characterization of professions is consistent with many others. From this account, I will claim that there are, at the very least, six characteristics of professional learning that set the terms for the challenge of preparing people to "profess." These characteristics are 1) service, 2) understanding, 3) practice, 4) judgment, 5) learning, and 6) community.

○ First, the goal of a profession is *service;* the pursuit of important social ends. Professionals are those who are educated to serve others using bodies of knowledge and skill not readily available to the man or woman in the street. This means that, fundamentally, a mature professional or someone learning a profession must develop *moral understanding* to aim and guide their practice. The ultimate rationale for their work is, in Tawney's words, "that they make health or safety or knowledge or good government or good law." They must develop both technical and moral understanding.

○ Second, a profession is a practice rooted in bodies of knowledge that are created, tested, elaborated, refuted, transformed, and reconstituted in colleges, universities, laboratories, libraries, and museums. To call something a profession is to claim that it has a knowledge base in the academy broadly construed. It has research and *theories*. Therefore, professions change not only because rules of practice change, or circumstances change, or policies change, but because the process of knowledge growth, criticism, and development in the academy leads to the achievement of new understandings, new perspectives, or new ways of interpreting the world.

○ Third, although a significant portion of the knowledge base of a profession is generated by scholars in the academy, it is not professional knowledge unless and until it is enacted in the crucible of "the field." The field of *practice* is the place where professions do their work, and claims for knowledge must pass the ultimate test of value in practice. Thus, the arenas for theory and practice in a profession are quite disparate, and this constitutes one of the defining problems for professional education. There is always a wide and troublesome gap between theory and practice.

○ Fourth, professions are nevertheless not simply conduits for taking knowledge from the academy and applying it to the field. If that were all that were necessary, professions would not be as complex, interesting, and respected as they are. What intervenes between knowledge and application is the process of *judgment*. The challenge of understanding the complexities of judgment defines another of the essential puzzles of professional education. Human judgment bridges the universal terms of theory and the gritty particularities of situated practice. And human judgment always incorporates both technical and moral elements.

○ Fifth, up to this point my analysis has implied that all of the movement of knowledge is, as it were, from left to right, from the academy to the field. But the most formidable challenge for anyone in a profession is *learning from experience*. While an academic knowledge base is necessary for professional work, it is far from sufficient. Therefore, members of professions have to develop the capacity to learn not only from the academy but, even more importantly, from the experience and contemplation of their own practice. This is true not only for individual professionals, but equally for the entire community of practice. Lessons of practice must have a way of getting back to inform and to render problematic knowledge development in the academy itself.

○ Sixth and finally, professions are inherently public and communal. We speak of someone not only *being a professional*, but also being a *member of a profession*. Professional knowledge is somehow held by a community of professionals who not only know collectively more than any individual member of the community ("distributed expertise" is a distinctive feature of a professional community, even though each member is thought to possess a substantial common core of skill and knowledge), but also have certain public responsibilities and accountabilities with respect to individual practice. Thus, professionals operate within their particular communities under privileges granted by virtue of their recognition by the broader society. Such autonomy and privilege is granted when the profession is viewed as holding specialized knowledge whose warrant only its own members can evaluate, and when its members are trusted to take responsibility for such evaluation.

## Elaborating on the Principles: Educating for Profession

What can we say about the challenges of professional education in light of these six principles?

### Profession as Service

As Brint observed, the starting point for professional preparation is that the aims of professionalism involve social purposes and responsibilities that are grounded both technically and morally. The core meaning of a profession is the organized practice of complex knowledge and skills in the service of others. The professional educator's challenge is to help future professors develop and shape a robust moral vision that will guide their practice and provide a prism of justice and virtue through which to reflect on their actions.

### Theory for Practice

Second, the notion that formal professional knowledge is rooted in academic knowledge bases creates the essential pedagogical problem of professional education. That is, the recurrent challenge of all professional learning is the unavoidable gap between theory and practice. There are at least two versions of the problem. Theory achieves its power through simplification and narrowing of the field of study. In that sense, theories deal with the world in general and, for the most part, making rough places smooth and messy settings neat. A second characteristic of theories is that they generally operate within identifiable disciplines while practical problems cross disciplinary boundaries with the abandon of rum-runners and meandering streams. Theories are extraordinarily powerful, which is why they are the treasure of the academy and valued by the professions; they are also frequently so remote from the particular conditions of professional practice that the novice professional-in-training rarely appreciates their contributions.

Any reader who has been educated for one of the professions, say in the two with which I am most familiar, medical education or teacher preparation, will immediately recognize the problem. My teacher, Joseph Schwab, devoted most of the last 20 years of his life and career to the problems of practical knowledge and its relations to theory. One need only try to connect the Krebs cycle with the intricacies of a particular clinical diagnosis, or the Loop of Henley with some specific aspect of kidney failure, to appreciate the problem. As a teacher educator, I have tried to help students see how one traverses the gap between Piaget's developmental theory and what to teach on Monday morning, or between Vygotsky's zones of proximal development and the pedagogical potential of group work. We who have tried to educate future professionals understand the challenge that is created when your starting point for a learned profession is bodies of academic knowledge. We prepare professionals in universities because we make the strong claim that these are *learned* professions and that academic knowledge is absolutely essential to their performance.

Now, this may be a false claim. It may well be that academic knowledge is essential only as an *entitlement* to practice and is not functionally necessary for practice. My point is that the claim of rootedness in a theoretical, empirical, and/or normative knowledge base is central to all of the professions. This is a crucial issue for the liberal arts, both conceptually and fiscally. The uniquely American view that a liberal education of some sort is a prerequisite for the study of medicine, law, teaching (foundations), and the like sets an interesting problem for the liberal arts at two levels: defining the foundation for understanding and practicing a profession on the one hand, and stipulating the liberal arts and sciences *per se* whose grasp would identify an individual as "educated" or "learned" and therefore entitled to pursue a learned profession. Only the second of these concerns is uniquely American, because the United States is nearly unique in treating most professions as graduate rather than undergraduate domains.

Third, while the theoretical is the foundation, practice is the end to which all the knowledge is directed. Student teaching, medical residencies, architects' apprenticeships, student nursing, all are examples of carefully designed pedagogies to afford eased entry into practice accompanied by intensive supervision. This is why in all professional preparation we find some conception of a supervised clinical experience. In medicine it seems to go on forever. One of the things that makes law so interesting is that legal educators have somehow managed to avoid the responsibility for introducing a serious clinical component into legal education, expecting the employing law firm to assume that burden.

The apprenticeship, the practice, the application that goes on in the field is not only a nearly universal element of professional learning, but typically, once a professional reaches the field of practice, he or she looks back on the theoretical preparation and begins to devalue it. There are always interesting tensions between the clinical and the theoretical.[2]

One of the sources of those tensions is that theoretical preparation, in spite of the conservatism of the academy, tends to be more radical and reform-oriented than is practice itself. Indeed, academicians often see themselves as the critical conscience of professional practice, taking upon themselves the responsibility for criticizing current practice and developing a vision for the future. And it is, again, almost universally the case in professional preparation that the students arrive at their clinical experiences only to hear the nursing supervisor, or the veteran teacher in the fifth grade where they're student teaching, or the chief of clinical services in the hospital admonish them to forget all the b.s. they were taught at the university because now they will learn the way it is really done. So, interestingly, the academy is the source of radical ideas. The field is where you encounter the bungee cord that pulls things back to the conservation of habits of practice. This kind of tension is, as I say, generally characteristic of professional education.

## The Role of Judgment

Another complication of professional learning is that the academy, to the extent that it addresses problems of practice at all, presents them as *prototypes*—simplified and schematized theoretical representations of the much messier and variable particularities of everyday life. When student-professionals move out to the fields of practice, they find inevitably that nothing quite fits the prototypes. The responsibility of the developing professional is not simply to apply what he or she has learned to practice, but to transform, to adapt, to merge and synthesize, to criticize and to invent in order to move from the theoretical knowledge of the academy to the kind of practical clinical knowledge needed to engage in the professional work. One of the reasons judgment is such an essential component of clinical work is that theoretical knowledge is generally knowledge of what is true universally. It is true in general and for the most part. It is knowledge of regularities and of patterns. It is an invaluable simplification of a world whose many variations would be far too burdensome to store in memory with all their detail and individuality. Yet the world of practice is beset by just those particularities, born of the workings of chance. To put it in Aristotelian terms, theories are about *essence,* practice is about *accident,* and the only way to get from there to here is via the exercise of *judgment.*

## Experience

As Dewey observed in his classic essay on the influence of Darwinism on philosophy, chance, error, and accidents present both the sciences and the fields of practice with their most fascinating puzzles.[3] The great challenge for professional learning is that *experience* occurs where design and intention collide with chance. Without the violation of expectations, it is impossible to learn from experience. Learning from experience, therefore, requires both the systematic prototype-centered, theoretical knowledge characteristic of the academy and the more fluid, reactive, prudential reasoning characteristic of practice. The professional must learn how to cope with those unpredictable matters, and how to reflect on his or her own actions. Professionals incorporate the consequences of those actions into their own growing knowledge base, which ultimately includes unique combinations of theoretical and moral principles, practical maxims, and a growing collection of narratives of experience.

In comparing John Dewey and George Herbert Mead with Jane Addams, all of whom were good friends in Chicago in the first five years of this century, Ellen Lagemann observed that for Dewey and Mead, the tools of their trade were the scientific hypothesis and the investigation; for Jane Addams it was the anecdote and the biography. In professional practice, the hypothesis rapidly gives way to the narrative. Jane Addams's Hull House was the setting in which the academic perspectives of Dewey and Mead were brought into collaborative contact with the truly professional practice embodied by Addams and the settlement movement.[4] The ideals of service clearly dominated the thinking of those who were inventing the professions of social work and community development, but the desire to ground those practices in the academic disciplines of social philosophy, sociology, and a professional school of social service administration were already a serious challenge.[5]

In Jerome Bruner's terms, in these situations the paradigmatic way of knowing shares space with the narrative. To foreshadow the concluding section of this essay, when we seek a pedagogy that can reside between the universal principles of theory and the narratives of lived practice, we invent something called a *case method* that employs cases as ways of capturing experience for subsequent analysis and review, and then creating a pedagogy of theoretically grounded experience. We render individual experiential learning into community property when we transform those lessons from personal experience into a literature of shared narratives. Connections between theoretical principles and case narratives are established when we not only ask, "what's the case?" but more critically, "what is this a case of?" In developing those connections between the universal and the particular, between the universal and the accidental, we forge professional knowledge. Such knowledge cannot be developed and sustained adequately by individuals experiencing and reflecting in isolation.

### Community

The sixth and final term is the notion of a community of practice. Although individual professionals carry the responsibility for practice, the assumption is that they are members of a community that defines and regulates the standards for that practice and that, as a community, knows more than does any individual practitioner. The public can turn to the professional community when questions of the quality of practice are at stake. From the perspective of professional pedagogy, the community of practice plays a critical role. The academic discipline serves the academy as a learning community whose invisible colleges ensure that knowledge gained is vetted for its warrant through peer review and then distributed among members of the community through journals and other forms of scholarly communication. The community of practice for a profession plays a similar role with regard to learning from experience, accumulating and critiquing the lessons gained and subsequently codified, and, in general, helping practitioners overcome the limitations of individual practice and individual experience. Without a community of practice, individual professionals would be trapped in a solipsistic universe in which only their own experiences were potentially educative. When the work of communities of practice is created and fostered, individual experience becomes communal, distributed expertise can be shared, and standards of practice can evolve.[6]

## Professing and Liberal Learning

I began by asking what liberal learning would look like if we treated it as a profession. If we said, that is, that liberal learning has as its end professional practice, doing something of service to the community in a manner that is both technically defensible and morally desirable. If we, therefore, saw the theory/practice problem as an inherent problem, as an inherent challenge in all liberal learning. If we recognized that taking theory and moving it into practice may not only be the challenge for theoretical understanding, but also the crucible in which merely theoretical understanding becomes meaningful, memorable, and internalizable. Indeed, what if we argued that theoretical understanding is inherently incomplete, even unrequited, until it is "practiced"? To address those questions I will begin by asking what are the major impediments in liberal learning now? That is, what challenges do liberal educators currently confront that define some of the perennial problems of that endeavor?

## The Challenges of Liberal Learning

What are the challenges of liberal learning? I will rather dogmatically suggest that liberal learning, as all learning for understanding (that endangered species of cognition), confronts three central challenges: the loss of learning, or *amnesia;* the illusion of learning, or *illusory understanding;* and the uselessness of learning, or *inert ideas.* These states can be exemplified by three student exclamations: "I forgot it," "I thought I understood it," and "I understand it but I can't use it." If we were ever to conduct proper evaluations of the long-term benefits of liberal education, I suspect we would encounter all three of these with painful frequency.

The first challenge of liberal learning is the problem of *amnesia.* It is a problem exemplified by the fact that, after having participated in a wide variety of courses and programs in colleges and universities, it is very sobering to discover that students rapidly forget much of what we have taught them or that they have ostensibly learned. Let me suggest a depressing exercise: conduct an exit interview with students at the end of their senior year (or a couple of years beyond) in which you sit them down with the transcript of the four years they have spent with you in the institution and say: "Treat the transcript as a kind of itinerary that you have followed for the last four or five years. Why don't you simply go course by course and just tell me what you remember doing and learning." This is not a test of deep understanding, but if students don't even remember the experience, it's quite hard for them to learn from it. This is one of the reasons that nearly every one of the professions, with the stunning exception of teaching, spends an incredible amount of time and energy teaching future professionals to develop habits of documentation and recording their practice. In medicine, in law, in nursing, in social work, in architecture, there are incredible archives of practice because amnesia is the great enemy of learning from experience. Yet in liberal learning, one of the ubiquitous problems we face is the fragility of what is learned. It's like dry ice. It just evaporates at room temperature and is gone. Students seldom remember much of what they've read or heard beyond their last high-stakes exam on the material. The first problem, therefore, is how do we address the problem of amnesia?

A second enemy of liberal learning is *illusory understanding.* It's far more dangerous and insidious than amnesia, because it is the kind of understanding where you think you do remember and understand, but you don't. A great problem of liberal learning is the confidence with which our graduates imagine that they understand many things with which they have only superficial acquaintance and glib verbal familiarity. They thus can throw around phrases like "supply and demand" or "survival of the fittest" with marvelous agility, albeit without substantial comprehension. There is a wonderful video that begins with graduating students at a Harvard commencement being asked two questions by faculty: Why do we have seasons and what accounts for the phases of the moon? In every case the respondent replied with great confidence. With little hesitation, and very few exceptions, respondents offered a similar theory of the seasons. They explained that we had summer when the elliptical orbit of the earth brought it closer to the sun, and winter when we were further away. When asked to explain the phases of the moon, similarly mistaken accounts were put forward. Here were well-educated students, many of whom had taken courses in the sciences, including astronomy and astrophysics, who were confidently expounding quite misconceived theories of how the solar system functioned. The illusion of understanding is as frequently encountered as it is infrequently detected by educators. The study and documentation of these kinds of misconceptions before and after formal education has become one of the most fascinating aspects of research in science and mathematics learning.

Some of the most interesting work in the history of philosophy deals with the philosophers' concern with illusory understanding. Nearly every one of the Socratic dialogues is an example. The Socratic dialogue is a form of pedagogy designed to confront the knower with what he was sure he knew but indeed doesn't understand. Socratic wisdom is said, therefore, to begin with the unveiling of Socratic ignorance. The whole metaphor of the cave in Plato's *Republic* is a metaphor about illusory understanding. And it is no accident that the way Socrates attempts to diagnose and treat illusory understanding is through an active, interactive process of dialogue in a social setting. Similarly, one of Francis Bacon's most memorable essays is about "the idols of the mind," all the ways in which we, as human intelligences, come to believe we know things that, in fact, we just don't understand.

Alfred North Whitehead warned us that "above all we must beware" of *"inert ideas,"* thus punning on Plato's reverence for the innate variety. Such ideas, he said, "are merely received into the mind without being utilized, or tested, or thrown into fresh combinations." Ideas escape inertness by being used, tested, or thrown into fresh combinations. Application is not only the ultimate test, it is the crucible within which ideas come alive and grow. Whitehead observes, "Pedants sneer at an education which is useful. But if education is not useful, what is it? Is it a talent, to be hidden away in a napkin?"[7]

## Principles of Professional Learning

If the three horsemen of the liberal learning apocalypse are amnesia, illusion, and inertness, what kinds of pedagogical strategies can we invoke to fend them off? The salvation of understanding is in our grasp. *The key to preserving the liberal arts is to profess the liberal arts.*

The principles through which we overcome amnesia, illusory understanding, and inertness are the same as those that enumerate the conditions of profession: activity, reflection, collaboration, passion, and community. These principles not only derive from current research in cognitive science and social learning, they also map very nicely onto the wisdom of practice in professional education. At the risk that an overly dogmatic rhetoric may give the lie to the very points I am making, I shall briefly explain these principles.

The first is *activity.* Students who are learning in professional settings are remarkably active most of the time in that they are engaged in clinical or practical work. They are designing, diagnosing, and arguing. They are writing; they are investigating; they are in the library or at the computer getting information. They are talking to one another, sharing information, and challenging one another's ideas. At every opportunity, the level of activity of the students is higher than in the average college classroom. The outcome should not surprise anyone. We all know from our practice as well as from theory that active learning results in more enduring learning than does passive learning. It is one of the key principles of all human learning, equally relevant for young adults as for children.

As a first principle, authentic and enduring learning occurs when the learner is an *active* agent in the process. Student learning becomes more active through experimentation and inquiry, as well as through writing, dialogue, and questioning. Thus, the college settings in which the students work must provide them with the opportunities and support for becoming active agents in the process of their own learning.

The second thing we know about effective learners is that they are not merely active, because activity alone is insufficient for learning. As Dewey observed many years ago, we do not learn by doing; we learn by thinking about what we are doing. Successful students spend considerable time, as Bruner calls it, "going meta," that is, thinking about what they are doing and why. Their teachers give them plenty of opportunities to talk about how they are learning, why they are learning in these ways, why they are getting things wrong when they get them wrong and right when they get them right. A very high level of carefully guided *reflection* is blended with activity.

Activity and reflection are hard work. If you are a typical learner, you often find yourself working alone, intending to read an article or a book. You sit down after dinner with a good reading light on, with good music playing softly in the background, and with no distractions in the room. Ten minutes later, you find yourself in the middle of a chapter with absolutely no recollection of what you have read up to that point. It can be very hard for anyone to engage in active and reflective learning alone. For college students, it is even harder.

One of the most important inventions of Ann Brown (with Annemarie Palinscar) was called "reciprocal teaching"—a process of enhancing young students' reading comprehension as they work with one another, scaffolding each others' learning; helping each other focus, attend, and question, actively, critically, and reflectively as they jointly read complicated text.[8] Active, reflective learning thus proceeds best in the presence of a third principle, which is *collaboration*.

College students can work together in ways that scaffold and support each other's learning, and in ways that supplement each other's knowledge. Collaboration is a *marriage of insufficiencies,* not exclusively "cooperation" in a particular form of social interaction. There are difficult intellectual and professional challenges that are nearly impossible to accomplish alone, but are readily addressed in the company of others.

Sandy Astin discusses the educative functions of collaboration—the educational advantages enjoyed through the juxtaposition and confrontation of perspectives for people to rethink, to reflect on what they thought they already knew, and through collaborative exchange *eventually to deepen their understanding of an idea.* So when we say that reflection is important, that collaboration is important, these aren't just pieties. These are essential elements of a pedagogical theory, a theory of learning and teaching that explains why it is that even if your goal is liberal learning, per se, and if what you want is people to learn ideas and concepts and principles that will be robust, that will be deep, that will be not merely inert ideas, shadows on the wall of the cave—the way you temper those ideas is through reflection and through interaction and collaboration. Otherwise it may well be just the illusion of understanding. These are some of the things we're learning about liberal learning.

This kind of learning is not exclusively cognitive or intellectual. Indeed, there is a significant emotional and affective component that inheres in such work. Authentic and enduring learning occurs when students share a *passion* for the material, are emotionally committed to the ideas, processes, and activities, and see the work as connected to present and future goals. Although the language of liberal learning is heavily intellectual, the importance of emotion, enthusiasm, and passion is central to these efforts, for both students and for their teachers. And there is a special quality to those affective responses that develop within individuals who have become interdependent members of well-functioning, cohesive groups. Simply observe the spirit that develops among the members of an athletic team, or the cast of a play, or residents of a cabin at camp, and you can begin to discern the special emotional qualities associated with working collaboratives that function as learning communities.

In that same vein, authentic and enduring learning works best when the processes of activity, reflection, emotion, and collaboration are supported, legitimated, and nurtured within a *community* or *culture* that values such experiences and creates many opportunities for them to occur and to be accomplished with success and pleasure. Such communities create "participant structures" that reduce the labor intensity of the activities needed to engage in the most daunting practices that lead to teaching and learning. Put another way, this kind of learning can rarely succeed one course at a time. The entire institution must be oriented toward these principles, and the principles must be consistently and regularly employed throughout each course and experience in a program. One of the "secrets" of the remarkable impact of the Hutchins College was probably the persistent and all-encompassing effect—course after course—of critical dialogue within small seminars as *the* pedagogical practice of the college.

Consistent with the centrality of teaching and learning, professional education programs that are characterized by activity, reflection, and collaboration in learning communities are inherently uncertain, complex, and demanding places. Both learning and teaching in such settings entails high levels of risk and unpredictability for the participants. Students and faculty both require a school and a community that support and reward those levels of risk taking and invention characteristic of such approaches to learning for understanding and commitment.

If we take these principles seriously as instruments for overcoming the major challenges to liberal learning, then, with Whitehead, I would assert that the kind of pedagogy that we associate with, say, service learning, is not simply a cocurricular extravagance. It may actually be central to the kind of pedagogy that would make a liberal education more professional, in the case of service learning, a pedagogy that would give the liberal arts a clinical component or the equivalent of an internship experience. Moreover, it may well be one of the ways in which we overcome the triple pathologies of amnesia, illusory understanding, and inert ideas. How might that sort of thing go on?

## A Pedagogy for Professing

### Cases as Conduits Between Theory and Practice

I shall now discuss a pedagogy of cases as an example of the kind of teaching and learning that begins to address the central problems of academic learning, in general, and professional learning, in particular. I am *not* arguing that all liberal and professional learning should immediately become case based!

For me, what is so alluring about a case is that it resides in that never-never land between theory and practice, between idea and experience, between the normative ideal and achievable real. One of the interesting things about cases is that they capture pieces of experience that initially existed solely within the life of a single individual and transform that solitary experience into text. You can do all kinds of things when you've rendered something into a text that can be shared by members of a group, all of whom are trying to make sense of the text. The function of the case as a means for preserving and communicating experience is clear given the persistent problems of amnesia.[9]

The great challenge for professionals who wish to learn from experience is the difficulty of holding experiences in memory in forms that can become the objects of disciplined analysis and reflection. Consider the possibility that cases are ways of parsing experience so that practitioners can examine and learn from it. Professionals are typically confronted with a seamless continuum of experience from which they can think about individual episodes or readings as cases, but rarely coordinate the different dimensions into meaningful experiential chunks. Case methods thus become strategies for helping professionals to "chunk" their experience into units that can become the focus for reflective practice. They therefore can become the basis for individual professional learning as well as a forum within which communities of professionals, both local and extended, as members of visible and invisible colleges, can store, exchange, and organize their experiences. How is case learning related to the principles we reviewed above? I will describe a situation—not infrequent in professional education—where the learners not only study and discuss cases written by others, but are actively participating in some sort of field experience around which they also write cases that document and analyze their own practice.

First, whether as case analyst or as case writer, the case learner becomes an active agent in his or her own understanding. When a student is wrestling with a case, whether as an occasion for analysis or a stimulus to reflect on his or her own experience as a prelude to writing, active agency is engaged. Second, cases are inherently reflective. They begin with an act of cognition, of turning around one's own lived experiences and examining them to find events and episodes worthy of transformation into telling cases. Even when the goal of case learning is not case writing, the discussion of cases eventually stimulates reflection on one's own experiences and reactions. Third, case methods nearly always emphasize the primacy of group discussion, deliberation, and debate. The thought process of cases is dialogic, as members of a group explore different perspectives, the available elective actions, or the import of the consequences. In case-based teaching, the interaction of activity, reflection, and collaboration is apparent. But what of community or culture?

Teaching and learning with cases is not an easy pedagogy. Active learners are much more outspoken and assertive than are passive learners. They are less predictable than their more passive counterparts, as they investigate their options, explore alternative interpretations, and challenge prevailing views. Because cases encourage connections between personal experiences and those vicariously experienced through narratives, the directions in which discussions might develop are rather difficult to anticipate, further complicating the pedagogy. Finally, the collaborative mode of instruction once again reduces the authority of the teacher and vests a growing proportion in the initiatives of students. Taken together, the enhancement of agency, reflection, and collaboration makes teaching more complex and unpredictable, albeit by reducing the authority of teachers and their ability to plan for contingencies. When uncertainty increases and power is distributed, the need for a supportive culture or community becomes paramount for teachers and students alike. A supportive culture helps manage the risk of contemplating one's failures and reduces the vulnerability created when one candidly discusses a path not taken. A supportive culture engages each member of the community in parallel risks. It celebrates the interdependence of learners who rely on one another for both insights and reassurance. A learning environment built on activity, reflection, and collaboration—which is an apt characterization of a well-functioning case-learning and case-writing community—proceeds smoothly only in the presence of a sustaining culture and community.

## An Example

How might we envision a clinical component to a liberal education? Consider the possibility that there are forms of service learning that could perform the function. One of the most frequently encountered forms of service learning is tutoring. Although only one among many activities that are quite appropriately classified as legitimate service learning, I want to offer the hypothesis that the tutoring of young children, of adults, or of peers has some uniquely powerful characteristics with regard both to the objectives of offering service and the objectives of making liberal learning more meaningful, more memorable, and more useful, that is, less inert.

In this regard I share the values of the medieval university, which viewed the ability to teach something to someone else as the highest, most rigorous, and final test of whether a scholar understood his discipline or profession deeply. It based this view on Aristotle's observation in the *Metaphysics* that it is the distinctive sign of a man who knows deeply that he can teach what he knows to another. Aristotle recognized that, in order to teach something to someone else, you have to engage in an act of reflection on and transformation of what you know, and then connect those insights to the mind, experience, and motives of somebody else. Teaching is a dual act of intelligence and empathy. It entails both technical and moral reason. By the same token, in order to make your own learning more meaningful and memorable, you have to somehow interconnect the many things you know in an intrapersonal network of associations and implications. Each time you can make a connection, whether in your own mind or with the minds of others, amnesia becomes less likely. Each connection serves as both anchor and springboard. Every time you can figure out a new way to take what you know and apply it, connect it, teach it to someone else, you've not only rendered a service, but you have deepened and enriched your own understanding.

I propose that one of the ways in which we can combine the notion of service and the notion of liberal learning is with the expectation that every one of our undergraduates who is engaged in liberal learning undertake the service of teaching something they know to somebody else. They also undertake writing about the experience as a case, describing both teaching and student learning. For me this isn't hypothetical. It's the way I prepare people to teach. They write cases of their own practice. But they don't write them for me. They write them for the other members of their community, because our argument is that experience is too precious to be limited in its benefits solely to the person who experienced it. We need to move from individual experiential learning to a scholarly community of practice.

Then we form small case conferences where groups of students come together and exchange their cases. Case discussions are very interesting. When the discussions are well managed, participants can move the case discussion in two directions. One is exploring the facts of the case. Here, participants are pressed to describe the context more richly and in greater detail. They are urged to elaborate on their accounts of what actually happened, what was said and done, how all that occurred made them feel. They are pressed to dig deeply into the particularity of the context, because it is in the devilish details that practice dramatically differs from theory.

Yet, at the same time that the participants are being sucked into depths of the particular, the skillful pedagogue (and eventually the students themselves) begins to build in a second-order genre of question which is, "what is the case an exemplar of?" What are some other principles, concepts, or ideas that link these two or three cases together or that make you think about your case in relation to some more general principle?[10]

Sitting astride theory and practice, the case both enriches the grasp of practice and at the same time links back to the world of theory and the world of principle. I already do that kind of work with prospective and veteran teachers, and can readily imagine being able to do something similar with undergraduates. Such a strategy would be an example of professing the liberal arts, in having students teach others what they know, in providing service in conjunction with our academic learning which was then captured in written cases. Those cases would then become the curriculum for seminars whose purpose was to link the experiences of application back to the theoretical understanding.

There is a powerful strategic value in writing and analyzing cases that have been written by the members of a case forum, and in systematically exploring the tough question "what is this a case of?" When I write a case describing my own practice, I am the protagonist in the plot. This means that I'm writing not only *what* I did, but I am writing about *why* I did it. I am writing not just about my strategies and actions, but about my intentions, goals, and values. I write, in Martin Buber's terms, not only about "I" and "thou," but reflexively about "I." In that sense, by injecting the self as protagonist into the deliberations around one's academic learning, we bring the moral dimensions of liberal learning back to center stage. This is only proper; the ultimate rationale for treating liberal learning as a worthy end in itself is a moral argument, not an instrumental one.

If we were to professionalize in these terms, if we were actively to connect learning with service, with practice, with application, and were further to capture that practice in a kind of pedagogy that uses cases and case methods in ways analogous to some of the ways we use them for professional preparation, we would not only achieve the moral ends of service, we would very likely do better at overcoming the challenges to liberal understanding. Through service, through application, through rendering their learning far more active, reflective, and collaborative, students would actually learn more liberally, understand what they have learned more deeply, and develop the capacity to use what they have learned in the service of their communities.

NOTES

1. Steven Brint, *In an Age of Experts: The Changing Role of Professionals in Politics and Public Life* (Princeton, NJ: Princeton University Press, 1994), 7.

2. It is also quite interesting when the supervised clinical experience affords such opportunities in only part of a future role, as when the future university professor is heavily mentored in the scholarship of discovery but receives little or no supervised clinical experience in the scholarship of teaching.

3. John Dewey, "The Influence of Darwinism on Philosophy," in Martin Gardner, editor, *Great Essays in Science* (Buffalo: Prometheus, 1994).

4. Ellen Condliffe Lagemann, "The Plural Worlds of Educational Research," *History of Education Quarterly* 29 (1988), 184–214.

5. William Rainey Harper, first president of the University of Chicago, wrestled with questions of how the professional school could fit into the new research university. Chicago had schools of theology, pedagogy, and social service. Dewey wrote a short paper on the topic of how the university-based school of pedagogy must be distinct from the traditional normal school, most particularly in its relationships with academic disciplines and research.

6. At least that's the theory. Professions are not equally successful in creating communities of practice that effectively play this role. Thus, medicine and engineering probably do it rather well. Law does it well for court cases but badly for the daily practice of law. Teaching, both K–12 and postsecondary, has barely scratched the surface of transforming the experiences of pedagogy into scholarship and community property.

7. Alfred North Whitehead, *The Aims of Education and Other Essays* (New York: Macmillan, 1929).

8. A. S. Palinscar and A. L. Brown, "Reciprocal Teaching of Comprehension—Fostering and Monitoring Activities," *Cognition and Instruction* 1 (1984), 117–75.

9. Sibling to amnesia is the challenge of *nostalgia,* in which forgetting is replaced by mis-remembering, usually in the service of reinforcing the mnemonist's interests, needs, or preferences. Nostalgia is not identical to illusory understanding, but it is likely to be a significant contributing condition.

10. Although I am using the example of tutoring, it should be apparent that this strategy for case-based liberal learning could be applied to a variety of other clinical experiences as well, both those that entail service and others that are more traditional—applied research and the like.

# INTRODUCTION

# TAKING LEARNING SERIOUSLY
## (1999)

ADAPTED FROM LEE SHULMAN's keynote address at the
American Association for Higher Education's 1999 National
Conference in Washington, D.C., this piece explores three
"pedago-pathologies" that result when teaching and learning
fail to connect: amnesia, fantasia, and inertia. Shulman also
used the talk to lay out a vision of the scholarship of teaching and learning and of Carnegie's program, in partnership
with AAHE, for infusing its principles into academic culture
as a way of "taking learning seriously." An edited version of
the presentation was then published in *Change* in the summer of 1999.

# TAKING LEARNING SERIOUSLY

WHAT DO WE MEAN BY "taking learning seriously?" Five interesting questions reflect what's involved in taking up that challenge. I shall ask and answer these briefly to begin this article. I shall then elaborate on those answers.

First, What does it mean to take anything seriously? I answer that when we take something quite seriously, we *profess* it.

Second, What do we mean by learning? I argue that learning is far more than bringing knowledge from outside the person to inside. Indeed, learning is basically an interplay of two challenging processes—getting knowledge that is inside to move out, and getting knowledge that is outside to move in.

Third, What does learning look like when it's not going well? I ask this question because I've spent much of my career in medical education, so I'm concerned not only with health but with pathology as well. I propose that the major pathologies of learning involve malfunctions of memory, understanding, and application and can be called *amnesia, fantasia,* and *inertia.*

Fourth, What do you need to create in order to take learning so seriously that you take active responsibility for understanding and treating its pathologies as well as enhancing its successes? I claim that you must create a *scholarship of teaching* to pursue those goals.

And fifth, What is the new partnership between The Carnegie Foundation for the Advancement of Teaching (CFAT) and the American Association for Higher Education (AAHE), designed to help us deal with the challenges of taking learning seriously? The Carnegie Academy for the Scholarship of Teaching and Learning (CASTL) has been created to respond to these challenges.

Let us now examine each of these core questions and elaborate on their answers.

## Professing Introduced

When we take something seriously, we often talk about *professing* it. The deepest, oldest meaning of the word "profess" is to take religious orders in a public and visible way. When one professes faith, it means taking on a set of obligations that will serve as the first principles for controlling one's life, no questions asked. Professing one's faith, behaviorally and emotionally, is an impressive example of taking something seriously.

Another sense of the word is that we *profess* our love—for our spouses and partners, our parents, our children, our dearest friends. We profess a kind of commitment that has within it a willingness to sacrifice on behalf of the other. Also in a public manner, we declare our devotion to another. Here is yet another example of taking something quite seriously.

A more contemporary meaning of the word, a meaning more closely associated with the work of those who read this magazine, is to profess one's understanding, one's expertise: to be professional, or to be a "professor." Members of professions take on the burden of their understanding by making public commitments to serve their fellow beings in a skilled and responsible manner. "Professors" take on a special set of roles and obligations. They profess their understanding in the interests of nurturing the knowledge, understanding, and development of others. They take learning so seriously that they profess it. This brings us to the topic of *learning*.

## Professing Learning

What is learning? Thirty-five years ago, I taught my first course as a college teacher at Michigan State University. It was a course on the psychology of learning. I can almost trace my career by saying that before I studied psychology, I had only the sketchiest understanding of what learning was. After I finished graduate school and first began teaching the psychology of learning, I was confident that I really understood what the process of learning entailed. However, over the past 35 years, I have systematically studied learning and understanding in many contexts, and I have taught many courses on the subject. Alas, my understanding has now become more complex, vague, and somewhat ambiguous.

When I began teaching learning theory, our conception of learning was fairly simple. For any given learning situation, the "inside" of the learner was treated as more or less empty; learning was understood as a process of getting the knowledge that was outside the learner—in books, theories, the mind of the teacher—to move inside. We tested for the success of learning by giving tests to look inside the heads of our students to see if what had previously been outside was now there. I exaggerate, but there was a comforting simplicity to our psychological behaviorism in those days.

We now understand that learning is a *dual* process in which, initially, the inside beliefs and understandings must come out, and only then can something outside get in. It is not that prior knowledge must be expelled to make room for its successors. Instead, these two processes—the inside-out and the outside-in movements of knowledge—alternate almost endlessly. To prompt learning, you've got to begin with the process of going from inside out. The first influence on new learning is not what teachers do pedagogically but the learning that's already inside the learner.

David Ausubel was one of the pioneering cognitive educational psychologists. He wrote a lovely epigraph at the beginning of his 1968 textbook *Educational Psychology: A Cognitive View:* "If I had to reduce all of educational psychology to just one principle, I would say this: The most important single factor influencing learning is what the learner already knows. Ascertain this and teach him accordingly."

We've come to understand more clearly the extent to which learners construct meaning out of their prior understanding. Any new learning must, in some fashion, connect with what learners already know. Of course, that is an oversimplification, but it is what I mean by "getting the inside out." As teachers, unless we can discover ways of getting the inside out and looking jointly at their prior knowledge with our students, taking seriously what they already know and believe, instruction becomes very difficult. Our first principle, therefore, begins with the assertion that we must take seriously what the students have already learned. To take *learning* seriously, we need to take *learners* seriously.

An interesting surprise is that once what is inside gets out, it seldom just sits there; in a setting where serious activity and/or discussion is possible, that knowledge is enriched and elaborated by social interactions with people who have also experienced their own processes of getting what's inside out. Thus, learners construct their sense of the world by applying their old understandings to new experiences and ideas. That new learning is enriched enormously by the ways in which people wrestle with such ideas on the "outside," before they bring those ideas back inside and make them their own. This explains why one of the most important remedies for combating the illusion of understanding and the persistence of misconceptions is to support learners in the active, collaborative, reflective reexamination of ideas in a social context.

Learning is least useful when it is private and hidden; it is most powerful when it becomes public and communal. Learning flourishes when we take what we think we know and offer it as community property among fellow learners so that it can be tested, examined, challenged, and improved before we internalize it.

## What Does It Look Like When Learning Doesn't Go Well?

I call this topic the "epidemiology of mislearning," or the "taxonomy of pedago-pathology." As I indicated earlier, there are three such pathologies: we forget, we don't understand that we misunderstand, and we are unable to use what we learned. I have dubbed these conditions *amnesia, fantasia,* and *inertia.*

*Amnesia* is one of the most frequent pathologies of learning—perhaps the most frequent. Students ordinarily and regularly forget what they have learned in their classes. Indeed, at times they forget that they even attended some classes.

More than 30 years ago, medical educators conducted a study on what first-year medical students remembered of the thousands of new terms that they'd memorized in their first-year gross anatomy course. They were tested and retested over time. The curve that matched most closely to their forgetting of gross anatomy was the same shape as discovered in Hermann Ebbinghaus's classic study of memory for nonsense syllables a century ago. The publication of data like these made a mark in the world of medical education. The teaching of anatomy has since changed radically in schools of medicine.

My colleagues and I at Stanford conducted a study in which we asked graduate students who were preparing to become high school teachers to bring their undergraduate college transcripts to an interview. We were trying to understand the connections between what and how they had learned in college, and the ways they themselves would teach in high school. We asked them to walk us through their college transcript course by course, and tell us what they remembered about each course. Certainly, they remembered the contents, teachers, and the activities of many courses vividly. On the other hand, a depressing number of courses had faded from memory. At times, students did not even recollect having taken them. Is that evidence that they learned nothing from those courses? Of course not. Should we be concerned by reports like that? Absolutely.

Are we satisfied with the notion that students forget a significant amount of what we once held them responsible for knowing? If we take learning seriously, we must take responsibility for the ubiquity of amnesia. We need to reexamine much of what we teach, and how we teach it.

*Fantasia* is the name we have given to what otherwise might be called illusory understanding or persistent misconceptions. Fantasia is potentially far more insidious than amnesia. With amnesia my attitude is to let by-gones be bygones. What you have simply forgotten may be harmless. But fantasia can be dangerous. It is that state in which students are absolutely confident that they understand something, but they don't.

You may have seen a short video in which graduating Harvard students were asked to explain why there are changes in the seasons. Nearly every student responded with supreme self-confidence that the orbit of the earth is elliptical and that, therefore, the earth is sometimes closer to the sun, hence summer, and sometimes farther from the sun, hence winter. They exemplified the condition of fantasia, the confident grasp of an idea or ex-planation that is fundamentally at odds with the most warranted con-ceptions held by experts. These illusions may have been based on widely accepted folklore that had become a prevailing preconception. They may have developed from a formal lesson that had been assimilated, memo-rized, but never accurately understood. These misconceptions are impor-tant for several reasons. New learning rests on old learning. A strategically held misconception can interfere with significant amounts of later good teaching. In that sense, misconceptions become insidious, a sort of intel-lectual land mine (or perhaps a "mind mine"?).

There is plenty of research—especially in science education—about the impact of illusory understandings. Many of them may not be a cause for alarm. An entire population can live happy and responsible lives bearing the heavy burden of illusions of understanding about the causes of sea-sons. But fantasia may also cause serious problems. Medical students who took literally the explanation that the heart functioned just like a pump later displayed frequent misunderstandings of how to deal with serious forms of cardiopathology.

Biology teachers must wrestle with the durability of student miscon-ceptions of evolution and natural selection. Most students in courses that emphasize evolution and natural selection enter these courses as intuitive Lamarckians. They are convinced that any characteristics acquired by one generation are then transmitted to the next generation. The formal in-struction emphasizes the Darwinian refutation of that position. These stu-dents may earn A's and B's in the course, demonstrating that they now understand the Darwinian perspective, but quiz them three months later and they're once again dedicated intuitive Lamarckians—as indeed are many of the rest of us. I suspect that forms of fantasia are endemic among students and graduates of higher education, many lying in wait for years before manifesting themselves at critical moments.

What about *inertia?* I take the word "inertia" from Alfred North White-head's lovely pun about "inert ideas" that occupy much of the space in our well-educated minds. A play on Plato's concept of "innate ideas," inert ideas are those that simply lie there, doing nothing. They are not forgotten; nor are they in some intrinsic sense wrong. They are simply not in a form that lends them to any useful purpose beyond being remembered.

For me, the best example of inertia is documented in research conducted in the 1950s by one of my mentors at the University of Chicago, Benjamin Bloom, on problem-solving processes in college students. Bloom was serving as the University Examiner, a role that led to his well-known contributions to the Taxonomy of Educational Objectives. Using the taxonomy, he identified a number of students who had acquired substantial amounts of "knowledge" of a subject, but could not apply that knowledge, or use it to analyze or synthesize new understandings.

Bloom identified two groups of students who had completed an American History course. Both groups had performed equivalently on the test items that measured knowledge of the facts of history, but one of the groups had excelled in measures of higher-order understanding while the other had floundered on problem-solving questions that required them to apply that knowledge to new situations. Bloom wanted to understand how two groups of people, who apparently knew roughly the same things, could be so very different in what they could *do* with their knowledge.

Bloom invited the students to think aloud when confronted with a question like this: "What do you think would have been the attitudes of Virginia tobacco farmers toward the new Constitution of 1789?" That particular "fact" was nowhere to be found in the students' reading or lecture materials. The students who had performed well on the problem-solving questions would say things like, "Well, I don't remember anything in particular about that, but let me work my way through it. The Virginia tobacco farmers, well, what would they have had a stake in? Let's see, they would have been very dependent on both interstate and international trade because they'd want to be able to sell their crop. A strong federal government might well be in their interest." As students reasoned their way through reviewing what they knew about the differences between the Articles of Confederation and the new Constitution, the consequences for the relationships among the states, and so on, they would weave together conjectures about the attitudes of tobacco farmers that were well grounded in evidence.

The students who "knew" the information but had not performed well in application would say things that would sum up to: "You want to know about the *attitudes* of these farmers? Hey, I'm sorry. We didn't study that." Those students are probably the ones likely to complain about how unfair it was for teachers to test them on things they had never been taught.

I emphatically am not saying that the "facts" don't matter. Absent the facts, any of these students would simply be fabricating. They wouldn't have a clue. You *need* facts to make sense; they are the basis for understanding, but they are never enough. Inertia as pathology describes those states of mind where people come to know something but simply can't go beyond the facts, can't synthesize them, think with them, or apply them in another situation. Since the ultimate purpose of any education is to help students to go well beyond the limitations of any formal instruction, the epidemiology of inertia should comprise a serious domain of institutional inquiry for higher education. Any institution that claims to take learning seriously must systematically monitor the circumstances of amnesia, fantasia, and inertia associated with its programs. Alas, most of our institutions are similar to hospitals that proceed blithely along well-traveled paths oblivious to the mortality and morbidity rates experienced by their patients.

In our attempts to understand the conditions that foster amnesia, fantasia, and inertia, and in trying to understand how to combat those problems, we unexpectedly stumbled over *nostalgia*. We found nostalgia not so much among students as among teachers, administrators, critics of education, and political leaders. This condition is marked by a common symptom—the firm belief that whatever the educational problem, the best way to combat it is by reinstating the ways through which the observers had been taught when they were the same age as their students. To teachers, the problem with modern education was that it was somehow riddled with new fads like group work, project-based learning, and—oh my!—service learning. Why can't we just get back to lectures, with an occasional discussion session? Why can't we just emphasize important facts, basic skills, fundamental principles, and the universal moral values? To the lay critics and policymakers, the solution involved returning to the rigor of yesteryear: tougher standards, punitive grading systems, and less tolerance for the mushy, politically correct additions to the bedrock of the traditional curriculum.

One of the problems is that those who are trying to remedy the aforementioned afflictions usually believe that the reason people forget, misunderstand, or go inert is that they haven't been taught *enough,* and that the answer is to teach them *more.* You can often see aspects of this "solution" in the one piece of pedagogy that is a true partnership between higher education and K–12: advanced placement. "AP" is exemplary in many ways. It is a lovely example of standards-based teaching and learning in which the teacher truly serves as a coach who supports all the students in their quest for the highest levels of performance. The test is external to the classroom and does not interfere with that cooperation between teacher and students. However, many AP exams such as Biology and U.S. History seem driven not by the principle that "less is more," but "much more is more." The content coverage of those courses is astounding in its magnitude.

We were shocked by the results of the publication of the Third International Math and Science Studies, where for the first time we compared our advanced placement students—the *crème de la crème* of American students—against the best students in other countries. We learned that the coverage strategy just doesn't work. Our kids don't match up well with their international counterparts. The very best explanation for the differences in performance lies in our very different ways of teaching. We define rigor as teaching our students more, however superficially. Other countries bring a much smaller set of ideas to students, then elaborate and deepen them pedagogically. They don't cover as much material, but the students understand more robustly what they have studied. If we are to take learning seriously, we will have to find another strategy to replace nostalgia. This leads to the fourth question.

## What Do We Do About These Pathologies?

We return to the essence of professing. It is certainly not sufficient to cast doubt on nostalgia and regression-to-the-familiar as adequate responses to the problems of learning. We need more vigorous strategies for the future. We have finally begun to recognize that when we confront serious problems in education, we must embark on systematic research to help us cope with them. Educational research is a powerful resource for educational improvement at all levels, from the preschool to the graduate school. One product of educational research is the elucidation of general principles useful to guide and critique current and future practices. I have written elsewhere about how the principles of *activity, reflection, collaboration,* and *passion* among learners, combined with *generative content* and the creation of powerful learning *communities,* can support general designs for instruction. The encouraging news is that such research can be conducted and adapted to fundamental variations among disciplines, levels of schooling, backgrounds of students, and educational purposes. The sobering news is that although we can learn a great deal from traditional forms of research at the level of general principles, education is not a science; it is a complex set of practices that is grounded and principled but not rule-governed. As the late Donald Schön wrote eloquently, the principles of technical rationality are necessary for this work to proceed, but these principles must be joined with reflective practice.

Far too many interpreted Schön's writings as advocating a rejection of scholarly research in the professions or applied fields. Far from it. The strategy we must pursue is an approach to scholarship that legitimates more than one kind of research. Research that renders one's own practice as the problem for investigation is at the heart of what we mean by *professing* or *profession*.

At the very core of any field that we call a profession is an inherent and inescapable uncertainty. Professions deal with those parts of the world that are characterized by unpredictability. Teachers can teach in the same manner to three classes in a row and experience different consequences each time. Professions (like teaching) deal with that part of the universe where design and chance collide. One cannot resolve that uncertainty by writing new rules. The way forward is to make that collision, that unpredictability in our fields, itself an object of individual and collective investigation. We will never fully remove the uncertainty from teaching any more than we can from such other professions as clinical medicine, architecture, economic planning, or clinical social work. But as a profession, we can grow much wiser about how to anticipate and deal with uncertainty. We can develop new forms of inquiry that both learn from and support the "wisdom of practice."

## Taking Teaching Seriously

My answer to the fourth question—How do we combat these pathologies?—is that we must commit ourselves professionally to a scholarship of teaching.

What do we mean when we call something "scholarship"? Certainly, all acts of intelligence are not scholarship. An act of intelligence or of artistic creation becomes scholarship when it possesses at least three attributes: it becomes public; it becomes an object of critical review and evaluation by members of one's community; and members of one's community begin to use, build upon, and develop those acts of mind and creation.

Think about what happens in the scholarship we create when we're doing traditional forms of research. We publish our findings and ideas because we have a responsibility to make our acts of mind available to our colleagues. Yes, a few of us want to get promoted, too. But the real reason that publication is important is that scholarly acts must be made available for public scrutiny. They have to become community property or they will not contribute to the larger profession, as scholarship must.

We cannot treat all acts of scholarship indiscriminately. We have to ask which of them meet certain standards and genuinely contribute to knowledge. We care about standards of quality because we recognize that scholars are engaged in work that none can accomplish alone. Since we can't do it alone, we depend on the scholarship of others as the building blocks for our own scholarship. Thoughtless critics often ridicule the fact that our acts of scholarship usually end with long lists of references. A list of references is a set of thank-you notes. It is our way of acknowledging that, without the people whom we reference, we could not have done the work we did. We are members of a community of scholars. References permit our readers to trace our research back to its sources.

For a scholarship of teaching, we need scholarship that makes our work public and thus susceptible to critique. It then becomes community property, available for others to build upon.

How many professional educators, when engaged in creating a new course or a new curriculum, can turn to a published, peer-reviewed scholarship of teaching in which colleagues at other colleges and universities present their experiments, their field trials, or their case studies of instruction and its consequences? Where is the scholarly literature through which higher educators study exemplars of teaching and can build upon that work? With precious few exceptions, we don't have such a literature.

In this respect, the scholarship of teaching is dramatically different from the scholarship of investigation. It's one of the reasons why any sort of progress is so hard to come by pedagogically—because blindness and amnesia are the state of the art in pedagogy. We just don't know what our colleagues before or elsewhere have done. We don't even document and analyze our own efforts. Indeed, we often don't know what our colleague in the next office is doing pedagogically, although we are thoroughly familiar with the research of colleagues a continent (and an e-mail click) away.

We are committed at the Carnegie Foundation to infusing into academic culture a profound commitment to the scholarship of teaching. This scholarship is a way of recording, displaying, examining, investigating, and building more powerful pedagogies for dealing with the challenges presented by the pathologies of learning, which are pandemic in our classrooms and institutions. (This brief taxonomy does not begin to exhaust the prevailing pathologies. We need scholarly investigations of such undeniable problems as the disconnection between intellectual learning and moral or civic learning in higher education. We also need investigations of the troubling absence of intellectual passion and commitment to ideas within our student populations.)

## A New Partnership

I now turn to question five, which is about the AAHE and CFAT collaboration to move the "scholarship of teaching" from rhetoric to action. We have designed a joint project called the Carnegie Academy for the Scholarship of Teaching and Learning (CASTL). It will have three parts that together exemplify what we mean by taking learning and teaching seriously.

## Part 1

If you do traditional kinds of scholarship in your field, you can be invited to places that give you a chance to do even more of that scholarship under wonderful conditions. These include the Center for Advanced Study in the Behavioral Sciences at Stanford, the National Humanities Center at the Research Triangle, the legendary Rockefeller think tank at Bellagio on Lake Como, and many more "think tanks" from Aspen to Berlin, from Woods Hole to Waasenar. For traditional kinds of scholarship, these perquisites can be quite alluring and conducive to further scholarly and artistic excellence.

There are few if any rewards for being equally gifted, committed, and effective as a scholar of teaching in one's discipline, interdiscipline, or profession. We have thus initiated an advanced study center for outstanding teachers—a Carnegie Academy for teachers who engage in the scholarship of teaching in ways that make their work public and available for critical evaluation, in a form that others can use, build upon, and transcend.

Outstanding university, college, and community college faculty members designated as "Pew Scholars" come to the Carnegie Academy each summer. They serve for a year as a Fellow, including two successive summers in residence at the Academy. Over a period of five years, more than 100 such Fellows will be selected to participate in the Academy. A parallel program is under way for scholars of teaching from the worlds of precollegiate education and teacher education. Eventually, when appropriate facilities are available, the two groups will interact extensively.

The Academy has a larger purpose than honoring scholars of teaching, enhancing their individual scholarship, and making them more visible. We intend to contribute to building a field of study, in addition to developing the capacities of individual scholars. We have only begun to understand the full range of inquiries entailed in a scholarship of teaching, much less in defining its standards of quality or conditions for aggregation. The Pew Scholars, individually and collectively, will be expected to create ideas and materials for a scholarship of teaching in their respective disciplines. Their efforts, and those of similarly engaged colleagues, will become the exemplars of this emerging field. These exemplars will be gathered together in the Carnegie Knowledge Media Laboratory, where we will attempt to understand how best to classify, display, understand, and distribute the kinds of work pursued and the kinds of knowledge created. We will study how to compress such inquiries into more economical forms so that others can readily build upon them. It is a long-term effort, which must involve both scholars and their institutions.

## Part 2

A second critical part of the Academy is the Campus Academies Program, coordinated by AAHE. This will be a national network of community colleges, liberal arts colleges, and comprehensive and doctoral institutions that commit themselves to taking learning and teaching seriously by creating conditions on their own campuses that reflect in their own way the values, culture, and principles of the core Academy. We envision these campus teaching academies as support systems and sanctuaries within their institutions to sustain the scholarship of teaching within departments and programs.

In time, we hope to witness a new kind of campus that nurtures the scholarship of teaching, and defines the pursuit of that kind of intellectual work by faculty members as central to its institutional mission. More than 120 institutions have already registered for this program. More are added each month.

## Part 3

Finally, we have begun to develop collaborative relationships with disciplinary and professional societies. Every postsecondary faculty member holds dual citizenship. We are citizens in our local institution; at the same time, we hold citizenship in a discipline or profession, which often gains at least as much allegiance from us as our home institution. If we're going to change academic culture, we need to work with both our visible and invisible colleges. We must expand the focus of journals, academic conferences, and hiring processes to give a higher profile to the scholarship of teaching.

We already have begun working with over 20 disciplinary and professional societies, such as the American Historical Association, the Mathematical Association of America, and the American Sociological Association. Many disciplinary groups are interested in such efforts because they recognize that the scholarship of teaching is important to the future of their fields.

## Professing Revisited

I have argued in this article that if we are to take learning seriously, we must profess teaching, and take our profession as teachers seriously. At the heart of the concept of a profession is a public and moral commitment to learning from pedagogical experience and exchanging that learning in acts of scholarship that contribute to the wisdom of practice across the profession.

A contradiction lies at the very heart of the notion of profession. Once appreciated, the contradiction helps us further understand the educational challenge we face. As I said earlier, when we take something seriously, we profess it—our faith, our love, our understanding. But notice how fundamentally different those kinds of professing are from one another.

When I profess my understanding, I am urged by my teachers to use critical reasoning, to demand evidence, and to make my arguments clear—always to ask, How do you really know? Skepticism, questioning, the demand for proof are at the heart of professing one's understanding.

But when I profess my love or my faith, at the heart of that professing is the requirement that I suspend disbelief. I do not typically ask for proof or demand evidence. I am asked to take some things on faith. Indeed, some of the great tragedies of our dramatic literature are accounts of protagonists who fail to grasp the differences between a profession of love or faith and a profession of skeptical, reasoned, evidence-based understanding. Othello is a tragic figure because he was incapable of professing his love for Desdemona unconditionally and took Iago's proffered evidence of her infidelity too credulously. Lear's tragedy was self-initiated, when he felt that he had to ask his three daughters for further evidence of their love. Cordelia's candor was misconstrued as absence of devotion.

To be deeply educated, I believe, is to understand both when skepticism and evidence are appropriate, and when faith and suspension of disbelief are appropriate. There are no rules or principles for knowing this distinction. Only through studying the examples in both scientific and humanistic sources—through wrestling with that inherent contradiction between faith and reason—can we and our students come to terms with the essential uncertainties that define our roles as professionals and as human beings.

As professors, we are asked to be rational and empirical, to demand evidence. On the other hand, as teaching professionals, we expect ourselves to believe what much empirical evidence says we shouldn't: that all our students can learn. We express our faith in our students' potential and in our ability to teach them. As professors, we do not choose between the skepticism of reason and the hope grounded in faith. Our students demand both. And we must learn, as professional educators, to do both.

RELATED READINGS

A number of sources elaborate on the ideas presented in this article.

*For further analysis of the commonplaces of the professions and how this analysis of the professions and professional education affects our roles as educators, see*

Shulman, Lee S. "Professing the Liberal Arts," in Robert Orrill, ed., *Education and Democracy.* New York: The College Board, 1997.

———. "Theory, Practice, and the Education of Professionals," *The Elementary School Journal,* Vol. 98, No. 5, 1998, pp. 511–526.

———. "The Wisdom of Practice: Managing Complexity in Medicine and Teaching," in D. C. Berliner and B. V. Rosenshine, eds., *Talks to Teachers: A Festschrift for N. L. Gage.* New York: Random House, 1987.

———. "Just in Case: Reflections on Learning from Experience," in J. A. Colbert, P. Desberg, and K. Trimble, eds., *The Case for Education: Contemporary Approaches for Using Case Methods.* Boston: Allyn & Bacon, 1996.

*For a contemporary conception of the processes of learning, see*

Bransford, John D., Ann L. Brown, and Rodney R. Cocking, eds. *How People Learn: Brain, Mind, Experience, and School.* Committee on Developments in the Science of Learning, National Research Council. Washington, D.C.: National Academy Press, 1999.

*For a fuller discussion of the scholarship of teaching, see*

Shulman, Lee S. "Course Anatomy: The Dissection and Analysis of Knowledge Through Teaching," in Pat Hutchings, ed., *The Course Portfolio.* Washington, D.C.: AAHE, 1998.

# INTRODUCTION

# PROBLEM-BASED LEARNING: THE PEDAGOGIES OF UNCERTAINTY (2000)

IN OCTOBER 2000, Lee Shulman delivered the opening keynote address to a conference on problem-based learning sponsored by Samford University as part of a project funded by The Pew Charitable Trusts. Drawing on both the research literature and his own experience designing "a pedagogy of problems" for Michigan State University's College of Human Medicine in the 1970s, Shulman examines six claims about problem-based learning and other "engaged pedagogies." In keeping with his growing interest in the scholarship of teaching and learning, he looks at the impact of such approaches not only on student learning but also on the learning of faculty as they seek to improve their practice as teachers. The essay has not been published previously.

# 3

# PROBLEM-BASED LEARNING

## THE PEDAGOGIES OF UNCERTAINTY

---

IT ONCE WOULD HAVE BEEN DIFFICULT to imagine an international conference on problem-based learning. As someone who has worked in this field since the 1960s, my colleagues and I at that time would never in our wildest, most enthusiastic dreams have believed that an event such as this were possible—more than six hundred people from all over the United States and around the world, gathered together for two and half days to exchange serious scholarly work about this very interesting genre of pedagogy.

I would like to engage in some nostalgic recollections to provide historical and educational context for the work on problem-based learning represented here. I'll then make some observations about the relationship between the pedagogies of problems and their likely impact on learning. I will direct your attention to look not only at the learning of our students but also at the concomitant learning of teachers and scholars of teaching who engage in the design and execution of problem-based pedagogies.

I begin by clarifying that my remarks today will broadly construe problem-based learning (PBL). That is, I will be talking not about a single model of a single pedagogy but about *a family of approaches*. Rather than limiting myself to the procedures and approaches that Howard Barrows began as a teacher of neurology at McMaster University in the early 1970s, I will treat problem-based pedagogy as a generic envelope, which, if opened and turned upside down, would rain down a diverse array of approaches to teaching. They bear, as I say, a family resemblance—some siblings, some perhaps more like distant fourth cousins—but all share some similar assumptions and make similar claims about learning.

## Origins: Bruner, Dewey, and Others

I begin with nostalgia. My starting point is the "learning by discovery" hypothesis framed by Jerome Bruner back in the fifties and sixties. In *The Process of Education* (and mind you, this was before we knew the word "constructivism" and before most of Piaget was even translated), Bruner (1960) argued that what he referred to as "learning by discovery" would be more engaging and more powerful and bring results more persistent and enduring than learning of the traditional, didactic kind. Of course, Bruner was not the first one to say this. Dewey had made essentially the same argument very powerfully, beginning in about 1895 and continuing throughout his long life. Rousseau made a similar argument, and I'm sure there were even earlier antecedents, for as Alfred North Whitehead once observed, "Everything of importance has been said before by somebody who did not discover it" (quoted in Merton, 1967, p. 1). My point is that the idea of learning through discovery is one that emerged early and has been often repeated. In fact, I would claim it is an idea that has especially needed to be repeated and reiterated, because it's a difficult idea, inherently problematic and even counterintuitive. This family of problem-based pedagogies—as many of you know up close and personal—doesn't gain traction easily.

Bruner's statement of the "learning-by-discovery hypothesis" rapidly attracted both advocates and critics and became even more important during the post-Sputnik rush to create new curricula in the sciences and mathematics so that our students could successfully compete with the Russians. I thus found myself in late January 1966 serving as the youthful "rapporteur" for a five-day conference held by the Social Science Research Council in which Bruner, Robert Gagné, Lee Cronbach, David Hawkins, Jerome Kagan, Richard Atkinson, Robert Glaser, and others came together to examine the state of our knowledge regarding Bruner's hypothesis about the potential of learning by discovery. A book, titled *Learning by Discovery: A Critical Appraisal,* resulted from the conference (Shulman & Keislar, 1966). I assume it will be no surprise that the verdict of the book was mixed, declaring that the power of approaches like discovery learning or problem-centered learning varies enormously—depending on what you're teaching, to whom, to what end, and in what kind of context.

For instance, in Bruner's (1966) chapter in the volume, he begins with an observation that will surprise you if you consider him to be the patron saint of problem-centered discovery learning. He opens with the observation that if we think seriously about the evolution of our species, it would be ludicrous to imagine that discovery is the primary means by which each generation acquired the wisdom of its predecessors. Discovery is hopelessly inefficient and uneconomical. You don't, Bruner tells us, want every generation to have to rediscover the hard-won understandings of all those that preceded it; you don't want every generation to reinvent the Bible or rediscover calculus. Bruner points out that we have to recognize that culture is transmitted not in a Darwinian manner but in a Lamarckian one: we transmit acquired characteristics from generation to generation because we have language, because we have modes of symbolic representation, because we don't have to rely on the chance processes of biological natural selection to pass on important things from one generation to the next.

Bruner nevertheless then went on to describe and extol a variety of examples of discovery learning. But his initial caveat set a tone: discovery learning (or PBL, in the language of this meeting) is not a panacea, and it may not even be the wisest primary means of transmitting what we know from one generation to the next. It must be understood strategically, contextually, and selectively.

In this way, PBL is both different from and like the modern prototype of panaceas, penicillin. It's different because penicillin has a very specific impact on a particular domain of microorganisms, whereas the impact of PBL is varied. But it's like penicillin in the sense that we do not want to go to a physician whose only drug is penicillin—or work with a teacher whose only method is PBL. What's needed, Bruner was reminding us, is an understanding of where such pedagogies can best be used, and how and where they need to be combined with other quite different approaches. What is needed, argued Lee Cronbach (1966, p. 91) is a "judicious blend" of pedagogical strategies.

## Recollections: Medical Education at Michigan State

I now move on to another personal recollection, this time as faculty member at Michigan State University, where I participated in the invention of a new medical school. At the College of Human Medicine, as we called it, we designed a program of instruction for the traditionally *preclinical* first two years of medical school that we called a "focal problems curriculum." (Howard Barrows and Geoffrey Norman, our colleagues and good friends at McMaster University, were beginning their PBL curriculum at about the same time, and we were in constant communication with them during this period.) The opening course, which we creatively dubbed "Phase One," set the tone.

It was the fall term, 1968. On the first day of the first week of the first year of medical school, I was wearing my social scientist hat and team teaching with an M.D. and Ph.D. physiologist; we had ten students in our section. And on this first day of study in the program, we handed our ten students a problem, a case if you will—very short, practically a vignette— of a patient with a sore throat. Nothing exotic. We simply said to the students, "You are the physician. What do you want to know?" and "What do you need to know?" and off we went. That was the structure of much of the medical education program at Michigan State. It was powerful, labor-intensive, exhausting, and exhilarating.

One of the obstacles we faced was that medical students were supposed to take Part One of the National Board of Medical Examiners examination at the end of the first two years of medical school. If students didn't pass those tests, your school didn't get accredited. But there was a problem with the National Board exam; it was predicated on a different set of assumptions about the structure of medical learning and medical understanding than the set of assumptions we had made in inventing this medical school. Indeed, the curriculum assumed by the National Board was the curriculum that was nearly universal across all medical schools in the United States and Canada—a curriculum based on the landmark study by Abraham Flexner.

Flexner, as many of you know, produced one of the earliest reports for The Carnegie Foundation for the Advancement of Teaching, the organization I now head. The Foundation was chartered in 1906, and Flexner's report was begun in 1908 and originally published in 1910 (Flexner, 1972). Based on visits to every medical school in the United States and Canada at that time, Flexner evaluated the extent to which each was a reasonable place to learn medicine, and most of the schools got D's and F's. Indeed, half of the medical schools in North America closed within the next decade. Flexner's report was not the only cause of their demise, but it surely contributed.

The "Flexner curriculum" began with two years of basic science, delivered didactically and with appropriate labs, to be studied by all medical students and organized disciplinarily: a year of each of the basic biological sciences, for example, anatomy, biochemistry, physiology, pharmacology, and the like, and two more years in rotating clinical clerkships. Flexner's model soon became the canonical curriculum, and by the 1960s there were only a few places (like Western Reserve, which used the first two years for basic science but organized them by organ system rather than by discipline) that deviated from Flexner's model. Flexner was, for us at Michigan State, the ultimate enemy.

He was the enemy because we were convinced that students had to learn medicine as a problem-centered activity from the very beginning of medical school. As I mentioned earlier, our move in the problem-based direction put accreditation very much at risk, because we initially told our students not to take the first part of the National Board exam; it was measuring something they were not taught and wouldn't know until the end of four years. We went eyeball-to-eyeball with the National Board on this point, and we lost. Over the subsequent five years, the curriculum was rendered less innovative because of the power of accreditation. The problem focus was retained, but it was much moderated.

I tell this story about the Flexner curriculum because it is associated with a puzzling historical contradiction that I have called the Flexnerian Paradox. Flexner was not, as you might expect, a physician; he was a schoolmaster—the head of a very successful prep school in Louisville, Kentucky. Lawrence Cremin (1961) in his classic history of progressive education, *The Transformation of the School*, recounts how in 1917 Flexner's ideas, in parallel with John Dewey's, became the basis for creating one of the most exciting laboratory schools in the history of America, called the Lincoln School of Teachers College, Columbia University. And what had characterized the Lincoln School? It wasn't organized around disciplines but around themes and problems! So the Flexnerian Paradox is this: Who was the real Flexner? The "evil genius" who created the discipline-based medical curriculum that we at Michigan State were desperately trying to overcome, or the progressive educator who designed a form of elementary education that disdained the disciplines and made themes and problems the organizing framework?

My answer to this puzzle is that both Flexners were real and not so much in conflict as it seems, because his ideas about both medical education and elementary education were *themselves* problem-initiated and problem-based. Medical education, as Flexner encountered it in 1908, was apprenticeship-based, problem-based, contextually rich, and *utterly* undisciplined. The kind of experience that physicians got as they learned medicine was totally out of touch with the scientific progress that was revolutionizing the practice of medicine. And the solution to that problem was not dogmatically to apply a one-size-fits-all theory of education but to establish a discipline-based approach that provided greater rigor and a substantive foundation for practice. After all, the Flexner curriculum did not forgo clinical experience; it merely deferred it for a couple of years.

Ten years later, when Flexner (1916) wrote "A Modern School," an essay that became the basis for the Lincoln School, he looked out at elementary education and saw a stagnant, uninspiring, semiparalyzed activity in which the division of subject areas into feudal fiefdoms called disciplines had sapped all the inspiration and creativity out of both teachers and students. And so, with this problem in mind—a problem distinctly different from the problem he was tackling in medical education—he proposed something very different. My point here is that though we are gathered here at this conference to celebrate problem-based learning, we would be remiss if we treated this potentially powerful pedagogy as a panacea or as a solution to all of education's problems. Instead, it behooves us constantly to ask if this approach is a good one (and I think it is), to ask when it is good, for what, for whom, and in what kind of mix or context.

Indeed, it's useful to recall what Ellen Condliffe Lagemann (2000)—a historian of education—writes about the battle between the psychologist Edward L. Thorndike and John Dewey. In the history of education, Lagemann asserts that Thorndike (representing the tradition of more didactic instruction, with a heavy emphasis on standardized tests) won and Dewey (and the progressive, child-centered pedagogy he advocated) lost. Dewey lost because the more active, problem-based approach was hard to execute well but also because his advocates tended to become zealots, insisting that their way was the *only* way. They wanted to define and dominate the entire curriculum, but in fact, as I will argue here, there may be strong reasons why you don't want PBL (or any other methodological orthodoxy) to write the entire story.

## Six Claims About Problem-Based Learning and Other Pedagogies of Engagement

All this leads me to my second topic: What do those of us who are enthusiastic about problem-based learning and its family of related pedagogies claim that these approaches can accomplish?

In 1997 Russ Edgerton wrote an essay, which was not widely enough disseminated, wherein he characterized this family of problem-centered, student-centered, activity-centered pedagogies with the phrase "pedagogies of engagement." That's a lovely and apt phase because these are indeed pedagogies whose means and end are engagement. And let me commend his idea not only by citing it but by building on it and suggesting that our claims about such pedagogies go well beyond their power to engage. In fact, I believe they are characterized by six features. Problem-based pedagogies are pedagogies of engagement, understanding, performance, reflection, generativity, and finally, commitment. Let me explain what I mean by each of these.

First, when we make the claim that these are powerful forms of teaching and learning, we are claiming that beginning with real problems *engages* students. It engages them in a way that draws them in, stimulates their attention, and holds that attention over a longer period of time than traditional pedagogies. Pedagogies of engagement do exactly what the phrase implies: they engage students. There's a kind of common sense here, for most teachers, because what's the first indicator we use to tell us whether things are going well in class? If students are snoring, or reading the paper, or whispering in the back of the room, we can feel pretty sure that things aren't going very well, and we begin casting about for an approach that will more directly engage students.

But the forms of engagement you can easily observe are not enough; they don't assure that *understanding* is occurring. Most of us have had the sobering experience of discovering on the midterm exam that those three students in the first row who looked so "engaged" (they laughed at our jokes and nodded in all the right places) just didn't get it. As you look at the midterm, you realize that all those alert looks have not translated into understanding of the material. The converse is familiar, as well, because the student who looked totally out of it for weeks turns out to have been paying exquisite attention, to have "gotten it" at a deep level. So pedagogies of understanding are not simply synonymous with pedagogies of engagement; understanding is not independent, but is an additional standard. In the best of all worlds, we have both; that is, I want to find a way to have students both visibly engaged and learning deeply. The claim we wish to make is that these pedagogies not only engage but also promote understanding.

A third claim about these pedagogies is that they lead to *performance.* They take the form not of a didactic discourse on the key ideas of, say, the cardiovascular system, but of the problem of a patient arriving at two o'clock in the morning in the emergency room, reporting shortness of breath, tingling and painful sensations up and down the left arm, pressure-like pain in the middle of the chest. The question is *what to do,* and the problem requires a decision, a judgment, an action—a performance, if you will. The point here is that these pedagogies can take learners beyond understanding as a cognitive phenomenon to understanding that gets linked to or enacted in performance. In this way, PBL means the private is made public—learning that comes out of the closet as performance, in the presence of peers and others, raises the stakes, sharpens the attention, and yes, deepens the learning. That's the claim.

The fourth claim we make is paradoxically the opposite of the third one, namely, that PBL is a pedagogy of *reflection.* That is, we want performance but we also want performance to stop, to be interrupted, and to be reflected upon. We want learners to ask, How did I reach this decision or judgment? Am I going in the right direction? What did I do that makes this performance effective? I call these reflective questions, but in my view, the term *reflection* is overused today; it seems everyone is a reflective practitioner (Schön, 1987) or its synonym. Perhaps we should instead refer to "pedagogies of interruption." Interestingly, many teacher evaluation forms identify (or classify or code) interruptions to the flow of classroom life as negative indicators, regardless of whether those interruptions are truly disruptive or indeed pedagogically useful. And yet we have a growing body of evidence that interruption is as important as flow, that active performance must be balanced with strategic and intentional cessation of performance.

A lovely piece of research in the social anthropology of science helps clarify the power of a pedagogy of interruption. Some of you may have heard me talk in other settings about the wonderful research conducted by Elinor Ochs, a linguistic anthropologist at UCLA. Several years ago, Ochs (Ochs and Jacoby, 1997) studied a group of physicists doing research in high-energy physics, some of them in a lab somewhere in California, others with an affiliated group in France. They were a "distributed" working group. She observed them in the "flow" of their work—writing, doing experiments, making calculations, the things that physicists do. But periodically that flow would be interrupted, because an important physics meeting was approaching, and the working group had to stop and figure out how to condense their complicated, collective work into a ten-minute paper. (In physics, it apparently doesn't matter if you've got a Nobel Prize or $50 million from the Department of Energy, you still have to observe the time limits for giving a paper.) Ochs observed that the conversations among the physicists, as they worked together to summarize and sort out and diagram their work in order to report on it publicly, brought to the surface interesting, different perspectives and assumptions, prompting a new round of "meaning making." Suddenly, they were not just "doing physics" but making sense of their doing, a shift caused by the need to be very explicit with one another about things they had, each of them, taken for granted for months. It was the interruption in the flow of their work that caused this very productive deliberation and reflection, which might otherwise not have occurred. The interruption required that they express their intuitions in public language, which often entailed the use of quite different lenses of interpretation and analysis than they had been using earlier.

The fifth characteristic on my list for these pedagogies is *generativity*. Those of us who are enthusiastic about problem-centered, student-centered kinds of pedagogy harbor the belief that there is something more natural about this kind of learning, that it is generative in the sense that what propels it is engagement with the problem, not the desire simply to pass the next test. The claim here is about the relationship between values and learning and about the power of a personal, deep-seated hunger to know. It is part of a related claim that learning ought to entail a learning-to-learn dimension as well, which brings me to the last of my dimensions, *commitment*.

Here we encounter the overtly emotional and moral component of learning and development. It's clear that many of us who are committed to student-centered pedagogies feel that engagement is not simply attention to the task—it's not just being "on task," to use that once-useful but now-hackneyed phrase we now all use; it's part of a much broader development of emotional and moral commitment to the enterprise of learning. We're interested not only in cognitive growth but also in a new set of dispositions, habits, values, and commitments that lead us to value learning and the process of learning. Such outcomes speak to the deepest passions and hopes that we have for our students.

## Thinking About Impact

I have described six features of problem-based learning and its related family of pedagogies that represent, I think, the claims that are often associated with such approaches. Let us now look at the evidence that might substantiate these claims. What kinds of evidence do we have that PBL moves us and our students in the directions we hope and claim? This is a tough question, and as suggested by my earlier comments, I believe the answers are mixed. Some of the claims can be supported, still others may be clearly refuted, and most remain equivocal, with no clear advantage for problem-based approaches over their alternatives. So, what I'd like to do instead is to explore a slightly different question, not about the effects of problem-based pedagogies on students but about their effects on teachers. We of course expect that teachers are learners, too. Indeed, in most of our settings, teachers are around a lot longer than students, and the impact of these pedagogies of engagement, understanding, and so forth on teachers has the potential to affect our educational institutions and programs in long-term ways.

One hypothesis I'd like to explore in this regard is that involvement with problem-based learning promotes teacher learning far more dramatically than engaging in traditional forms of pedagogy. I believe this is true, paradoxically, because PBL is so very hard to do, to sustain, and to persuade our colleagues to do. In fact, if you wanted to invent a pedagogy that was inherently uncertain, risky, unpredictable, and guaranteed to surprise you,

you would invent some version of discovery or problem-based learning. One of the things that characterizes a really good PBL approach is that students generate ideas you never saw before; they take the class in directions you could never have predicted or planned for. Of course, this is at first deeply unsettling for many faculty, but such uncertainty is precisely the condition that generates learning, which does not, after all, occur when the world goes exactly as you designed it but rather when intention collides with chance and accident. That's when learning occurs. Problem-based pedagogies thus create the conditions that stimulate us to ask, "What in the world just happened?" If what happened was wonderful, you want to "interrupt" the flow of the activity to reflect on how to replicate what was wonderful. And if what happened was a disaster, you want to reflect on how to avoid its repetition. But it's precisely because you were doing something risky and new in the first place that you paid attention to whether it was working or not. In contrast, our established routines become invisible to us. You know the quip that lecture is a way of getting ideas from the notes of the teacher to the notes of the student, without passing through the minds of either. Mind you, I don't mean to demonize lecture, because in the right circumstance it's a highly effective pedagogy. My hypothesis is simply that problem-based learning is a better stimulus to *teacher* learning than are its more didactic, controllable, and predictable alternatives.

I cannot imagine any better evidence for that final claim than this conference, where scholars of teaching and learning from across a wide variety of fields have come together to exchange experiences, reflections, insights, and findings with respect to the deployment of the variety of problem-based pedagogies across your disciplines, institutions, nations, and students. As scholars of such teaching and learning, you are here to learn from each other, and to go public with your own learning, submitting your work and findings for the critical appraisal of your peers. That is precisely what we, at the Carnegie Foundation, call engaging in the scholarship of teaching and learning.

Some of you may know a wonderful observation by the famous Russian psychologist, Ivan Pavlov. Pavlov likened ideas and theories to a bird's wings, because they permit us to soar to the heavens. But facts, observations, and data are like the air, the atmosphere against which those wings must beat, and without which even the most perfect wings will not prevent the bird from plummeting back to earth. You come here inspired by a set of ideas and theories but you come prepared, as well, with evidence— to test, examine, explore, and critique those ideas and theories. Together these two elements give rise to the kind of pedagogical flight we need in order to engage successfully in problem-based learning.

Let me end, as I began, with Jerome Bruner. In one of his classic essays on discovery, Bruner (1965) responds to the question "What is a problem?" by referring to the work of a British philosopher named T. D. Weldon, who distinguished among difficulties, puzzles, and problems. Difficulties are the sources of discomfort, annoyance, and pain that we encounter all the time; life is made up of difficulties, which are by their nature inchoate, fuzzy, ill-defined. Puzzles, on the other hand, are neat, clean, structured, organized; they have a beginning, middle, and an end. If you figure out the rules, you can figure out the puzzle. And then there are problems. A problem is what you have when you find a puzzle whose form you can use to frame and give order to your difficulties.

That, I think, is one way to think about our engagement with problem-based pedagogies. The difficulties are what set off and inspire the problems we present to our students. But the disciplines they learn are like puzzles. Disciplines without authentic difficulties are mere exercises, and difficulties without discipline are just shooting the breeze. But if you can somehow put them together, if difficulties can meet puzzles in the right way, you have moved to a kind of teaching that is truly problem-based. And at that point, the process of deep education begins.

REFERENCES

Bruner, J. *The Process of Education.* Cambridge, Mass.: Harvard University Press, 1960.

Bruner, J. "On Learning Mathematics." In J. Bruner (ed.), *On Knowing: Essays for the Left Hand.* New York: Atheneum, 1965.

Bruner, J. "Some Elements of Discovery." In L. S. Shulman and E. R. Keislar (eds.), *Learning by Discovery: A Critical Appraisal.* Skokie, Ill.: Rand McNally, 1966.

Cremin, L. A. *The Transformation of the School.* New York: Random House/Vintage, 1961.

Cronbach, L. J. "The Logic of Experiments on Discovery." In L. S. Shulman and E. R. Keislar (eds.), *Learning by Discovery: A Critical Appraisal.* Skokie, Ill.: Rand McNally, 1966.

Edgerton, R. *Higher Education* (unpublished white paper). Philadelphia: The Pew Charitable Trusts Education Program, 1997.

Flexner, A. "A Modern School." *American Review of Reviews,* 1916, *53,* 465–474.

Flexner, A. *Medical Education in the United States and Canada: A Report to the Carnegie Foundation for the Advancement of Teaching.* Stanford, Calif.:

Carnegie Foundation for the Advancement of Teaching, 1972. (Originally published 1910.)

Lagemann, E. C. *An Elusive Science: The Troubling History of Education Research*. Chicago: University of Chicago Press, 2000.

Merton, R. K. *On Theoretical Sociology: Five Essays, Old and New*. New York: Free Press, 1967.

Ochs, E., and Jacoby, S. "Down to the Wire: The Cultural Clock of Physicists and the Discourse of Consensus." *Language in Society*, 1997, 26(4), 479–505.

Schön, D. A. *Educating the Reflective Practitioner*. San Francisco: Jossey-Bass, 1987.

Shulman, L. S., and Keislar, E. R. (eds.). *Learning by Discovery: A Critical Appraisal*. Skokie, Ill.: Rand McNally, 1966.

INTRODUCTION

# MAKING DIFFERENCES:
# A TABLE OF LEARNING (2002)

EXERCISING WHAT HE CALLS the "categorical imperative"—
the irresistible urge to classify—Shulman proposes a new
taxonomy geared to the growing interest in pedagogies of engagement in higher education generally and in the work of
The Carnegie Foundation for the Advancement of Teaching
in particular. The taxonomy reflects a highly integrated vision
of learning and also the variety of paths such learning can
take. Relevant to both liberal and professional education, the
table of learning has attracted the interest of many faculty
and campuses. Originally delivered as the opening keynote
address at the American Association for Higher Education's
National Conference in March 2002, the essay was subsequently published in *Change* magazine.

## 4

# MAKING DIFFERENCES

## A TABLE OF LEARNING

---

*At the beginning of God's creating of the heavens and the earth,
when the earth was wild and waste, darkness over the face
of ocean, rushing spirit of God hovering over the face of the
waters—God said: Let there be light! And there was light. God
saw the light: that it was good. God separated the light from the
darkness. God called the light: Day! And the darkness he called:
Night! There was setting, there was dawning, one day.*

—Gen. I:1–5, Everett Fox (1995 translation)
*The Five Books of Moses*, Schocken Books, Inc.

*Some things exist by nature, some from other causes.
Animals and their bodily organs, plants, and the physical
elements—earth, fire, air, and water—such things as these
we say exist by nature.*

—Aristotle, *Physics*, Book 2

*All the world's a stage.*
*And all the men and women merely players,*
*They have their exits and their entrances,*
*And one man in his time plays many parts,*
*His acts being seven ages . . .*
*That ends this strange eventful history,*
*Is second childishness and mere oblivion,*
*Sans teeth, sans eyes, sans taste, sans everything*

—*As You Like It,* 2.7.139–167

ONE OF THE CENTRAL WAYS we make sense of experience is by making differences. The world presents itself without inherent order, and our impulse is to place things in piles, count them, and name them. In the act of creation, day is divided from night. Aristotle classifies just about everything. Shakespeare gives us the seven ages of man, Dante maps the circles of hell, Burton anatomizes melancholy . . . In ways that Kant never intended by the phrase, we are driven by a "categorical imperative," the irresistible impulse to place things in categories.

This is not an irrational impulse. Distinctions and taxonomies are tools for thought. We make distinctions for the same reasons we carve a turkey or write our books in chapters—to make the world more manageable. And it's only natural that we further order our distinctions and categories into systems, tables, and taxonomies.

The systems sometimes entail stages or hierarchies that imply a sequence of merit or maturity (for example, the biological phyla progressing from single cells to human beings). Sometimes there is no implied hierarchy (as in libraries, university catalogues, and the four basic food groups). We may propose systems that look like a call for balance and new priorities, as in Ernest Boyer's four scholarships.

Categories and distinctions also can call attention to ideas, principles, or values that hitherto have been ignored. In my own work on knowledge for teaching, for example, I once argued that it was insufficient merely to distinguish between content knowledge and pedagogical knowledge of teaching methods. I proposed a new category, *pedagogical content knowledge,* as a way of signaling that there was a missing component in our theories of teaching.

That concept, often called PCK, became a tool for thought, an analytic category, a mnemonic, and even a call to action. As a new category, it was like a new piece of furniture in the living room. It changed the landscape and created both new opportunities and new barriers. In short, for all the post-modern criticisms and deconstruction of distinctions and taxonomies, they sometimes come in quite handy. Indeed, as educators, one of the ways we can make a difference is by making distinctions.

## A New Table of Learning

There is no such thing as a "new" taxonomy; all the likely taxonomies have been invented, and in nearly infinite variety. Probably the single most famous list in the world of educational thought is the Taxonomy of Educational Objectives devised by my one-time teacher Benjamin Bloom. I can't begin to talk about a new taxonomy without acknowledging the invaluable contributions of Bloom and his colleagues—as well as other taxonomic pioneers including Lawrence Kohlberg, Grant Wiggins, and William Perry, among others, who have attempted to create a system for classifying the kinds of learning we seek for our students. Here then, stark and unadorned, is what I will call Shulman's Table of Learning:

Engagement and Motivation

Knowledge and Understanding

Performance and Action

Reflection and Critique

Judgment and Design

Commitment and Identity

That's all there is. If you ask what comes after commitment and identity, I will suggest it is new engagements and motivations. Like the brave souls whose job it is to paint the Golden Gate Bridge, when you reach the end you return to the beginning. The table meets the mnemonic criterion of seven items plus or minus two, so it's a list you can probably remember without notes. It's also a list you can forget when forgetting, as I'll suggest later, is appropriate.

In a nutshell, the taxonomy makes the following assertion: Learning begins with student engagement, which in turn leads to knowledge and understanding. Once someone understands, he or she becomes capable of performance or action. Critical reflection on one's practice and understanding leads to higher-order thinking in the form of a capacity to exercise judgment in the face of uncertainty and to create designs in the presence of constraints and unpredictability. Ultimately, the exercise of judgment makes possible the development of commitment. In commitment, we become capable of professing our understandings and our values, our faith and our love, our skepticism and our doubts, internalizing those attributes and making them integral to our identities. These commitments, in turn, make new engagements possible—and even necessary.

## The Roots of This Work

About five years ago, when Russ Edgerton was serving as education officer for The Pew Charitable Trusts, he produced a terrific white paper, which has propelled many of the most interesting initiatives in higher education today. One of Russ's arguments focused on something he called "pedagogies of engagement"—approaches that have within them the capacity to engage students actively with learning in new ways. He wasn't talking only about service learning, though service learning was an example; he was talking about an array of approaches, from problem-based and project-based learning to varieties of collaborative work and field-based instruction. Russ used the rubric "pedagogies of engagement" to describe them all.

For me, there was an intriguing ambiguity associated with Edgerton's phrase and the claims implicit in it. Is engagement a means to an end, a proxy, or an end in itself? Are pedagogies of engagement a way to involve the minds, the hearts, the hands and feet, the passions and interests of students who are otherwise inclined to learn passively? Is the hallmark of these pedagogies the fact that they grab the student's interest? Or is their purpose not only to grab but to hold that interest, not only to entice but to instruct?

Or—a third possibility—did Edgerton intend to claim that engagement is a worthwhile end in itself, and that often an educator's responsibility is to make it possible for students to engage in experiences they would never otherwise have had? After all, we attend a chamber music concert as an end in itself, not as a means to some other end. These questions in response to Edgerton's discussion of pedagogies were one source of my thinking about the relationship between engagement and other dimensions of learning.

A second stimulus for the taxonomy was the study of professional education that The Carnegie Foundation for the Advancement of Teaching is now undertaking, looking concurrently at preparation for law, engineering, teaching, and the clergy. One emerging theme in this work is that learning to be a professional isn't a purely intellectual endeavor. To become a professional, one must learn not only to think in certain ways but also to perform particular skills, and to practice or act in ways consistent with the norms, values, and conventions of the profession. Thus, to learn to be a lawyer one needs to *think* like a lawyer, *perform* like a lawyer, and *act* like a lawyer.

*Acting* is more than knowing something or performing well; it seems to involve the development of a set of values, commitments, or internalized dispositions. It reminds me of what theological educators talk about as *formation*—the development of an identity that integrates one's capacities and dispositions to create a more generalized orientation to practice. Moreover, professionals cannot, in principle, learn all that they will need while they remain in school. Professional education must have at its core the concept of ongoing individual and collective learning, because the experiences of engaging, understanding, and acting must become the basis for subsequent learning and development.

These and other reflections about Carnegie's work on professional education triggered a "categorical imperative," and I responded by trying to invent a more ordered system, a table of learning or a taxonomy of educational ends.

## What Are the Uses of Taxonomies?

To answer this question, and to say something about the history and nature of taxonomies, I want to return to the work of Benjamin Bloom. What motivated Bloom and his colleagues to create taxonomies in the first place?

It was the late 1940s, and, partially in response to the needs of veterans returning from World War II eager to get a superb education, undergraduate liberal education was experiencing yet another renaissance (they occur rather regularly). "General education" was the mantra of the day, and it posed interesting problems for practitioners. One problem was that everyone agreed that general education should be about more than putting discrete items of knowledge into students' heads, that knowledge wasn't enough; the question was, "What more is there? Knowledge and *then what?*" Educators needed a language, a set of terms for making sense of the general education world.

About the same time, some campuses that were developing new general education programs made the very interesting decision to distinguish the roles of teacher, mentor, and instructor from those of evaluator, judge, and grader. The result was an arrangement such as I encountered as a student at the University of Chicago—the Examiner's Office, directed by Bloom, designed to develop assessments that would measure and evaluate how well students had learned what the general education program intended to teach.

The challenge was to ensure that what was assessed was compatible with what was taught. It made no sense at all to have instruction and assessment marching to different drummers (even though we now do that as a matter of public policy in K–12 and are in danger of doing so in post-secondary education). Educators needed a new language, a lexicon, to connect and align teaching and assessment. Bloom and his colleagues spent a number of years developing this common language, and because the concern for its existence was shared across institutions, dozens of institutions collaborated.

So what did this common language look like? Many educators across the world know the six categories of Bloom's Taxonomy of Educational Objectives by heart: knowledge, comprehension, application, analysis, synthesis, and evaluation. Complicating things further, Bloom recognized that the cognitive domain was only part of the picture, so, several years later, the Affective Domain Taxonomy was added by Krathwohl, Bloom, and Masia. It depicts how learners move from a willingness to receive an experience, to beginning to respond to it, to valuing what is taught, to organizing it within their larger set of values and attitudes, and ultimately to internalizing those values such that they no longer need an external stimulus to trigger the associated affective and emotional responses.

| THE COGNITIVE TAXONOMY | THE AFFECTIVE TAXONOMY |
|---|---|
| Knowledge | Receiving |
| Comprehension | Responding |
| Application | Valuing |
| Analysis | Organizing |
| Synthesis | Internalizing |
| Evaluation | |

What can we learn from Bloom about the uses and perhaps abuses of taxonomies? One thing that happened is that the categories quickly became far more than rubrics for assessment. Taxonomies exist to classify and to clarify, but they also serve to guide and to goad. People rapidly began to use Bloom (and related schemes) as frameworks for designing courses and programs. They used the taxonomies to determine if they were putting too much emphasis on knowledge; if they were teaching for comprehension; if they were teaching for analysis or synthesis; if students at the end of a course were able to evaluate and make critical judgments about the relative value of alternative ways of making sense of the world.

Quickly, then, the taxonomies moved from being a scoring rubric and vehicle for communicating about test items, to being a heuristic for instructional design. (It's worth noting that although William Perry's model became as central to discussions of higher education and its goals as Bloom's has been in elementary and secondary education, the two literatures have developed quite independently. Between 1972 and 2002, Social SciSearch listed 1687 citations of Bloom, and 692 of Perry, but only 30 items that cite both.)

Moreover, we see that these heuristics are not value-free; indeed, they rapidly become ideologies, a form of collective conscience. Disciples of Bloom soon switched from asking, "Do we have the right balance between higher- and lower-order thinking in the design of our course?" to asking, "Shouldn't we be teaching more higher-order thinking?" A moral obligation to teach synthesis (not to mention evaluation) was created, and the taxonomies evolved from an ostensibly dispassionate framework into ideologies that had real, normative implications (though not necessarily bad ones). This is how taxonomies often work: They become ideologies. A taxonomy's rapid progression from analytic description to normative system—literally becoming a pedagogical conscience—warrants caution.

Another thing that happens to taxonomies, and it happened to Bloom's, is that they come to be understood as making a theoretical claim about sequentiality and hierarchy, suggesting that the only legitimate way to learn something is in *this particular order*. The implication of sequence and hierarchy within taxonomies obscures their true value because taxonomies are not and should not be treated as theories. They are *certainly* not grand theories. At their best, they are what Robert Merton has called, coining a very useful concept, "theories of the middle range."

A theory of the middle range can be thought about in many ways: as an extended metaphor, a limited explanatory principle, or even a story. Thus, Bloom's cognitive taxonomy tells the story of education beginning with the acquisition by rote of facts that someone else has taught you and which you are only expected to reproduce or repeat. The story becomes more exciting as knowing matures into understanding and application, and then even more adventurous as ideas are subjected to analysis, as new ideas can be created and synthesized, and finally, at the highest level, as the learner becomes capable of judging and evaluating the truth or usefulness of the ideas themselves. That's the narrative version of Bloom's taxonomy.

Here then (I cannot resist) is a possible taxonomy (or is it a typology?) of the uses of taxonomies:

USES OF TAXONOMIES

Lexicon; working vocabulary; language

Classification (library, catalogue, Carnegie Classification)

Elements to be balanced (food groups; Boyer's scholarships)

Assessment and design framework; protocol for analysis

Middle-range theory

Master narrative

Mnemonic; checklist; heuristic

Ideology; conscience; moral code

Elements to be played with

## A Table of Learning: Elaborating the Elements

Now let us return to the Table of Learning, which I introduced earlier as a taxonomy of liberal and professional learning. What do its six elements mean, and how are they related?

The first item on the list, *engagement,* is one of the most interesting and important aspects of learning. We rarely paid enough attention to it in the past, but higher education is now much more focused on "active learning" and on evidence that students are engaged in worthwhile educational experiences. Indeed, it's interesting that one of the instruments receiving the most attention in the last couple of years has been the National Survey of Student Engagement (NSSE)—another product of Russ Edgerton's work at Pew and an intended antidote to the reputational ranking systems that many of us find so infuriating.

The argument NSSE makes is that we want to know about student engagement because it serves as a proxy for learning, understanding, and postgraduation commitments that we cannot measure very well directly, or that we would have to wait 20 years to measure. As noted earlier, however, I would argue that engagement is not solely a proxy; it can also be an end in itself. Our institutions of higher education are settings where students can encounter a range of people and ideas and human experiences that they have never been exposed to before. Engagement in this sense is not just a proxy for learning but a fundamental purpose of education.

*Understanding* is the category we spend most of our time as educators worrying about, as well we should. It includes knowledge, and it includes the ability to restate in one's own words the ideas learned from others. In fact, one way of putting it is to say that understanding means knowing the difference between paraphrase and plagiary. It also means knowing when we can claim an understanding for ourselves, when we can claim an understanding of the work of those whose sources we acknowledge, and when we can say, "I didn't know this, but somebody else did and here it is." In contrast to knowledge and information, understanding connotes a form of ownership.

Next we come to *performance, practice,* or *action.* For me the difference between understanding and practice lies in the fact that acts of understanding are always based on what's in our heads. Even performances of understanding, such as writing an essay, are still about the ideas themselves. But as we move toward performance or practice we start to act in and on the world, to change things in it, and therefore a different set of consequences are associated with performance than with understanding.

We in the academy would love to believe that one can't practice or perform without first understanding. Alas, we all know that's not true (those of us who've raised children certainly know it's not true, neither for the raiser nor the raisee). During my decade of work in medical diagnosis, I studied gifted internists to understand how they made diagnostic judgments. A good friend, the Australian surgeon Ken Cox, came to me one day and said, "Lee, you're doing pioneering work on internists, trying to learn how their diagnoses lead to courses of action, but there's a big difference between internists and surgeons."

"Internists," he said, "make a diagnosis in order to act. Surgeons act in order to make a diagnosis." That may be a frightening thought for anyone facing surgery, but if you're wheeled into the emergency room with severe abdominal pain, and the physician treating you says he needs to do three days of tests before he acts, your family may want to begin saying their farewells to you. There are times when action is absolutely necessary in order to figure out what's going on, rather than waiting to figure out what's going on in order to act. My point is that the directionality of the taxonomy is situational; it isn't always the same. Practice may be the crucible in which understanding is tested, or in which commitment is affirmed; it's the pivot point, one might argue, around which most of education revolves.

I've already commented on the relationship between *critical reflection* and action. But let me add that the connection between critical reflection and action is in some ways a paradoxical one because in order to act in the most effective ways, we sometimes must cease action. Eleanor Ochs, an anthropologist, studied a team of physicists working on a large-scale collaborative research project. It was, she found, when they had to stop their research in order to prepare papers for a conference (which felt to them like an interruption) that they made important discoveries about how to move forward with the next stage of research. At the Carnegie Foundation, we often talk about our work as attempts to provide mirrors and lenses that can assist others to pause, reflect, and see their work differently as they move into a next stage of activity. Thus, action without reflection is unlikely to produce learning.

*Judgment and design* are like understanding—only different. They're what happens when understanding meets the constraints and complexities of a world with respect to which we can no longer say (as we might in a world of ideas alone), "all other things being equal . . . " When I design a home, I work within constraints of budget, terrain, and lifestyle of the person for whom I'm designing it. I'm limited, too, by codes and regulations of the county in which it's being built; a home will look different in a tectonically challenged part of the world like Palo Alto, California, as opposed to one that is challenged by tornadoes, like East Lansing, Michigan. Design is a matter of exercising understanding, as well as applying skills, under a variety of constraints and contingencies.

By the same token, when we're asked to exercise judgment—and I think this is why Bloom put evaluation so high on his taxonomy—we are being asked to take into consideration multiple factors and constantly to compare those factors to values and standards that may themselves be shifting, in order to make some evaluative judgment about quality, courses of action, or people. So, while judgment is like understanding, it's also *not* the same, and, as educators, we need to go beyond teaching and assessing for understanding in order to foster judgment and design. Of course, the training of engineers is mostly about design, and education in areas like law, music, and art is often about judgment. There's much to be learned from these disciplines.

Finally, we come to *commitment.* As noted earlier, we experience commitment as we internalize values, develop character, and become people who no longer need to be goaded to behave in ethical, moral, or publicly responsible ways. We also commit ourselves to larger groups, larger communities, larger congregations, and professions at large—and by doing so, we make a statement that we take the values and principles of that group seriously enough to make them our own.

Therefore, commitment is both moving inward *and* connecting outward; it is the highest attainment an educated person can achieve, and it is also the most dangerous—I don't think I have to explain why, given the state of world affairs these days. An educated person, I would argue, is someone whose commitments always leave open a window for skeptical scrutiny, for imagining how it might be otherwise.

So, what does the Table of Learning look like with all of its elements working in concert, as a narrative? I proposed one for Bloom earlier, and here is mine.

Once upon a time someone was engaged in an experience of learning. And that engagement was so profound that it led to her understanding things she didn't understand before, and therefore gave her the capacity to practice and to act in the world in new ways. But once she started acting in the world, she realized that action doesn't always work out as intended, so she had to start looking at what she was doing and at the consequences of her actions. This meant re-examining her actions to see whether she might want to act differently.

Through that kind of reflection on her own performance and under-standing, she became wiser and capable of making judgments and devis-ing designs in situations that were progressively more uncertain. And as she did so, she began to internalize the values that she had been exposed to, at which point she was no longer merely engaged but truly commit-ted. Those commitments, in turn, disposed her to seek out new engage-ments, which led (of course the story is a circle) to new understandings and practices . . .

Isn't that a lovely story? Well, we can tell a similar story using Perry's Model, Kohlberg's Stages of Moral Development, or the levels of Dante's *Inferno* (indeed, learning is what Dante's epic poem is all about). And again, these are not trivial narratives because they offer us coherent ways of thinking about why we do what we do, where we're coming from, and where we're going as educators.

What is important about these taxonomies is that they are indeed heuristics. They help us think more clearly about what we're doing, and they afford us a language through which we can exchange ideas and di-lemmas. They point to the mutually interdependent facts of an educated person's life of mind, of emotion, and of action. They are powerful in these ways as long as we don't take them too seriously, as long as we don't trans-form mnemonic into dogma or heuristic into orthodoxy.

## Shuffling the Deck: Playing at the Table

One way to forestall premature cementing and misuse of the categories is to recognize from the beginning that there is no single "first stage." For example, while the Table of Learning lists *commitment* as the terminal stage of a sequence, the closing chapter of the narrative as it were, it's possible to imagine a situation in which commitment is itself the starting point for new learning.

Several years ago, I had the wonderful experience of visiting Messiah College as part of the Carnegie Foundation's work on moral and civic education. One thing that struck me was that Messiah's students arrive already committed. As a faith-based institution, the college naturally attracts students from religious families—students who are members of congregations and who already have a deep-seated set of commitments.

Our site-visit team talked to students about the goal of the first-year experience at Messiah, and they said, as with one voice, "The faculty is out to challenge our faith." And the reason, as our interviews with faculty made clear, is that students' prior commitments need to be exposed to the crucible of engagement with texts and people with different views. Only then, only through new engagements, can stronger commitments be formed. For Messiah, therefore, the Table of Learning might well look like this:

Commitment (to religious beliefs and practices)

Performance (of rituals and prosocial actions)

Engagement (with new texts and ideas)

Understanding (of new ideas and doubt of certainty)

Reflection (on tension between faith and "reason")

Judgment (deliberations, dialectics, debates)

New commitment (to beliefs, practices, faith, and reason)

New engagements . . . .

What's interesting is the cyclical quality of all this. Successfully committed people are more disposed to engage—they don't just sit home and feel committed (although that depends on whether it's an intransitive or transitive verb, doesn't it?). Commitment is a powerful stage in the learning process because it engenders new engagements, which in turn engender new understandings, and so forth.

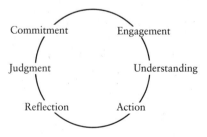

If commitment and engagement have a potentially paired relationship with one another, might this be the case for other learning goals as well? For example: How do we get understanding to lead to the capacity for judgment and design when the conditions in which understanding can be displayed become fuzzier, more variable, more ambiguous, less readily controlled? And how, once we have engendered in people the disposition to act in the world, do we get them to stop acting and to step back in order to think about what they're doing? The next diagram emphasizes those particular pairings within the cycle of learning.

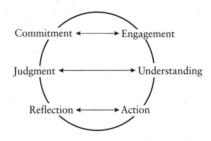

Which leads me to another observation about these taxonomies, which is that taxonomies exist to be played with, not to be read devotionally. Let me give you an example of playing with a taxonomy.

What this version of the table suggests is that knowledge, understanding, analysis, and design each need, on the one hand, to be worked upon in a critical and reflective manner via judgment and, on the other hand, to be enacted in practice as a crucible or reality test for the ideas. You may think of yet other ways to relate the central terms. My point is that once we feel comfortable with a set of terms, we can begin to play with them. They are, after all, propositions and not received wisdom; they are ideas that become useful when we treat them seriously and yet with a bit of skepticism, disrespect, and playfulness—which, interestingly, is an attitude that we try to foster in our students, as well, with regard to much of what we teach them.

In short, I propose the Table of Learning not because it's theoretically valid or true—no taxonomy is—but because I find it practically and theoretically useful, conceptually robust, and fun. (My categories are evocative of the classic Greek standards of good architecture: commodity, firmness, and delight.) Having these terms and ideas in front of me, in a small enough number so that I can actually hold them in my mind (which gets harder as I get older), is helpful because they serve as a mnemonic, a heuristic, a way of helping me think about a wide range of educational conditions and situations.

I find the taxonomy valuable, as well, because I can use it to think not only about students but also about *institutions*. NSSE is relevant here again because it recognizes that engagement may apply not only to individual students but to their institutions. One now regularly hears the phrase "the engaged university." It rolls trippingly off the tongue, but it's important to begin defining more precisely what it means.

Is an engaged university one where certain patterns of engagements are characteristic of individuals or groups of students? Or is an engaged university one where students are highly motivated to engage with the texts and experiences that the institution deems valuable? Of course these are not mutually exclusive meanings. And one might ask the same question about other elements of the taxonomy. For example, what might it mean to be an "understanding university"?

With respect to "commitment," can we speak of an institution that matures from being merely engaged to one that is committed—and how would we know the difference? Here's one possible basis for knowing: If an institution becomes engaged because of its leadership and key people, from the president's office to the faculty, then what happens to the institution when those key people leave?

I might argue that at an engaged institution one would soon see a return to what was happening before, but at an institution that had moved from engagement to commitment, the culture of the place would remain changed. A committed institution's culture has been internalized in some fashion, so that even when the original perpetrators move on, the institution remains committed to continuing engagement. One of the great challenges for leadership is how to create this kind of committed institution, and it's one of the great challenges for us as teachers.

I can also use the Table of Learning to think about myself. A framework that leaves no room for describing the work of the person who created it should make us suspicious. This is what Merton meant when he talked about the need for theories to be "self-exemplifying." Similarly, Joseph Schwab, my teacher at the University of Chicago, once left us on a Friday with this little question: "And where is Plato on Plato's divided line? Where is Plato sitting in the cave when he is thinking about the cave?" It *killed* my entire weekend. And so the Table of Learning invites me to think about my own learning as a teacher and a scholar. Indeed, I would argue that it can, in some ways, serve as a model for faculty development across the career, reminding us that *all* education is continuing education.

## Antinomies and the Concordance of Opposites

Nancy Cantor and Steven Schomberg have written eloquently about their concept of education, and they pose a couple of intriguing antinomies. One is that undergraduate education involves a critical balance between playfulness and responsibility. On one hand, students come to our campuses to learn to play with ideas, which, paradoxically, means that they must take ideas seriously enough to consider playing with them. On the other hand, students come to our campuses to learn that education is also about developing a sense of obligation and responsibility to the society that will benefit from their capacity to play with ideas ever more creatively and insightfully. In a similar vein, they see the university as simultaneously a place apart—the ivory tower is needed because it's hard to play in the middle of Times Square—*and* a place connected to communities and to society.

As we look at our purposes for education, and at the taxonomies that aim to give language and shape to those purposes, we need to keep front and center our recognition of the contrasts, the tensions, the antinomies—seeing them not as problems but as opportunities to define our roles. Engagement on the part of students is a goal, and we ought to stipulate it and measure it and take responsibility for it, but there are times and purposes for which we will instead seek *dis*engagement.

These are not contradictions; they are mutually supportive, compatible, and interdependent. We seek understanding for the pleasure and confidence it brings, and we seek puzzlement or self-conscious ignorance for the mental itching and scratching it engenders. We want students who will leave our institutions deeply committed to values and civic and moral responsibility; yet we must never forget that they must also be committed to skepticism and doubt. We foster the transformation of thought into action, but we also strive to educate for delay, self-criticism, and reflection. These equally important goals must be taught and assessed in ways that taxonomies, properly understood and used, can help us do in powerful ways.

## A Look in the Mirror

In the spirit of self-critical reflection, I want to conclude by expressing some misgivings I have about the elements that appear in the Table of Learning—and about what's missing. In particular, I'm sensitive to the potential or apparent absence of emotion, collaboration, and the centrality of trust.

Although engagement and commitment are certainly constructs intended to convey a strong component of emotion and feelings, I worry that the table as a whole feels overly cognitive. How might it be revised or interpreted to remind those who use it of the centrality of the emotions in the motivation to learn, the exercise of reason, and the development of character—all legitimate and necessary aspects of any vision of the well-educated person? This is something I will continue to think about.

The table may also seem to convey a strongly individual orientation. Yet engagement is often collaborative with others, and commitment frequently involves the development of, and membership in, communities. Moreover, the exercise of understanding, practice, reflection, and judgment or design is increasingly collaborative in character, drawing upon distributed expertise adroitly combined, rather than on the power of solo performances.

In both the emotional and collaborative aspects of learning, the development of trust becomes central. Learners must learn both to trust and to be worthy of trust. If learners are to employ their achievement of the goals of liberal and professional education to take on the responsibilities of leadership in a democratic community and society, their good judgment needs to be exercised in a context of trust and interdependence. Are these perspectives utterly missing in the table? Or are they embedded in the ideas, if only those who use them are conscious of them?

Taken together, these concerns about missing or underemphasized features of the table remind us that although a taxonomy is not a theory, it shares many of the virtues and liabilities of theory. A system of categories is an attempt to simplify and order a complex and chaotic world. The unavoidable price of simplification is to make some views salient while others fade into the background. That is why all such systems need to be used with a combination of reverence and skepticism.

What then do I hope for this Table of Learning? I hope it will be useful precisely because its parts are so familiar. It offers us familiar blocks to rearrange, with its echoes of Bloom and Perry, of Krathwohl and Kohlberg. I hope that it will serve as a set of heuristics, as a stimulus for thinking about the design and evaluation of education, and as the basis for creative narratives about the learning process. Indeed, I hope it will variously contribute to all the functions I described earlier as the uses of taxonomies. I hope it will guide and inform both invention and critique. And I certainly hope that it will be used playfully rather than devotionally or dogmatically.

When speaking of the goals of science, Alfred North Whitehead once declared, "Seek generalizations—and distrust them!" In the same spirit, I urge you, "Seek taxonomies—and play with them!"

## RESOURCES

Anderson, Lorin W., and David R. Krathwohl, Eds., *A Taxonomy for Learning, Teaching and Assessment: A Revision of Bloom's Taxonomy of Educational Objectives*. New York: Longman, 2001.

Anderson, Lorin W., and Lauren A. Sosniak, Eds., *Bloom's Taxonomy: A Forty-Year Retrospective, Ninety-Third Yearbook of the National Society for the Study of Education*. Chicago: University of Chicago Press, 1994.

Bloom, Benjamin S., and collaborators, *The Taxonomy of Educational Objectives: Cognitive Domain*. New York: David McKay, 1956.

Edgerton, Russ, *Higher Education* (unpublished white paper). Philadelphia: The Pew Charitable Trusts Education Program, 1997.

Krathwohl, David R., Benjamin S. Bloom, and Bertram B. Masia, *Taxonomy of Educational Objectives: Affective Domain*. New York: David McKay, 1964.

"National Survey of Student Engagement: The College Student Report," www.indiana.edu/~nsse/.

Perry, William G., Jr., *Forms of Intellectual and Ethical Growth During the College Years: A Scheme*. New York: Holt Rinehart and Winston, 1970.

Rhem, James, "Of Diagrams and Models: Learning as a Game of Pinball," *National Teaching and Learning Forum*, Vol. 11, No. 4, 2002, www.ntlf.com/html/ti/diagrams/htm.

Wiggins, Grant, *Educative Assessment: Designing Assessments to Inform and Improve Performance*. San Francisco: Jossey-Bass, 1998.

## PART TWO

# THE PROFESSION
# OF TEACHING

# INTRODUCTION

# KNOWLEDGE AND TEACHING: FOUNDATIONS OF THE NEW REFORM (1987)

THIS ESSAY, the earliest piece in the collection, was originally published in the February 1987 issue of the *Harvard Educational Review*. Intended for a specialized audience of scholars in teacher education, "Knowledge and Teaching" appears in the companion volume, *The Wisdom of Practice: Essays on Teaching, Learning, and Learning to Teach,* but is included here as well because it sets the stage for Shulman's work on teaching in higher education more generally. In contrast to prevailing views of teaching as generic technique, he argues for a more substantive, knowledge-based model in which the discipline plays an essential role.

# KNOWLEDGE AND TEACHING

## FOUNDATIONS OF THE NEW REFORM

---

## Prologue: A Portrait of Expertise

Richly developed portrayals of expertise in teaching are rare. While many characterizations of effective teachers exist, most of these dwell on the teacher's management of the classroom. We find few descriptions or analyses of teachers that give careful attention not only to the management of students in classrooms, but also to the management of *ideas* within classroom discourse. Both kinds of emphasis will be needed if our portrayals of good practice are to serve as sufficient guides to the design of better education. Let us examine one brief account.

---

○

---

A twenty-five-year veteran English teacher, Nancy, was the subject of a continuing study of experienced teachers that we had been conducting. The class was nearing the end of the second week of a unit on *Moby Dick*. The observer had been well impressed with the depth of Nancy's understanding of that novel and her skill as a pedagogue, as she documented how Nancy helped a group of California high school juniors grasp the many faces of that masterpiece. Nancy was a highly active teacher, whose classroom style employed substantial interaction with her students, both through recitations and more open-ended discussion. She was like a symphony conductor, posing questions, probing for alternative views, drawing out the shy while tempering the boisterous. Not much happened in the classroom that did not pass through Nancy, whose pacing and ordering, structuring and expanding, controlled the rhythm of classroom life.

Nancy characterized her treatment of literature in terms of a general theoretical model that she employed.

> Basically, I break reading skills into four levels:
>
> *Level 1* is simply translation. . . . It is understanding the literal meaning, denotative, and frequently for students that means getting a dictionary.
>
> *Level 2* is connotative meaning and again you are still looking at the words. . . . What does that mean, what does that tell us about the character? . . . We looked at *The Scarlet Letter.* Hawthorne described a rose bush in the first chapter. Literal level is: What is a rose bush? More important, what does a rose bush suggest, what is it that comes to mind, what did you picture?
>
> *Level 3* is the level of interpretation. . . . It is the implication of Levels 1 and 2. If the author is using a symbol, what does that say about his view of life? In *Moby Dick,* the example I used in class was the boots. The boots would be the literal level. What does it mean when he gets under the bed? And the students would say, he is trying to hide something. Level 3 would be what does Melville say about human nature? What is the implication of this? What does this tell us about this character?
>
> *Level 4* is what I call application and evaluation and I try, as I teach literature, to get the students to Level 4, and that is where they take the literature and see how it has meaning for their own lives. Where would we see that event occur in our own society? How would people that we know be behaving if they are doing what these characters are doing? How is this piece of literature similar to our common experiences as human beings? . . . So my view of reading is basically to take them from the literal on the page to making it mean something in their lives. In teaching literature I am always working in and out of those levels. (Gudmundsdottir, in preparation)

Nancy employed this conceptual framework in her teaching, using it to guide her own sequencing of material and formulation of questions. She taught the framework explicitly to her students over the semester, helping them employ it like a scaffolding to organize their own study of the texts, to monitor their own thinking. Although as a teacher she maintained tight control of the classroom discourse, her teaching goals were to liberate her students' minds through literacy, eventually to use great works of literature to illuminate their own lives. Whichever work she was teaching, she understood how to organize it, frame it for teaching, divide it appropriately for assignments and activities. She seemed to possess a mental index for these books she had taught so often—*The Red Badge of Courage, Moby Dick, The Scarlet Letter, The Adventures of Huckleberry Finn*—with key episodes organized in her mind for different pedagogical purposes, different levels of difficulty, different kinds of pupils, different themes or emphases. Her combination of subject-matter understanding and pedagogical skill was quite dazzling.

When the observer arrived at the classroom one morning, she found Nancy sitting at her desk as usual. But her morning greeting elicited no response from Nancy other than a grimace and motion toward the pad of paper on her desktop. "I have laryngitis this morning and will not be able to speak aloud," said the note. What's more, she appeared to be fighting the flu, for she had little energy. For a teacher who managed her classroom through the power of her voice and her manner, this was certainly a disabling condition. Or was it?

Using a combination of handwritten notes and whispers, she divided the class into small groups by rows, a tactic she had used twice before during this unit. Each group was given a different character who has a prominent role in the first chapters of the novel, and each group was expected to answer a series of questions about that character. Ample time was used at the end of the period for representatives of each group to report to the whole class. Once again the class had run smoothly, and the subject matter had been treated with care. But the style had changed radically, an utterly different teaching technology was employed, and still the students were engaged, and learning appeared to occur.

Subsequently, we were to see many more examples of Nancy's flexible style, adapted to the characteristics of learners, the complexities of subject matter, and her own physical condition. When learners experienced serious problems with a particular text, she self-consciously stayed at the lower levels of the reading ladder, helping the students with denotative and connotative meanings, while emphasizing literary interpretations somewhat less. When teaching *Huck Finn,* a novel she saw as less difficult than *Moby Dick,* her style changed once again. She gave much more autonomy to the students and did not directly run the classroom as much.

For *Huck Finn,* she abandoned the stage early on and let the students teach each other. She had the students working independently in eight multi-ability groups, each group tracing one of eight themes: hypocrisy; luck and superstition; greed and materialism; romantic ideas and fantasy; religion and the Bible; social class and customs; family, racism, and prejudice; freedom and conscience. There were only two reading checks at the beginning and only two rounds of reporting. Once the groups were underway, Nancy took a seat at the back of the class and only interacted with students when she was called upon, and during group presentations. (Gudmundsdottir, in preparation)

Thus Nancy's pattern of instruction, her style of teaching, is not uniform or predictable in some simple sense. She flexibly responds to the difficulty and character of the subject matter, the capacities of the students (which can change even over the span of a single course), and her educational purposes. She can not only conduct her orchestra from the podium, she can sit back and watch it play with virtuosity by itself.

○

What does Nancy believe, understand, and know how to do that permits her to teach as she does? Can other teachers be prepared to teach with such skill? The hope that teaching like Nancy's can become typical instead of unusual motivates much of the effort in the newly proposed reforms of teaching.

## The New Reforms

During the past year the U.S. public and its professional educators have been presented with several reports on how to improve teaching as both an activity and a profession. One of the recurring themes of these reports has been the professionalization of teaching—the elevation of teaching to a more respected, more responsible, more rewarding and better rewarded occupation. The claim that teaching deserves professional status, however, is based on a more fundamental premise: that the standards by which the education and performance of teachers must be judged can be raised and more clearly articulated. The advocates of professional reform base their arguments on the belief that there exists a "knowledge base for teaching"—a codified or codifiable aggregation of knowledge, skill, understanding, and technology, of ethics and disposition, of collective responsibility—as well as a means for representing and communicating it. The reports of the

Holmes Group (1986) and the Carnegie Task Force (1986) rest on this belief and, furthermore, claim that the knowledge base is growing. They argue that it should frame teacher education and directly inform teaching practice.

The rhetoric regarding the knowledge base, however, rarely specifies the character of such knowledge. It does not say what teachers should know, do, understand, or profess that will render teaching more than a form of individual labor, let alone be considered among the learned professions.

In this paper, I present an argument regarding the content, character, and sources for a knowledge base of teaching that suggests an answer to the question of the intellectual, practical, and normative basis for the professionalization of teaching. The questions that focus the argument are: What are the sources of the knowledge base for teaching? In what terms can these sources be conceptualized? What are the implications for teaching policy and educational reform?[1]

In addressing these questions I am following the footsteps of many eminent scholars, including Dewey (1904), Scheffler (1965), Green (1971), Fenstermacher (1978), Smith (1980), and Schwab (1983), among others. Their discussions of what qualities and understandings, skills and abilities, and what traits and sensibilities render someone a competent teacher have continued to echo in the conference rooms of educators for generations. My approach has been conditioned, as well, by two current projects: a study of how new teachers learn to teach and an attempt to develop a national board for teaching.

First, for the past three years, my colleagues and I have been watching knowledge of pedagogy and content grow in the minds of young men and women. They have generously permitted us to observe and follow their eventful journeys from being teacher education students to becoming neophyte teachers. In this research, we are taking advantage of the kinds of insights Piaget provided from his investigations of knowledge growth. He discovered that he could learn a great deal about knowledge and its development from careful observation of the very young—those who were just beginning to develop and organize their intelligence. We are following this lead by studying those just learning to teach. Their development from students to teachers, from a state of expertise as learners through a novitiate as teachers, exposes and highlights the complex bodies of knowledge and skill needed to function effectively as a teacher. The result is that error, success, and refinement—in a word, teacher-knowledge growth—are seen in high profile and in slow motion. The neophyte's stumble becomes the scholar's window.

Concurrently, we have found and explored cases of veteran teachers such as Nancy (Baxter, in preparation; Gudmundsdottir, in preparation; Hashweh, 1985) to compare with those of the novices. What these studies show is that the knowledge, understanding, and skill we see displayed haltingly, and occasionally masterfully, among beginners are often demonstrated with ease by the expert. But, as we have wrestled with our cases, we have repeatedly asked what teachers knew (or failed to know) that permitted them to teach in a particular manner.

Second, for much of the past year, I have engaged in quite a different project on the role of knowledge in teaching. In conjunction with the recent Carnegie initiative for the reform of the teaching profession, my colleagues and I have been studying ways to design a national board assessment for teaching, parallel in several ways to the National Board of Medical Examiners (Shulman & Sykes, 1986; Sykes, 1986). This challenge renders the questions about the definition and operationalization of knowledge in teaching as far more than academic exercises. If teachers are to be certified on the basis of well-grounded judgments and standards, then those standards on which a national board relies must be legitimized by three factors: they must be closely tied to the findings of scholarship in the academic disciplines that form the curriculum (such as English, physics, and history) as well as those that serve as foundations for the process of education (such as psychology, sociology, or philosophy); they must possess intuitive credibility (or "face validity") in the opinions of the professional community in whose interests they have been designed; and they must relate to the appropriate normative conceptions of teaching and teacher education.

The new reform proposals carry assumptions about the knowledge base for teaching: when advocates of reform suggest that requirements for the education of teachers should be augmented and periods of training lengthened, they assume there must be something substantial to be learned. When they recommend that standards be raised and a system of examinations introduced, they assume there must exist a body of knowledge and skill to examine. Our research and that of others (for example, Berliner, 1986; Leinhardt & Greeno, 1986) have identified the sources and suggested outlines of that knowledge base. Watching veterans such as Nancy teach the same material that poses difficulties for novice teachers helped focus our attention on what kinds of knowledge and skill were needed to teach demanding materials well. By focusing on the teaching of particular topics—*Huck Finn*, quadratic equations, the Indian subcontinent, photosynthesis—we learned how particular kinds of content knowledge and pedagogical strategies necessarily interacted in the minds of teachers.

What follows is a discussion of the sources and outlines of the required knowledge base for teaching. I divide this discussion into two distinct analyses. First, after providing an overview of one framework for a knowledge base for teaching, I examine the *sources* of that knowledge base, that is, the domains of scholarship and experience from which teachers may draw their understanding. Second, I explore the processes of pedagogical reasoning and action within which such teacher knowledge is used.

## The Knowledge Base

Begin a discussion on the knowledge base of teaching, and several related questions immediately arise: What knowledge base? Is enough known about teaching to support a knowledge base? Isn't teaching little more than personal style, artful communication, knowing some subject matter, and applying the results of recent research on teaching effectiveness? Only the last of these, the findings of research on effective teaching, is typically deemed a legitimate part of a knowledge base.

The actions of both policymakers and teacher educators in the past have been consistent with the formulation that teaching requires basic skills, content knowledge, and general pedagogical skills. Assessments of teachers in most states consist of some combination of basic-skills tests, an examination of competence in subject matter, and observations in the classroom to ensure that certain kinds of general teaching behavior are present. In this manner, I would argue, teaching is trivialized, its complexities ignored, and its demands diminished. Teachers themselves have difficulty in articulating what they know and how they know it.

Nevertheless, the policy community at present continues to hold that the skills needed for teaching are those identified in the empirical research on teaching effectiveness. This research, summarized by Brophy and Good (1986), Gage (1986), and Rosenshine and Stevens (1986), was conducted within the psychological research tradition. It assumes that complex forms of situation-specific human performance can be understood in terms of the workings of underlying generic processes. In a study of teaching context, the research, therefore, seeks to identify those general forms of teaching behavior that correlate with student performance on standardized tests, whether in descriptive or experimental studies. The investigators who conduct the research realize that important simplifications must be made, but they believe that these are necessary steps for conducting scientific studies. Critical features of teaching, such as the subject matter being taught, the classroom context, the physical and psychological characteristics of the students, or the accomplishment of purposes not readily assessed on standardized tests, are typically ignored in the quest for general principles of effective teaching.

When policymakers have sought "research-based" definitions of good teaching to serve as the basis for teacher tests or systems of classroom observation, the lists of teacher behaviors that had been identified as effective in the empirical research were translated into the desirable competencies for classroom teachers. They became items on tests or on classroom-observation scales. They were accorded legitimacy because they had been "confirmed by research." While the researchers understood the findings to be simplified and incomplete, the policy community accepted them as sufficient for the definitions of standards.

For example, some research had indicated that students achieved more when teachers explicitly informed them of the lesson's objective. This seems like a perfectly reasonable finding. When translated into policy, however, classroom-observation competency-rating scales asked whether the teacher had written the objective on the blackboard and/or directly told the students the objectives at the beginning of class. If the teacher had not, he or she was marked off for failing to demonstrate a desired competency. No effort was made to discover whether the withholding of an objective might have been consistent with the form of the lesson being organized or delivered.

Moreover, those who hold with bifurcating content and teaching processes have once again introduced into policy what had been merely an act of scholarly convenience and simplification in the research. Teaching processes were observed and evaluated without reference to the adequacy or accuracy of the ideas transmitted. In many cases, observers were not expected to have content expertise in the areas being observed, because it did not matter for the rating of teacher performance. Thus, what may have been an acceptable strategy for research became an unacceptable policy for teacher evaluation.

In this paper I argue that the results of research on effective teaching, while valuable, are not the sole source of evidence on which to base a definition of the knowledge base of teaching. Those sources should be understood to be far richer and more extensive. Indeed, properly understood, the actual and potential sources for a knowledge base are so plentiful that our question should not be, Is there really much one needs to know in order to teach? Rather, it should express our wonder at how the extensive knowledge of teaching can be learned at all during the brief period allotted to teacher preparation. Much of the rest of this paper provides the details of the argument that there exists an elaborate knowledge base for teaching.

## A View of Teaching

I begin with the formulation that the capacity to teach centers around the following commonplaces of teaching, paraphrased from Fenstermacher (1986). A teacher knows something not understood by others, presumably the students. The teacher can transform understanding, performance skills, or desired attitudes or values into pedagogical representations and actions. These are ways of talking, showing, enacting, or otherwise representing ideas so that the unknowing can come to know, those without understanding can comprehend and discern, and the unskilled can become adept. Thus, teaching necessarily begins with a teacher's understanding of what is to be learned and how it is to be taught. It proceeds through a series of activities during which the students are provided specific instruction and opportunities for learning,[2] though the learning itself ultimately remains the responsibility of the students. Teaching ends with new comprehension by both the teacher and the student.[3] Although this is certainly a core conception of teaching, it is also an incomplete conception. Teaching must properly be understood to be more than the enhancement of understanding; but if it is not even that, then questions regarding performance of its other functions remain moot. The next step is to outline the categories of knowledge that underlie the teacher understanding needed to promote comprehension among students.

## Categories of the Knowledge Base

If teacher knowledge were to be organized into a handbook, an encyclopedia, or some other format for arraying knowledge, what would the category headings look like?[4] At minimum, they would include:

- content knowledge;
- general pedagogical knowledge, with special reference to those broad principles and strategies of classroom management and organization that appear to transcend subject matter;
- curriculum knowledge, with particular grasp of the materials and programs that serve as "tools of the trade" for teachers;
- pedagogical content knowledge, that special amalgam of content and pedagogy that is uniquely the province of teachers, their own special form of professional understanding;
- knowledge of learners and their characteristics;

o knowledge of educational contexts, ranging from the workings of the group or classroom, the governance and financing of school districts, to the character of communities and cultures; and

o knowledge of educational ends, purposes, and values, and their philosophical and historical grounds.

Among those categories, pedagogical content knowledge is of special interest because it identifies the distinctive bodies of knowledge for teaching. It represents the blending of content and pedagogy into an understanding of how particular topics, problems, or issues are organized, represented, and adapted to the diverse interests and abilities of learners, and presented for instruction. Pedagogical content knowledge is the category most likely to distinguish the understanding of the content specialist from that of the pedagogue. While far more can be said regarding the categories of a knowledge base for teaching, elucidation of them is not a central purpose of this paper.

## Enumerating the Sources

There are at least four major sources for the teaching knowledge base: (1) scholarship in content disciplines, (2) the materials and settings of the institutionalized educational process (for example, curricula, textbooks, school organizations and finance, and the structure of the teaching profession), (3) research on schooling, social organizations, human learning, teaching and development, and the other social and cultural phenomena that affect what teachers can do, and (4) the wisdom of practice itself. Let me elaborate on each of these.

SCHOLARSHIP IN CONTENT DISCIPLINES. The first source of the knowledge base is content knowledge—the knowledge, understanding, skill, and disposition that are to be learned by school children. This knowledge rests on two foundations: the accumulated literature and studies in the content areas, and the historical and philosophical scholarship on the nature of knowledge in those fields of study. For example, the teacher of English should know English and American prose and poetry, written and spoken language use and comprehension, and grammar. In addition, he or she should be familiar with the critical literature that applies to particular novels or epics that are under discussion in class. Moreover, the teacher should understand alternative theories of interpretation and criticism, and how these might relate to issues of curriculum and of teaching.

Teaching is, essentially, a learned profession. A teacher is a member of a scholarly community. He or she must understand the structures of subject matter, the principles of conceptual organization, and the principles of inquiry that help answer two kinds of questions in each field: What are the important ideas and skills in this domain? and How are new ideas added and deficient ones dropped by those who produce knowledge in this area? That is, what are the rules and procedures of good scholarship or inquiry? These questions parallel what Schwab (1964) has characterized as knowledge of substantive and syntactic structures, respectively. This view of the sources of content knowledge necessarily implies that the teacher must have not only depth of understanding with respect to the particular subjects taught, but also a broad liberal education that serves as a framework for old learning and as a facilitator for new understanding. The teacher has special responsibilities in relation to content knowledge, serving as the primary source of student understanding of subject matter. The manner in which that understanding is communicated conveys to students what is essential about a subject and what is peripheral. In the face of student diversity, the teacher must have a flexible and multifaceted comprehension, adequate to impart alternative explanations of the same concepts or principles. The teacher also communicates, whether consciously or not, ideas about the ways in which "truth" is determined in a field and a set of attitudes and values that markedly influence student understanding. This responsibility places special demands on the teacher's own depth of understanding of the structures of the subject matter, as well as on the teacher's attitudes toward and enthusiasms for what is being taught and learned. These many aspects of content knowledge, therefore, are properly understood as a central feature of the knowledge base of teaching.

EDUCATIONAL MATERIALS AND STRUCTURES. To advance the aims of organized schooling, materials and structures for teaching and learning are created. These include: curricula with their scopes and sequences; tests and testing materials; institutions with their hierarchies, their explicit and implicit systems of rules and roles; professional teachers' organizations with their functions of negotiation, social change, and mutual protection; government agencies from the district through the state and federal levels; and general mechanisms of governance and finance. Because teachers necessarily function within a matrix created by these elements, using and being used by them, it stands to reason that the principles, policies, and facts of their functioning comprise a major source for the knowledge base. There is no need to claim that a specific literature undergirds this source, although there is certainly abundant research literature in most of these domains. But if a teacher has to "know the territory" of teaching, then it is the landscape of such materials, institutions, organizations, and mechanisms with which he or she must be familiar. These comprise both the tools of the trade and the contextual conditions that will either facilitate or inhibit teaching efforts.

FORMAL EDUCATIONAL SCHOLARSHIP. A third source is the important and growing body of scholarly literature devoted to understanding the processes of schooling, teaching, and learning. This literature includes the findings and methods of empirical research in the areas of teaching, learning, and human development, as well as the normative, philosophical, and ethical foundations of education.

The normative and theoretical aspects of teaching's scholarly knowledge are perhaps most important. Unfortunately, educational policymakers and staff developers tend to treat only the findings of empirical research on teaching and learning as relevant portions of the scholarly knowledge base. But these research findings, while important and worthy of careful study, represent only one facet of the contribution of scholarship. Perhaps the most enduring and powerful scholarly influences on teachers are those that enrich their images of the possible: their visions of what constitutes good education, or what a well-educated youngster might look like if provided with appropriate opportunities and stimulation.

The writings of Plato, Dewey, Neill, and Skinner all communicate their conceptions of what a good educational system should be. In addition, many works written primarily to disseminate empirical research findings also serve as important sources of these concepts. I count among these such works as Bloom's (1976) on mastery learning and Rosenthal and Jacobson's (1968) on teaching expectations. Quite independent of whether the empirical claims of those books can be supported, their impact on teachers' conceptions of the possible and desirable ends of education is undeniable. Thus, the philosophical, critical, and empirical literature which can inform the goals, visions, and dreams of teachers is a major portion of the scholarly knowledge base of teaching.

A more frequently cited kind of scholarly knowledge grows out of the empirical study of teaching effectiveness. This research has been summarized recently by Gage (1978, 1986), Shulman (1986a), Brophy and Good (1986), and Rosenshine and Stevens (1986). The essential goal of this program of research has been to identify those teacher behaviors and strategies most likely to lead to achievement gains among students. Because the search has focused on generic relationships—teacher behaviors associated with student academic gains irrespective of subject matter or grade level— the findings have been much more closely connected with the management of classrooms than with the subtleties of content pedagogy. That is, the effective-teaching principles deal with making classrooms places where pupils can attend to instructional tasks, orient themselves toward learning with a minimum of disruption and distraction, and receive a fair and adequate opportunity to learn. Moreover, the educational purposes for which these research results are most relevant are the teaching of skills. Rosenshine (1986) has observed that effective teaching research has much less to offer to the teaching of understanding, especially of complex written material; thus, the research applies more to teaching a skill like multiplication than to teaching critical interpretations of, say, the *Federalist Papers*.

There are a growing number of such generic principles of effective teaching, and they have already found their way into examinations such as the National Teachers Examination and into state-level assessments of teaching performance during the first teaching year. Their weakness, that they essentially ignore the content-specific character of most teaching, is also their strength. Discovering, explicating, and codifying general teaching principles simplify the otherwise outrageously complex activity of teaching. The great danger occurs, however, when a general teaching principle is distorted into prescription, when maxim becomes mandate. Those states that have taken working principles of teaching, based solely on empirical studies of generic teaching effectiveness, and have tendered them as hard, independent criteria for judging a teacher's worth, are engaged in a political process likely to injure the teaching profession rather than improve it.

The results of research on learning and development also fall within the area of empirical research findings. This research differs from research on teaching by the unit of investigation. Studies of teaching typically take place in conventional classrooms. Learning and development are ordinarily studied in individuals. Hence, teaching studies give accounts of how teachers cope with the inescapable character of schools as places where groups of students work and learn in concert. By comparison, learning and development studies produce principles of individual thought or behavior that must often be generalized to groups with caution if they are to be useful for schoolteaching.

The research in these domains can be both generic and content-specific. For example, cognitive psychological research contributes to the development of understanding of how the mind works to store, process, and retrieve information. Such general understanding can certainly be a source of knowledge for teachers, just as the work of Piaget, Maslow, Erikson, or Bloom has been and continues to be. We also find work on specific subject matter and student developmental levels that is enormously useful; for example, we learn about student misconceptions in the learning of arithmetic by elementary school youngsters (Erlwanger, 1975) or difficulties in grasping principles of physics by university and secondary school students (for example, Clement, 1982). Both these sorts of research contribute to a knowledge base for teaching.

WISDOM OF PRACTICE. The final source of the knowledge base is the least codified of all. It is the wisdom of practice itself, the maxims that guide (or provide reflective rationalization for) the practices of able teachers. One of the more important tasks for the research community is to work with practitioners to develop codified representations of the practical pedagogical wisdom of able teachers. As indicated above, much of the conception of teaching embodied in this paper is derived from collecting, examining, and beginning to codify the emerging wisdom of practice among both inexperienced and experienced teachers.

The portrait of Nancy with which this paper began is only one of the many descriptions and analyses of excellent teaching we have been collecting over the past few years. As we organize and interpret such data, we attempt to infer principles of good practice that can serve as useful guidelines for efforts of educational reform. We attempt to keep the accounts highly contextualized, especially with respect to the content-specificity of the pedagogical strategies employed. In this manner we contribute to the documentation of good practice as a significant source for teaching standards. We also attempt to lay a foundation for a scholarly literature that records the details and rationales for specific pedagogical practice.

One of the frustrations of teaching as an occupation and profession is its extensive individual and collective amnesia, the consistency with which the best creations of its practitioners are lost to both contemporary and future peers. Unlike fields such as architecture (which preserves its creations in both plans and edifices), law (which builds a case literature of opinions and interpretations), medicine (with its records and case studies), and even unlike chess, bridge, or ballet (with their traditions of preserving both memorable games and choreographed performances through inventive forms of notation and recording), teaching is conducted without an audience of peers. It is devoid of a history of practice.

Without such a system of notation and memory, the next steps of analysis, interpretation, and codification of principles of practice are hard to pursue. We have concluded from our research with teachers at all levels of experience that the potentially codifiable knowledge that can be gleaned from the wisdom of practice is extensive. Practitioners simply know a great deal that they have never even tried to articulate. A major portion of the research agenda for the next decade will be to collect, collate, and interpret the practical knowledge of teachers for the purpose of establishing a case literature and codifying its principles, precedents, and parables (Shulman, 1986b). A significant portion of the research agenda associated with the Carnegie program to develop new assessments for teachers involves the conducting of "wisdom-of-practice" studies. These studies record and organize the reasoning and actions of gifted teachers into cases to establish standards of practice for particular areas of teaching.[5]

A knowledge base for teaching is not fixed and final. Although teaching is among the world's oldest professions, educational research, especially the systematic study of teaching, is a relatively new enterprise. We may be able to offer a compelling argument for the broad outlines and categories of the knowledge base for teaching. It will, however, become abundantly clear that much, if not most, of the proposed knowledge base remains to be discovered, invented, and refined. As more is learned about teaching, we will come to recognize new categories of performance and understanding that are characteristic of good teachers, and will have to reconsider and redefine other domains. Our current "blueprint" for the knowledge base of teaching has many cells or categories with only the most rudimentary place-holders, much like the chemist's periodic table of a century ago. As we proceed, we will know that something can be known in principle about a particular aspect of teaching, but we will not yet know what that principle or practice entails. At base, however, we believe that scholars and expert teachers are able to define, describe, and reproduce good teaching.

## The Processes of Pedagogical Reasoning and Action

The conception of teaching I shall discuss has emerged from a number of sources, both philosophical and empirical. A key source has been the several dozen teachers whom we have been studying in our research during the past three years. Through interviews, observations, structured tasks, and examination of materials, we have attempted to understand how they commute from the status of learner to that of teacher,[6] from being able to comprehend subject matter for themselves, to becoming able to elucidate subject matter in new ways, reorganize and partition it, clothe it in activities and emotions, in metaphors and exercises, and in examples and demonstrations, so that it can be grasped by students.

As we have come to view teaching, it begins with an act of reason, continues with a process of reasoning, culminates in performances of imparting, eliciting, involving, or enticing, and is then thought about some more until the process can begin again. In the discussion of teaching that follows, we will emphasize teaching as comprehension and reasoning, as transformation and reflection. This emphasis is justified by the resoluteness with which research and policy have so blatantly ignored those aspects of teaching in the past.

Fenstermacher (1978, 1986) provides a useful framework for analysis. The goal of teacher education, he argues, is not to indoctrinate or train teachers to behave in prescribed ways, but to educate teachers to reason soundly about their teaching as well as to perform skillfully. Sound reasoning requires both a process of thinking about what they are doing and an adequate base of facts, principles, and experiences from which to reason. Teachers must learn to use their knowledge base to provide the grounds for choices and actions. Therefore, teacher education must work with the beliefs that guide teacher actions, with the principles and evidence that underlie the choices teachers make. Such reasons (called "premises of the practical argument" in the analysis of Green, 1971, on which Fenstermacher bases his argument) can be predominantly arbitrary or idiosyncratic ("It sure seemed like the right idea at the time!" "I don't know much about teaching, but I know what I like."), or they can rest on ethical, empirical, theoretical, or practical principles that have substantial support among members of the professional community of teachers. Fenstermacher argues that good teaching not only is effective behaviorally, but must rest on a foundation of adequately grounded premises.

When we examine the quality of teaching, the idea of influencing the grounds or reasons for teachers' decisions places the emphasis precisely where it belongs: on the features of pedagogical reasoning that lead to or can be invoked to explain pedagogical actions. We must be cautious, however, lest we place undue emphasis upon the ways teachers reason to achieve particular ends, at the expense of attention to the grounds they present for selecting the ends themselves. Teaching is both effective and normative; it is concerned with both means and ends. Processes of reasoning underlie both. The knowledge base must therefore deal with the purposes of education as well as the methods and strategies of educating.

This image of teaching involves the exchange of ideas. The idea is grasped, probed, and comprehended by a teacher, who then must turn it about in his or her mind, seeing many sides of it. Then the idea is shaped or tailored until it can in turn be grasped by students. This grasping, however, is not a passive act. Just as the teacher's comprehension requires a vigorous interaction with the ideas, so students will be expected to encounter ideas actively as well. Indeed, our exemplary teachers present ideas in order to provoke the constructive processes of their students and not to incur student dependence on teachers or to stimulate the flatteries of imitation.[7]

Comprehension alone is not sufficient. The usefulness of such knowledge lies in its value for judgment and action. Thus, in response to my aphorism, "those who can, do; those who understand, teach" (Shulman, 1986b, p. 14), Petrie (1986) correctly observed that I had not gone far enough. Understanding, he argued, must be linked to judgment and action, to the proper uses of understanding in the forging of wise pedagogical decisions.

## Aspects of Pedagogical Reasoning

I begin with the assumption that most teaching is initiated by some form of "text": a textbook, a syllabus, or an actual piece of material the teacher or student wishes to have understood. The text may be a vehicle for the accomplishment of other educational purposes, but some sort of teaching material is almost always involved. The following conception of pedagogical reasoning and action is taken from the point of view of the teacher, who is presented with the challenge of taking what he or she already understands and making it ready for effective instruction. The model of pedagogical reasoning and action is summarized in Table 5.1.

Given a text, educational purposes, and/or a set of ideas, pedagogical reasoning and action involve a cycle through the activities of comprehension, transformation, instruction, evaluation, and reflection.[8] The starting point and terminus for the process is an act of comprehension.

COMPREHENSION. To teach is first to understand. We ask that the teacher comprehend critically a set of ideas to be taught.[9] We expect teachers to understand what they teach and, when possible, to understand it in several ways. They should understand how a given idea relates to other ideas within the same subject area and to ideas in other subjects as well.

Comprehension of purposes is also central here. We engage in teaching to achieve educational purposes, to accomplish ends having to do with student literacy, student freedom to use and enjoy, student responsibility to care and care for, to believe and respect, to inquire and discover, to develop understandings, skills, and values needed to function in a free and just society. As teachers, we also strive to balance our goals of fostering individual excellence with more general ends involving equality of opportunity

## Table 5.1. A Model of Pedagogical Reasoning and Action.

*Comprehension*

Of purposes, subject matter structures, ideas within and outside the discipline

*Transformation*

Preparation: critical interpretation and analysis of texts, structuring and segmenting, development of a curricular repertoire, and clarification of purposes

Representation: use of a representational repertoire which includes analogies, metaphors, examples, demonstrations, explanations, and so forth

Selection: choice from among an instructional repertoire which includes modes of teaching, organizing, managing, and arranging

Adaptation and Tailoring to Student Characteristics: consideration of conceptions, preconceptions, misconceptions, and difficulties, language, culture, and motivations, social class, gender, age, ability, aptitude, interests, self concepts, and attention

*Instruction*

Management, presentations, interactions, group work, discipline, humor, questioning, and other aspects of active teaching, discovery or inquiry instruction, and the observable forms of classroom teaching

*Evaluation*

Checking for student understanding during interactive teaching

Testing student understanding at the end of lessons or units

Evaluating one's own performance, and adjusting for experiences

*Reflection*

Reviewing, reconstructing, reenacting and critically analyzing one's own and the class's performance, and grounding explanations in evidence

*New Comprehension*

Of purposes, subject matter, students, teaching, and self

Consolidation of new understandings, and learnings from experience and equity among students of different backgrounds and cultures. Although most teaching begins with some sort of text, and the learning of that text can be a worthy end in itself, we should not lose sight of the fact that the text is often a vehicle for achieving other educational purposes. The goals of education transcend the comprehension of particular texts, but may be unachievable without it.

Saying that a teacher must first comprehend both content and purposes, however, does not particularly distinguish a teacher from non-teaching peers. We expect a math major to understand mathematics or a history specialist to comprehend history. But the key to distinguishing the knowledge base of teaching lies at the intersection of content and pedagogy, in the capacity of a teacher to transform the content knowledge he or she possesses into forms that are pedagogically powerful and yet adaptive to the variations in ability and background presented by the students. We now turn to a discussion of transformation and its components.

TRANSFORMATION. Comprehended ideas must be transformed in some manner if they are to be taught. To reason one's way through an act of teaching is to think one's way from the subject matter as understood by the teacher into the minds and motivations of learners. Transformations, therefore, require some combination or ordering of the following processes, each of which employs a kind of repertoire: (1) preparation (of the given text materials) including the process of critical interpretation, (2) representation of the ideas in the form of new analogies, metaphors, and so forth, (3) instructional selections from among an array of teaching methods and models, and (4) adaptation of these representations to the general characteristics of the children to be taught, as well as (5) tailoring the adaptations to the specific youngsters in the classroom. These forms of transformation, these aspects of the process wherein one moves from personal comprehension to preparing for the comprehension of others, are the essence of the act of pedagogical reasoning, of teaching as thinking, and of planning—whether explicitly or implicitly—the performance of teaching.

Preparation involves examining and critically interpreting the materials of instruction in terms of the teacher's own understanding of the subject matter (Ben-Peretz, 1975). That is, one scrutinizes the teaching material in light of one's own comprehension and asks whether it is "fit to be taught." This process of preparation will usually include (1) detecting and correcting errors of omission and commission in the text, and (2) the crucial processes of structuring and segmenting the material into forms better adapted to the teacher's understanding and, in prospect, more suitable for teaching. One also scrutinizes educational purposes or goals. We find examples of this preparation process in a number of our studies. Preparation certainly draws upon the availability of a curricular repertoire, a grasp of the full array of extant instructional materials, programs, and conceptions.

Representation involves thinking through the key ideas in the text or lesson and identifying the alternative ways of representing them to students. What analogies, metaphors, examples, demonstrations, simulations, and the like can help to build a bridge between the teacher's comprehension and that desired for the students? Multiple forms of representation are desirable. We speak of the importance of a representational repertoire in this activity.[10]

Instructional selections occur when the teacher must move from the reformulation of content through representations to the embodiment of representations in instructional forms or methods. Here the teacher draws upon an instructional repertoire of approaches or strategies of teaching. This repertoire can be quite rich, including not only the more conventional alternatives such as lecture, demonstration, recitation, or seatwork, but also a variety of forms of cooperative learning, reciprocal teaching, Socratic dialogue, discovery learning, project methods, and learning outside the classroom setting.

Adaptation is the process of fitting the represented material to the characteristics of the students. What are the relevant aspects of student ability, gender, language, culture, motivations, or prior knowledge and skills that will affect their responses to different forms of representation and presentation? What student conceptions, misconceptions, expectations, motives, difficulties, or strategies might influence the ways in which they approach, interpret, understand, or misunderstand the material? Related to adaptation is tailoring, which refers to the fitting of the material to the specific students in one's classrooms rather than to students in general. When a teacher thinks through the teaching of something, the activity is a bit like the manufacture of a suit of clothing. Adaptation is like preparing a suit of a particular style, color, and size that can be hung on a rack. Once it is prepared for purchase by a particular customer, however, it must be tailored to fit perfectly.

Moreover, the activity of teaching is rarely engaged with a single student at a time. This is a process for which the special term "tutoring" is needed. When we speak of teaching under typical school circumstances, we describe an activity which brings instruction to groups of at least fifteen—or more typically, twenty-five to thirty-five—students. Thus, the tailoring of instruction entails fitting representations not only to particular students, but also to a group of a particular size, disposition, receptivity, and inter-personal "chemistry."

All these processes of transformation result in a plan, or set of strate-gies, to present a lesson, unit, or course. Up to this point, of course, it is all a rehearsal for the performances of teaching which have not yet oc-curred. Pedagogical reasoning is as much a part of teaching as is the actual performance itself. Reasoning does not end when instruction begins. The activities of comprehension, transformation, evaluation, and reflection con-tinue to occur during active teaching. Teaching itself becomes a stimulus for thoughtfulness as well as for action. We therefore turn next to the perfor-mance that consummates all this reasoning in the act of instruction.

INSTRUCTION. This activity involves the observable performance of the variety of teaching acts. It includes many of the most crucial aspects of pedagogy: organizing and managing the classroom; presenting clear ex-planations and vivid descriptions; assigning and checking work; and in-teracting effectively with students through questions and probes, answers and reactions, and praise and criticism. It thus includes management, ex-planation, discussion, and all the observable features of effective direct and heuristic instruction already well documented in the research litera-ture on effective teaching.

We have compelling reasons to believe that there are powerful rela-tionships between the comprehension of a new teacher and the styles of teaching employed. An example, based on the research of Grossman (1985), will illustrate this point.

○

Colleen had completed a master's degree in English before entering a teacher education program. She expressed confidence in her command of the subject matter and began her internship with energy and en-thusiasm. Her view of literature and its teaching was highly interpre-tive and interactive. She saw fine literature as layered communication, capable of many diverse readings and interpretations. Moreover, she felt that these various readings should be provided by her students through their own careful reading of the texts.

Colleen was so committed to helping students learn to read texts carefully, a habit of mind not often found among the young or old, that she constructed one assignment in which each student was asked to bring to school the lyrics of a favorite rock song. (She may have re-alized that some of these song lyrics were of questionable taste, but preferred to maximize motivation rather than discretion in this particular unit.) She then asked them to rewrite each line of the song, using synonyms or paraphrases to replace every original word. For many, it was the first time they had looked at any piece of text with such care.

When teaching a piece of literature, Colleen performed in a highly interactive manner, drawing out student ideas about a phrase or line, accepting multiple competing interpretations as long as the student could offer a defense of the construction by reference to the text itself. Student participation was active and hearty in these sessions. Based on these observations, one would have characterized Colleen's teaching style with descriptors such as student-centered, discussion-based, occasionally Socratic, or otherwise highly interactive.

Several weeks later, however, we observed Colleen teaching a unit on grammar. Although she had completed two university degrees in English, Colleen had received almost no preparation in prescriptive grammar. However, since a typical high school English class includes some grammar in addition to the literature and writing, it was impossible to avoid teaching the subject. She expressed some anxiety about it during a pre-observational interview.

Colleen looked like a different teacher during that lesson. Her interactive style evaporated. In its place was a highly didactic, teacher-directed, swiftly paced combination of lecture and tightly-controlled recitation: Socrates replaced by DISTAR. I sometimes refer to such teaching as the Admiral Farragut style, "Damn the questions, full speed ahead." Students were not given opportunities to raise questions or offer alternative views. After the session, she confessed to the observer that she had actively avoided making eye contact with one particular student in the front row because that youngster always had good questions or ideas and in this particular lesson Colleen really didn't want to encourage either, because she wasn't sure of the answers. She was uncertain about the content and adapted her instructional style to allay her anxiety.[11]

---

o

---

Colleen's case illustrates the ways in which teaching behavior is bound up with comprehension and transformation of understanding. The flexible and interactive teaching techniques that she uses are simply not available to her when she does not understand the topic to be taught. Having examined the processes of pedagogical reasoning and performance that are prospective and enactive in nature, we now move to those that are retrospective.

EVALUATION. This process includes the on-line checking for understanding and misunderstanding that a teacher must employ while teaching interactively, as well as the more formal testing and evaluation that teachers do to provide feedback and grades. Clearly, checking for such understanding requires all the forms of teacher comprehension and transformation described above. To understand what a pupil understands will require a deep grasp of both the material to be taught and the processes of learning. This understanding must be specific to particular school subjects and to individual topics within the subject. This represents another way in which what we call pedagogical content knowledge is used. Evaluation is also directed at one's own teaching and at the lessons and materials employed in those activities. In that sense it leads directly to reflection.

REFLECTION. This is what a teacher does when he or she looks back at the teaching and learning that has occurred, and reconstructs, reenacts, and/or recaptures the events, the emotions, and the accomplishments. It is that set of processes through which a professional learns from experience. It can be done alone or in concert, with the help of recording devices or solely through memory. Here again, it is likely that reflection is not merely a disposition (as in, "she's such a reflective person!") or a set of strategies, but also the use of particular kinds of analytic knowledge brought to bear on one's work (Richert, in preparation). Central to this process will be a review of the teaching in comparison to the ends that were sought.

NEW COMPREHENSION. Thus we arrive at the new beginning, the expectation that through acts of teaching that are "reasoned" and "reasonable" the teacher achieves new comprehension, both of the purposes and of the subjects to be taught, and also of the students and of the processes of pedagogy themselves. There is a good deal of transient experiential learning among teachers, characterized by the "aha" of a moment that is never consolidated and made part of a new understanding or a reconstituted repertoire (Brodkey, 1986). New comprehension does not automatically occur, even after evaluation and reflection. Specific strategies for documentation, analysis, and discussion are needed.

Although the processes in this model are presented in sequence, they are not meant to represent a set of fixed stages, phases, or steps. Many of the processes can occur in different order. Some may not occur at all during some acts of teaching. Some may be truncated, others elaborated. In elementary teaching, for example, some processes may occur that are ignored or given short shrift in this model. But a teacher should demonstrate the capacity to engage in these processes when called upon, and teacher education should provide students with the understandings and performance abilities they will need to reason their ways through and to enact a complete act of pedagogy, as represented here.

## Knowledge, Teaching Policy, and Educational Reform

The investigations, deliberations, and debates regarding what teachers should know and know how to do have never been more active. Reform efforts are underway: they range from raising standards for admission into teacher education programs, to establishing state and national examinations for teachers; from insisting that teacher preparation require at least five years of higher education (because there is so much to learn), to organizing elaborate programs of new-teacher induction and mentoring (because the most important learning and socialization can occur only in the workplace).

Most of the current reforms rest on the call for greater professionalization in teaching, with higher standards for entry, greater emphasis on the scholarly bases for practice, more rigorous programs of theoretical and practical preparation, better strategies for certification and licensure, and changes in the workplace that permit greater autonomy and teacher leadership. In large measure, they call for teaching to follow the model of other professions that define their knowledge bases in systematic terms, require extended periods of preparation, socialize neophytes into practice with extended periods of internship or residency, and employ demanding national and state certification procedures.

Implicit in all these reforms are conceptions of teacher competence. Standards for teacher education and assessment are necessarily predicated on images of teaching and its demands. The conception of the knowledge base of teaching presented in this paper differs in significant ways from many of those currently existing in the policy community. The emphasis on the integral relationships between teaching and the scholarly domains of the liberal arts makes clear that teacher education is the responsibility of the entire university, not the schools or departments of education alone. Moreover, teachers cannot be adequately assessed by observing their teaching performance without reference to the content being taught.

The conception of pedagogical reasoning places emphasis upon the intellectual basis for teaching performance rather than on behavior alone. If this conception is to be taken seriously, both the organization and content of teacher education programs and the definition of the scholarly foundations of education will require revision. Teacher education programs would no longer be able to confine their activity to the content-free domains of pedagogy and supervision. An emphasis on pedagogical content knowledge would permeate the teacher preparation curriculum. A national board examination for teachers would focus upon the teacher's ability to reason about teaching and to teach specific topics, and to base his or her actions on premises that can bear the scrutiny of the professional community.

We have an obligation to raise standards in the interests of improvement and reform, but we must avoid the creation of rigid orthodoxies. We must achieve standards without standardization. We must be careful that the knowledge-base approach does not produce an overly technical image of teaching, a scientific enterprise that has lost its soul. The serious problems in medicine and other health professions arise when doctors treat the disease rather than the person, or when the professional or personal needs of the practitioner are permitted to take precedence over the responsibilities to those being served.

Needed change cannot occur without risk, however. The currently incomplete and trivial definitions of teaching held by the policy community comprise a far greater danger to good education than does a more serious attempt to formulate the knowledge base. Nancy represents a model of pedagogical excellence that should become the basis for the new reforms. A proper understanding of the knowledge base of teaching, the sources for that knowledge, and the complexities of the pedagogical process will make the emergence of such teachers more likely.

## NOTES

1. Most of the empirical work on which this essay rests has been conducted with secondary-school teachers, both new and experienced. While I firmly believe that much of the emphasis to be found here on the centrality of content knowledge in pedagogy holds reasonably well for the elementary level as well, I am reluctant to make that claim too boldly. Work currently underway at the elementary level, both by Leinhardt (1983) and her colleagues (for example, Leinhardt & Greeno, 1986; Leinhardt & Smith, 1985) and by our own research group, may help clarify this matter.

2. There are several aspects of this formulation that are unfortunate, if only for the impression they may leave. The rhetoric of the analysis, for example, is not meant to suggest that education is reduced to knowledge transmission, the conveying of information from an active teacher to a passive learner, and that this information is viewed as product rather than process. My conception of teaching is not limited to direct instruction. Indeed, my

affinity for discovery learning and inquiry teaching is both enthusiastic and ancient (for example, Shulman & Keislar, 1966). Yet even in those most student-centered forms of education, where much of the initiative is in the hands of the students, there is little room for teacher ignorance. Indeed, we have reason to believe that teacher comprehension is even more critical for the inquiry-oriented classroom than for its more didactic alternative.

Central to my concept of teaching are the objectives of students learning how to understand and solve problems, learning to think critically and creatively as well as learning facts, principles, and rules of procedure. Finally, I understand that the learning of subject matter is often not an end in itself, but rather a vehicle employed in the service of other goals. Nevertheless, at least at the secondary level, subject matter is a nearly universal vehicle for instruction, whatever the ultimate goal.

3. This formulation is drawn from the teacher's perspective and, hence, may be viewed by some readers as overly teacher-centered. I do not mean to diminish the centrality of student learning for the process of education, nor the priority that must be given to student learning over teacher comprehension. But our analyses of effective teaching must recognize that outcomes *for teachers* as well as pupils must be considered in any adequate treatment of educational outcomes.

4. I have attempted this list in other publications, though, admittedly, not with great cross-article consistency (for example, Shulman, 1986b; Shulman & Sykes, 1986; Wilson, Shulman, & Richert, in press).

5. It might be argued that the sources of skilled performances are typically tacit, and unavailable to the practitioner. But teaching requires a special kind of expertise or artistry, for which explaining and showing are the central features. Tacit knowledge among teachers is of limited value if the teachers are held responsible for explaining what they do and why they do it, to their students, their communities, and their peers.

6. The metaphor of commuting is not used idly. The journey between learner and teacher is not one-way. In the best teachers, as well as in the more marginal, new learning is constantly required for teaching.

7. The direction and sequence of instruction can be quite different as well. Students can literally initiate the process, proceeding by discovering, inventing, or inquiring, to prepare their own representations and transformations. Then it is the role of the teacher to respond actively and creatively to those student initiatives. In each case the teacher needs to possess both the comprehension and the capacities for transformation. In the student-initiated case, the flexibility to respond, judge, nurture, and provoke student

creativity will depend on the teacher's own capacities for sympathetic transformation and interpretation.

8. Under some conditions, teaching may begin with: "Given a group of students." It is likely that at the early elementary grades, or in special education classes or other settings where children have been brought together for particular reasons, the starting point for reasoning about instruction may well be at the characteristics of the group itself. There are probably some days when a teacher necessarily uses the youngsters as a starting point.

9. Other views of teaching will also begin with comprehension, but of something other than the ideas or text to be taught and learned. They may focus on comprehension of a particular set of values, of the characteristics, needs, interests, or propensities of a particular individual or group of learners. But some sort of comprehension (or self-conscious confusion, wonder, or ignorance) will always initiate teaching.

10. The centrality of representation to our conception of pedagogical reasoning is important for relating our model of teaching to more general approaches to the study of human thinking and problem solving. Cognitive psychologists (for example, Gardner, 1986; Marton, 1986; Norman, 1980) argue that processes of internal representation are key elements in any cognitive psychology. "To my mind, the major accomplishment of cognitive science has been the clear demonstration of the validity of positing a level of mental representation: a set of constructs that can be invoked for the explanation of cognitive phenomena, ranging from visual perception to story comprehension" (Gardner, 1986, p. 383). Such a linkage between models of pedagogy and models of more general cognitive functioning can serve as an important impetus for the needed study of teacher thinking.

11. In no way do I wish to imply that effective lectures are out of place in a high school classroom. On the contrary, good lecturing is an indispensable teaching technique. In this case I am more interested in the relationship between knowledge and teaching. It might be suggested that this teaching style is more suited to grammar than to literature because there is little to discuss or interpret in a grammar lesson. I do not agree, but will not pursue the matter here. In Colleen's case, the rationale for a linear lecture was not grounded in such an argument, but quite clearly in her concern for limiting the range of possible deviations from the path she had designed.

REFERENCES

Baxter, J. (in preparation). *Teacher explanations in computer programming: A study of knowledge transformation.* Unpublished doctoral dissertation in progress, Stanford University.

Ben-Peretz, M. (1975). The concept of curriculum potential. *Curriculum Theory Network, 5,* 151–159.

Berliner, D. (1986). In pursuit of the expert pedagogue. *Educational Researcher, 15*(7), 5–13.

Bloom, B. S. (1976). *Human characteristics and school learning.* New York: McGraw-Hill.

Brodkey, J. J. (1986). *Learning while teaching: Self-assessment in the classroom.* Unpublished doctoral dissertation, Stanford University.

Brophy, J. J., & Good, T. (1986). Teacher behavior and student achievement. In M. C. Wittrock (Ed.), *Handbook of research on teaching* (3rd ed., pp. 328–375). New York: Macmillan.

Carnegie Task Force on Teaching as a Profession. (1986). *A nation prepared: Teachers for the 21st century.* Washington, DC: Carnegie Forum on Education and the Economy.

Clement, J. (1982). Students' preconceptions in introductory mechanics. *American Journal of Physics, 50,* 67–71.

Dewey, J. (1904). The relation of theory to practice in education. In C. A. McMurry (Ed.), *The relation of theory to practice in the education of teachers* (Third Yearbook of the National Society for the Scientific Study of Education, Part I). Bloomington, IL: Public School Publishing.

Erlwanger, S. H. (1975). Case studies of children's conceptions of mathematics, Part I. *Journal of Children's Mathematical Behavior, 1,* 157–283.

Fenstermacher, G. (1978). A philosophical consideration of recent research on teacher effectiveness. In L. S. Shulman (Ed.), *Review of research in education* (Vol. 6, pp. 157–185). Itasca, IL: Peacock.

Fenstermacher, G. (1986). Philosophy of research on teaching: Three aspects. In M. C. Wittrock (Ed.), *Handbook of research on teaching* (3rd ed., pp. 37–49). New York: Macmillan.

Gage, N. L. (1978). *The scientific basis of the art of teaching.* New York: Teachers College Press.

Gage, N. L. (1986). *Hard gains in the soft sciences: The case of pedagogy.* Bloomington, IN: Phi Delta Kappa.

Gardner, H. (1986). *The mind's new science: A history of cognitive revolution.* New York: Basic Books.

Green, T. F. (1971). *The activities of teaching.* New York: McGraw-Hill.

Grossman, P. (1985). *A passion for language: From text to teaching* (Knowledge Growth in Teaching Publications Series). Stanford: Stanford University, School of Education.

Gudmundsdottir, S. (in preparation). *Knowledge use among experienced teachers: Four case studies of high school teaching.* Unpublished doctoral dissertation in progress, Stanford University.

Hashweh, M. Z. (1985). *An exploratory study of teacher knowledge and teaching: The effects of science teachers' knowledge of subject-matter and their conceptions of learning on their teaching.* Unpublished doctoral dissertation, Stanford University.

The Holmes Group (1986). *Tomorrow's teachers: A report of the Holmes Group.* East Lansing, MI: Author.

Leinhardt, G. (1983). Novice and expert knowledge of individual students' achievement. *Educational Psychologist, 18,* 165–179.

Leinhardt, G., & Greeno, J. G. (1986). The cognitive skill of teaching. *Journal of Educational Psychology, 78,* 75–95.

Leinhardt, G., & Smith, D. A. (1985). Expertise in mathematics instruction: Subject matter knowledge. *Journal of Educational Psychology, 77,* 247–271.

Marton, F. (1986). *Towards a pedagogy of content.* Unpublished manuscript, University of Gothenburg, Sweden.

Norman, D. A. (1980). What goes on in the mind of the learner? In W. J. McKeachie (Ed.), *New directions for teaching and learning: Learning, cognition, and college teaching* (Vol. 2). San Francisco: Jossey-Bass.

Petrie, H. (1986, May). *The liberal arts and sciences in the teacher education curriculum.* Paper presented at the Conference on Excellence in Teacher Preparation through the Liberal Arts, Muhlenberg College, Allentown, PA.

Richert, A. (in preparation). *Reflex to reflection: Facilitating reflection in novice teachers.* Unpublished doctoral dissertation in progress, Stanford University.

Rosenshine, B. (1986, April). *Unsolved issues in teaching content: A critique of a lesson on Federalist Paper No. 10.* Paper presented at the meeting of the American Educational Research Association, San Francisco, CA.

Rosenshine, B., & Stevens, R. S. (1986). Teaching functions. In M. C. Wittrock (Ed.), *Handbook of research on teaching* (3rd ed., pp. 376–391). New York: Macmillan.

Rosenthal, R., & Jacobson, L. (1968). *Pygmalion in the classroom.* New York: Holt, Rinehart & Winston.

Scheffler, I. (1965). *Conditions of knowledge: An introduction to epistemology and education.* Chicago: University of Chicago Press.

Schwab, J. J. (1964). The structure of the disciplines: Meanings and significances. In G. W. Ford & L. Pugno (Eds.), *The structure of knowledge and the curriculum.* Chicago: Rand McNally.

Schwab, J. J. (1983). The practical four: Something for curriculum professors to do. *Curriculum Inquiry, 13,* 239–265.

Shulman, L. S. (1986a). Paradigms and research programs for the study of teaching. In M. C. Wittrock (Ed.), *Handbook of research on teaching* (3rd ed., pp. 3–36). New York: Macmillan.

Shulman, L. S. (1986b). Those who understand: Knowledge growth in teaching. *Educational Researcher, 15*(2), 4–14.

Shulman, L. S., & Keislar, E. R. (Eds.). (1966). *Learning by discovery: A critical appraisal.* Chicago: Rand McNally.

Shulman, L. S., & Sykes, G. (1986, March). *A national board for teaching?: In search of a bold standard* (Paper commissioned for the Task Force on Teaching as a Profession, Carnegie Forum on Education and the Economy).

Smith, B. O. (1980). *A design for a school of pedagogy.* Washington, DC: U.S. Department of Education.

Sykes, G. (1986). *The social consequences of standard-setting in the professions* (Paper commissioned for the Task Force on Teaching as a Profession, Carnegie Forum on Education and the Economy).

Wilson, S. M., Shulman, L. S., & Richert, A. (in press). "150 different ways" of knowing: Representations of knowledge in teaching. In J. Calderhead (Ed.), *Exploring teacher thinking.* Sussex, Eng.: Holt, Rinehart & Winston.

---

○

---

ACKNOWLEDGMENTS

Preparation of this paper was made possible, in part, by grants to Stanford University from the Spencer Foundation for the project, Knowledge Growth in a Profession, and from the Carnegie Corporation of New York for research on the development of new modes of assessment for teachers, Lee S. Shulman, principal investigator. Suzanne Wilson, Pamela Grossman, and Judy Shulman provided criticism and counsel when it was most needed. A longer version of this paper will be available from the Carnegie Forum on Education and the Economy. The views expressed are the author's and are not necessarily shared by these organizations or individuals.

# INTRODUCTION

# LEARNING TO TEACH (1987)

IN 1987 Shulman addressed a group of university presidents convened by the American Association for Higher Education as part of a family of initiatives sponsored by the Carnegie Corporation of New York. Prompted by the recent national report *A Nation Prepared: Teachers for the 21st Century,* the meeting was intended to engage higher education leaders more directly in the education of teachers, urging them to see teacher preparation as a responsibility of the entire university, not only of the teacher education program. Edited and reprinted in the *AAHE Bulletin* in November 1987 as "Learning to Teach," the essay represents one of Shulman's first attempts to translate his ideas about teacher knowledge for a broad higher education audience.

# 6

# LEARNING TO TEACH

INCREASINGLY, I SEE in both the press and in some of our discussions what is for me a worrisome tendency. It is a tendency that in some small manner I feel a responsibility for having helped initiate. Within the field of research on teaching and teacher education, one of the small contributions I've been able to make is to reintroduce the study of teaching with a strong emphasis on the disciplinary content of what is being taught. After all, while process is certainly central to our concern as educators, what is being taught is at least as important as how it is taught.

But in the spirit that besets this pendular field called education, we have once again overcompensated. National Endowment for the Humanities Director Lynne Cheney and her much publicized report, "American Memory," is a perfect example of that. Essentially, she and many others are now trying to come up with cures for teacher education that amputate pedagogy altogether. This is a serious mistake.

My colleagues and I have spent a great deal of time over the past several years studying how young men and women become teachers; how they undergo that metamorphosis from being an expert learner to becoming a novice teacher; how they learn to transform what they know into representations and presentations that make sense to other people. A nontrivial task. We have done this by taking these young men and women so seriously that we have, as it were, become Boswells to their Johnsons. We have interviewed them, observed them, followed them, written hundreds, even thousands of pages transcribing our discussions, and we have done intellectual biographies with them.

At the same time, we've also been doing some studies of mature, successful, experienced teachers to try to get a sense of what the finished product looks like when it both survives and flourishes. And, parenthetically, one of the things I like about the kind of work we've done is that, in principle, there is nothing about the methodology or the high-tech character of the data gathering that makes it a kind of inquiry that can only be carried out in a research university. In fact, these case studies of people learning to teach exemplify a kind of scholarship that could well be pursued in schools and departments of education all over the country. Not only would it contribute to a now almost totally missing research literature on learning to teach, but it has such an extraordinarily positive impact on those of us who teach teachers.

The primary purpose of our research is to determine why it is that, of all the professions, learning to teach is so difficult. Let me try to lay out some reasons and give some examples.

## Disciplines

One of the first reasons learning to teach is so difficult is because, unlike the other professions where you use the disciplines as a basis for your practice, in teaching the disciplines play a dual role. They are both the basis for practice, and they are *what* you practice. In other words, if I'm a physician and understand anatomy—I've learned well enough not to confuse the aorta with the superior vena cava—I'm OK. If I'm a teacher of anatomy, that's not enough. I've got to understand it enough to explain it to somebody else. So the disciplines are not only the grounds for practice, they are a big chunk of what the practice is about. And it is much more difficult to teach somebody something than merely to know that something.

Let me give you an example. In one of the studies we did at Stanford, we were trying to understand what some of the difficult things were that somebody transformed from knowing to teaching.

Imagine now a typical eleventh-grade English class. The curriculum for the year is made up of a series of books, short stories, plays, and poems, including *To Kill a Mockingbird, Huckleberry Finn, 1984, Gentleman's Agreement,* and others.

If you look through this list it strikes you that all of the readings deal with a very similar theme—the struggle of the individual seeking autonomy or liberty in the face of a somewhat restrictive society. Then you start studying the teacher in that classroom and you realize the incredible agenda that teacher is trying to pursue in that course. The teacher is trying to teach the reading of literary text, no small challenge. The teacher is trying to teach what is, in effect, a course in social criticism. *1984* is more than a literary text. *Huck Finn* is more than a literary text. *To Kill a*

*Mockingbird* is a very critical text with regard to the society that it describes. So, in addition to having to be able to teach the literature, the teacher is teaching social criticism and social analysis.

Then we look at the list in another way. Almost all of them deal with what is the prevailing problem in the lives of typical American teenagers—namely, their own sense of individuality and freedom in a society they find restrictive. So it is also a course in individual development for adolescents. And, by the by, the teacher has to teach them writing and usage as well. High school teachers have to do that five different times daily with five different groups of 30 to 35 kids, so at the end of the day they've done this with an aggregate of 170 kids, all of whose names they are supposed to know by the end of the first week.

And the beef about English teachers is that they don't give enough writing assignments? How could they?

Now let's take a small piece of that big picture. How do you teach somebody to read *To Kill a Mockingbird?* If you've been an English major, and just about every secondary English teacher in the country was an English major not an education major, one of the first things you do is ask the students the question, "OK, you've read this book, what is the theme?" If you don't know what the theme is, what are you going to discuss?

George, one of the teachers we were studying, went in to class and asked "What's the theme of this book?" And they told him what the story was about. They didn't know what a theme was. So George gave them the definition of a theme. No luck. He tried analogies, metaphors, examples. Still no luck.

There is no question that George knew what a theme was. But it's a very subtle concept and he really struggled with trying to figure out how to teach it to a group of eleventh graders.

One of the things we're doing in our teacher education program is to develop uses for case studies of teaching in a manner analogous to the ways in which business and law schools use them. Brian, a student in the methods course in the teaching of English, read the case about George and his unsuccessful attempts to teach theme and really got down on George. Four months later, in Brian's own course, he started trying to teach his students what a theme was. In the debriefing after the third day, he walked in, dropped into a chair, looked at his supervisor, and said, "My God, I'm George!"

Again, the point here is that one of the reasons learning to teach is so difficult is that teaching is simply far more than telling what you know. Teaching takes practice. It takes feedback. It takes instruction.

## Observation

A second reason it is so difficult to learn to teach is that, unlike many other professions, people who learn to teach learn it after having completed, in Dan Lortie's phrase, a seventeen-year "apprenticeship of observation." They have spent seventeen years, more or less, and nearly 20,000 hours as observers of teaching and they've learned an enormous amount about it. And now you've got a relatively few number of hours, often to try to overcome the accumulation of models of teaching that they have so assiduously, and often emotionally, observed.

What that means is, to the extent that we in the university have any control over the kinds of models they get, we must recognize that the teacher of Shakespeare in the English department may be having a more profound impact on how the future teacher of Shakespeare will teach in the high school than the English methods professor is having in the brief period in which he might discuss the teaching of Shakespeare. I don't want to emphasize this too strongly, because I think that we who prepare teachers can do some very powerful things if we can surface the underlying preconceptions students have. But it would be so much easier if we didn't have to overcome some sort of pedagogical immunity first before trying to prepare someone to teach.

## Learning from Experience

Another reason learning to teach is difficult is that much of learning to teach depends on learning from experience, and if there is something we have learned from psychologists it is how very difficult learning from experience is.

The whole idea of learning from experience is: I do something, it doesn't work, so I try something else until I finally find something that does work. It's a kind of thoughtful trial and error, but it's predicated on two assumptions: one, we have reasonably accurate access to what we do, and two, we are reasonably accurate in identifying the consequences of what we do. But it is very difficult to establish those two assumptions.

As part of our research into developing new approaches to teacher assessment, we took over a local school in Palo Alto for a couple of weeks in summer and designed and built an assessment center. We brought in teachers at different levels who came for four days each to go through a whole variety of simulations and exercises that were designed to give a veridical representation of teaching.

One of those exercises required the teachers to bring in a lesson that they had actually taught. Here's how the rest of the exercise goes: First you go through an interview where you explain to your interviewer what the lesson is about, what its purposes are, and how you plan to teach it. Then we bring in half a dozen kids you've never seen before and you have to teach the lesson to those six kids. Meanwhile, we're videotaping the whole business.

When that's over you go to one room, the kids go to another room, the kids are asked questions like "What was that lesson about? What was the point?" and so on. You get a chance to reflect on the lesson and then we debrief—Here's what I think happened, here is what I would do differently if I had a chance, etc. Then we ask questions: How would you describe your teaching in that class?

One teacher answered that he teaches using the Socratic method—a Socratic dialogue that is interactive and involves the students. Then we looked at the videotape. The teaching followed this pattern: The teacher asks a question . . . no response from the students. So the teacher answers the question. The same pattern continues without interruption. I call this a Socratic monologue. The teacher did not engage in a dialogue, Socratic or otherwise.

That teacher had no sense that he was not teaching in the way he had intended. The reason is fairly straightforward. It's incredibly difficult to maintain one's engagement with a group of students, be there six or thirty-six of them. And one of the things you are not monitoring very well is what you yourself are doing. You're focused on the students. So it's not at all surprising that you lose touch with what you are doing.

But if that's the case, what are you going to learn from experience? Whatever you are going to learn has got to be somewhat distorted because you often begin with an inaccurate notion of what you have done. A major purpose of teacher education is to provide candidates with the wherewithal to monitor their own performance.

What about consequences? It helps to know what the consequences of your teaching are. One of the methods we use in our teacher education program is what we call reciprocal observation. In a course I teach jointly with a philosopher, student teachers pair up and interview one another about lessons each is going to observe the other teaching. They then go to each other's classrooms, observe the teaching, and take notes on the teaching they have seen. If there is a difference between what you think you were doing and what you were observed to do, you'll find out. After class, the observer interviews two or three kids about what they thought went on in that class. And then there is a final debriefing.

A teacher of physics, who was a wonderful physics student and understands physics very well, was teaching the opening lesson in a unit on mechanics. The lesson dealt with four different conceptions of force and, as described by his observer, it was a beautifully crafted lesson. There was lecture, there was interaction, it was just lovely, highly conceptual. Then we interviewed two students afterwards; each was asked, "What was the class about?" Each student answered, "It was about something called vectors and how to calculate them." What?

Well, you go back and look at the notes taken on the lecture. Of the forty-five minutes of the active teaching that was going on, ten of those minutes were spent on a kind of subordinate clause, as it were, in which the teacher went to the board and, because he wanted to give the students some language for talking about forces, taught them how to represent forces as arrows with a certain length and a certain direction, called vectors. This was the only time he went to the blackboard; it was, therefore, the only time the students took notes.

What he didn't know as a novice teacher was that there are ways students pick up the cues about what is important and what is not, and in fact what he had seen as a mere example—a kind of technical footnote in his lecture on forces—the students immediately zoomed in on as the core concept being taught.

Had there not been that interview with the students immediately thereafter, neither the observer nor the teacher would have had a clue about what the students had actually learned in that session. While it was a shock, as often these exercises are to our student teachers, they realized how undependable their institutions can be about what students are learning, and how much more systematically they must gather information from their students about what in fact they are learning.

My purpose in giving these examples is to show how the learning from experience avenue for teachers is not simple—it does not occur automatically or easily. But people can be taught a variety of ways of getting a better fix on what they actually do and on how to tap into the consequences of their actions.

## Influence of Past Teachers

One of the things that comes out very clearly in the intellectual biographies of our students is the enormous influence content course teachers have on students' conceptions of teaching. Whether they like it or not, university and college teachers in the disciplines are teacher educators. They are educating future teachers every time they represent their subject in a particular way, every time they either do or do not make the evaluations they conduct compatible with the goals of the instruction in which they engage, every time they present their pedagogy in a particular way.

An example: you may recall that the first scene of the first act in *Romeo and Juliet* is absolutely filthy, filled with the dirtiest puns. One of our student teachers was helping the students understand the punning and told them: "Approach the uses of language in the play as Shakespeare's equivalent to special effects in modern movies. We're attuned to the visual, but the people who went to Shakespeare's plays were attuned to the auditory. Many of them couldn't read but they could hear nuances, puns, plays on words. Those were the special effects. Let's see how many special effects we can find."

Then there was another example of somebody who wanted to teach her students to get into the habit of very close reading. So she had them bring in the lyrics of their favorite rock songs and paraphrase them. Now there may not be all that much meaning in the lyrics of rock songs, but this was something the kids had some investment in. They analyzed them very closely and then she said, "OK, now let's take a piece of Shakespeare and see if we can paraphrase that in the same careful way."

In each of those cases, when we asked the student teachers where they learned to do that, the answer was: "That's one of the things that was done in my Shakespeare course. It seemed to work pretty well. So I tried it myself." They are constantly drawing on the exemplars of pedagogy provided by the teacher educators who call themselves professors of English or mathematics or physics.

## Students of Teachers

Those are some of the reasons learning to teach is so difficult. But how can we turn what we know into something positive? If we begin with the notion that content teachers are themselves teacher educators, then perhaps one of the ways we can improve the preparation of teachers is to make future teachers much more conscious students of teaching, even when they are still undergraduates.

This is something we are going to try this year with a group of undergraduates who will begin a three-year program leading to a teaching degree at Stanford. In their seminar, we'll ask them to begin to become students of the teaching they get, whether in biology, English, economics, or history, and to begin to try to understand that teaching. I'll be interested to see how my colleagues in the arts and sciences feel about being scrutinized in that way. But I think it is quite reasonable for students who want to be teachers to look at the teaching they are getting as a wonderful opportunity to get smarter about teaching.

What sorts of things should they be looking for? First, they should ask how, if at all, does the teacher or course provide a glimpse of the underlying discipline or field of study? We've had a lot of talk about the importance of disciplinary integrity in the undergraduate preparation of people who are going to be teachers. One sense of disciplinary integrity is: Does somebody who is teaching biology have a sense of what biology is? Can that person deal intelligently with questions like, what are the most important concepts in biology? Which are the ones you want to make sure students understand, and which are more peripheral to the field?

What are the few simple ideas that underlie the complexities of algebra or geometry? Can you help the students see the forest for the trees so they don't get overwhelmed by the volume of the material being taught? We know that so much of our curriculum is coverage of enormous amounts of material. Is the student getting a sense of what the discipline itself looks like, about what the major concepts and their relations are, or is that left for somewhere else in the curriculum? Does the teaching, through its presentation, its discussions, its projects, its assignments, provide a glimpse of how people gain knowledge in a given discipline?

If it's a course in history, is there a sense not only of core ideas in history—the French revolution as a period of great ferment and excitement—but of how the historiography of the French revolution is done? About how historians begin to have those ideas, and what historical evidence looks like, and whether there is controversy among honest men and women who practice in this field, and how those controversies are addressed? Similarly with English: Is Macbeth a good play or a poor play? We've all been taught that Macbeth is a good play. What about a Neil Simon play? How are the standards of taste in a field like English developed? Are the syntax of the field, the rules of evidence in the field, the ways knowledge is developed in the field, reflected at all?

These are the sorts of things that teachers in a field must understand. The teacher is someone who not only tells students what is so, but has to be able to deal with why it is so. Why am I asking you to believe this and not simply dogmatically saying this is a good play and this is a poor one?

Another thing one should look for is: Do courses involve the students in a sense of having accomplished something worthwhile? Are the teachers and their courses rigorous, challenging, and demanding? What are the characteristics that make them so?

Next: Is there anything at all unusual or unconventional about the pedagogy? The answer may be no. It may be that nearly every teacher is teaching in a very conventional way. But I would think about the pedagogy on two levels. First, is the teacher using small groups, bringing inside what is outside the classroom as interactive projects of some sort, or something other than the conventional lecture/recitation method? Second, is there anything unconventional about the way the teacher has transformed or framed or organized the material of the course, so that by juxtaposition of what would otherwise be surprising texts or events or materials, he or she has created a pedagogical opportunity that would normally be missed?

For example, I was discussing the teaching of the Declaration of Independence with a group of faculty from both the arts and sciences and education departments at one of the California state universities. A professor of physics said, "Before teaching the Declaration of Independence, I would want to have the students spend some time understanding the logic of physics in a Newtonian perspective." We were puzzled. He explained, "Well, what does it mean to say 'we hold these truths to be self-evident?' I would want my students to look at a piece of physics text, as it were, from that era and a piece of the Declaration of Independence side by side so they could begin to understand that both of them were emerging from a very similar matrix of understanding." This, by the way, was a physics teacher who worked in an inner-city school—not St. Paul's or Milton Academy.

Sometimes the juxtaposition of things, the way you frame and formulate the material, can be just as pedagogically adventurous and powerful as using some method or technique that is unusual but leaving the material in its pristine form. We must be open to alternative conceptions of what we mean by unconventional pedagogy.

Finally, what kind of sense does one get of the affective, motivational, personal, element of the teaching? Does the teacher display a sense of passion behind the teaching? I would distinguish between passion and charisma; some people communicate a deep set of feelings about what they teach that does not necessarily translate itself into the typical notion of a charismatic teacher, though the two may in fact go hand in hand. How, if at all, does the teacher communicate that he or she gives a damn or has deep feelings and considers the subject extremely important? If so, is there some way to teach this quality or at least to convey its importance?

All our research on learning to teach really revolves around the notion that teaching, that incredibly complex and demanding activity, is the central focus of everything we do in universities and colleges and it ought to be the primary concern for all of us. Currently, only one part of the university—the school of education or department of education—takes the responsibility for preparing people to engage in teaching. But, like it or not, the entire university is a participant in the teacher education process. All who teach are obliged to become more positive and helpful participants in teacher preparation, rather than randomly assigned accessories. And all who teach are obliged to think about how they teach, as well as the content of what they teach. The stakes are too high for us to tolerate anything less.

# INTRODUCTION

# TOWARD A PEDAGOGY
# OF SUBSTANCE (1989)

IN HIS WORK as a teacher educator, Shulman proposed what has become a foundational idea for the field, which he called *pedagogical content knowledge* (see Chapter Five, "Knowledge and Teaching"). This essay translates that idea for an audience of faculty and administrators from multiple disciplines assembled at the American Association for Higher Education's 1989 National Conference. Building on an address the previous evening by Jaime Escalante—the high school mathematics teacher whose work was made famous in the movie *Stand and Deliver*—Shulman advocates a "pedagogy of substance, rooted in the subject matter itself as well as in a connection with the lives and culture" of students. His argument for "a new kind of disciplinary scholarship" focused on teaching and learning prefigures a commitment to the scholarship of teaching and learning that becomes a hallmark of his leadership at the Carnegie Foundation when he assumes the presidency in 1997.

# 7

# TOWARD A PEDAGOGY
# OF SUBSTANCE

IT'S ALWAYS A PARTICULAR JOY for me to come back to my hometown. I took a cab ride last night, and in striking up a conversation with the driver found that he was a man of about my age who had grown up in the same Logan Square neighborhood on the near northwest side of Chicago that I had.

I asked him about the neighborhood, and he said, "Well, you wouldn't recognize it now. Different kinds of folks moved in. Not folks like us," and he was talking about *us* as first-generation, eastern European emigrants. That's what most of the neighborhood was when I was a kid. He said, "The wrong kind of people live in there now."

As I talked to this cabbie, I thought again, in sweet nostalgia, about my own life in Chicago and was so thankful that the folks on the admissions committee at the University of Chicago many years ago hadn't looked at my background and said, "Better not take a chance on him. Wrong kind of people." Because you know that fifty years ago somebody was riding around in a cab in Logan Square and saying, "Boy, this used to be one hell of a neighborhood, but now it's full of the wrong kind of people."

The reason I bring up this cab ride is because I sit on an elected faculty committee at Stanford University called the Advisory Board, where we have the responsibility of reviewing every appointment or promotion to tenure in the university.

We had an interaction in the committee just a couple of weeks ago in which we were reviewing the record of an extraordinary young scholar. A fellow in engineering. All the letters from outside said that this guy was the number one person of his age cohort in his field. But something about his record troubled me.

When you look at the student evaluations—because you've got to have a demonstration of the quality of teaching, not just the quality of scholarship—there was a recurrent pattern. They were bimodal—about half the class always thought that he was extraordinarily good, and a good half the class thought that he was absolutely horrible. "Goes too fast." "Doesn't explain what he's saying." "Isn't well organized." "Doesn't give good feedback."

One of my colleagues on the committee, who was from the natural sciences and mathematics side, said, "Now that's what I call a good teaching record."

And I said, "What do you mean? He's leaving half these kids in the dust."

He said, "Yeah, but those are probably the kinds of kids who shouldn't be studying physics anyway."

Wrong kind of students. They shouldn't be there.

I said to him, "My God, he's teaching undergraduates at Stanford. What if he were teaching in the real world? Do you know how hard it is to get into this place? And you're simply dismissing half the kids who take this guy's physics class because they're the 'wrong kind of students'?"

And yet, what struck me is what a facile, glib, pedagogical explanation that is for all of us, whether we're driving cabs or teaching in the university. When things just don't seem to go well, trouble is we're working with the wrong kind of people.

I think that this "stand and deliver" theme that AAHE has so aptly selected for this meeting is a theme that says, "That kind of account of why teaching doesn't work will no longer fly." We do not applaud the physician who heals all patients who come to her except those who are ill; we call that malpractice if done with a certain persistence or consistency.

And I dare say I do not call elite pedagogy the ability not to teach those whose learning is most valuable because, as I explained to my colleague on the Advisory Board, "You know, there are places in this country that feel a responsibility to educate by teaching and not just by selection. Not just by admitting in those who will learn whether you admit them or not."

I think that's what Jaime Escalante represents for us. He represents this sense of obligation, commitment, moral and ethical, as well as pedagogical responsibility, to teach all the youngsters who are entrusted to us.

"Stand and deliver" is a powerful metaphor, which captures the courage, the tenacity, of the teacher who will not give up. And yet, for our purposes I think it is also an incomplete metaphor, as are almost all metaphors and analogies if pushed as far as they should be. Because teaching, of course, is more than "stand and deliver." It's more than standing up and giving your very best lecture to those passive souls, those nodding heads, those kids who take pride in going through four years of college without ever taking an eight o'clock, even when they've got one.

I would like to expand, elaborate, go beyond, these notions of "stand and deliver" to discuss a broader notion of teaching, a notion that emerges from my own research, from an exciting and growing research literature in precollegiate as well as collegiate teaching, and from examples accessible to all of us if we would but pay some attention to them.

The example to which we can pay initial attention is Jaime Escalante himself, because an analysis of his teaching would make it very clear that the reason he is an extraordinary teacher is because he does not merely stand and deliver.

Many of you saw the movie about Escalante, *Stand and Deliver*. Of course, the movie is not Escalante, but data aren't reality either and we make a lot of those. So let me take a brief scene from that movie and revisit it with you.

Very early in the movie Escalante is having an encounter with this class of his. And he says to the class, "Let's talk about negative numbers." Remember that scene?

Negative numbers. Minus two, plus two. Minus two, plus two. He says, "Very important, negative numbers." Escalante understands that if you don't understand about negative and positive numbers, you are dead as you continue trying to study mathematics.

Does he go to the board and start writing equations? Hell no. He says, "You go to the beach. You dig a hole in the sand." Remember that scene? "You dig a hole and you put the sand next to the hole. The hole? Minus two. The pile of sand? Plus two."

He's talking to kids in L.A. who not only have a lot of experience at the beach but wish they were there at the moment they are sitting there with him. They know what holes in the sand look like. What happens if you put them back together again? The hole is minus two, the sand is plus two.

There's silence in the class, wait-time. He strolls to the back of the class, eyes riveted to this kid in the back row who's a gang member with one foot out the door. And he says, "What do you get? Minus two, plus two?"

Finally the kid very quietly says, "Zero." And Escalante says, "Right. Zero. The Greeks didn't understand zero. Your ancestors, the Mayans, they *invented* zero." End of the scene. Probably takes no more than forty-five seconds in the movie. I probably got parts of it wrong already, but as I said, it was like data.

What do we learn from that little clip about pedagogy? The first thing we learn is a good pedagogue understands the subject matter. Now that may seem trivially obvious, but it's not. It's not trivially obvious because it's difficult to understand the subject matter.

When a fifth grader goes up to an elementary school teacher and says, "When we divide fractions by fractions, we're supposed to invert and multiply, right?"

"Yeah."

"Why?"

Most fifth grade teachers don't know the reason. And do you know why? Among other things, because although she took three courses in mathematics during her university preparation—none of them in the School of Education, by the way—nobody ever taught her that. Or if they taught her that, they didn't take enough care and assessment and feedback to make sure she understood it. So knowing the subject matter is not trivially simple. Not at all.

The second thing that Escalante does in his knowledge of teaching is he understands the difference between what's in the book that you really have to know, and what's in the book that you can live without. Think about textbooks, both at the precollegiate and the collegiate level. Have you noticed that they aren't getting smaller?

The outstanding pedagogue recognizes that you can't teach everything, and so understands the subject matter deeply enough to be selective, to be simplifying, to be structuring and organizing. Escalante does not do what the typical pedagogue does, and do a chapter a week, relentlessly. No matter what.

A third thing that Escalante understands is that the heads of students are full, are rich, are variegated. And that teaching involves connecting not with their ignorance but with their prior knowledge.

Understanding the impact of prior knowledge on subsequent learning has been the most significant area of progress in cognitive science and cognitive psychology in the last ten years. I don't believe that Escalante reads that literature, but he understands the principles behind it, understands how exquisitely a teacher must connect with what students already know and come up with a set of pedagogical representations, metaphors, analogies, examples, stories, demonstrations, that will connect with those prior understandings, that will make them visible, will correct them when they are way off base, and will help the students generate, create, construct, their own representations to replace them. Because if the students don't get help using representations that are powerful and productive, they'll keep on using the ones they had at the beginning, which are often distortive and limiting.

Escalante understands about representations. If you see the movie, if you read about him, he's an extraordinary creator of physical representations, of models, of examples, of stories of all kinds to teach the stuff of mathematics. And yet he goes beyond that. He makes an extraordinary human connection with his students, a connection that is initiated by the expectation that they can and will learn.

That's one of the themes in the movie. The rest of the mathematics department says these are the wrong kinds of kids for mathematics. Teach them how to balance their checkbooks. His response implicitly is if all we teach them is how to balance their checkbooks, the sums will wind up being so small that it won't be much of a job to balance.

No. He expects, demands, challenges. He will not be satisfied with the explanation "they're the wrong kind of kids for calculus."

He is masterful in the way he organizes classroom life, and I suspect that he thinks hard about what he is doing, reflects on it, and learns from experience. He does not strike me as the kind of teacher who figures that he had it right the first time he did it and he'll keep on doing it that way again and again because it sure seemed to work okay the first time.

I urge you to read the book about Escalante that was written by Jay Matthews called *Escalante: Best Teacher in America,* a subtitle that, I think, embarrasses Escalante and actually embarrasses Matthews.

There are a couple of things that are really neat in the book. First of all, the book was begun before the movie was even a glimmer. It was a five-year project by Matthews, who's a correspondent for the *Washington Post* in California. One thing you see is that Escalante had years of experience teaching physics and mathematics in Bolivia before he came to the United States. And he wasn't an instant success. He had to learn from experience.

But there is something else that's extraordinary in the book that you never see in the movie. One of the worrisome things about the movie is that people conclude, sure, Escalante can succeed with the wrong kind of kids. He's charismatic. He's flamboyant. He's willing to teach himself into a heart attack. I guess that's what you need, a combination of P. T. Barnum and somebody in cardiac arrest. That's the great teacher.

Well, not all of us are a coronary P. T. Barnum. Therefore, Escalante is simply an anomaly, not someone to be taken seriously.

But when you read the book you learn something very interesting. Once Escalante created the precedent, broke the cycle of negative expectations, there were so many kids who wanted to study mathematics seriously at Garfield High that they had to hire a second teacher. The other teacher is also of Hispanic origin, younger than Escalante, and an utterly different personality and teaching style. Not flamboyant, apparently not charismatic. Never had a heart attack. But you know what? The results that his students get on AP calculus are exactly the same as those who study with Escalante. That's the most critical datum that's in the book and not in the movie.

It isn't just the charismatic oddball who can teach the wrong kind of kids. Good teaching can teach kids. And it's that kind of pedagogy—what I call a *pedagogy of substance*—rooted in the subject matter itself as well as in a connection with the lives and culture of the kids, that produces the sorts of results that we see so dramatically in the movie, but that we would see if we went out to many classrooms in the secondary level, the elementary level, the collegiate level all over the country.

What is fascinating is that as you analyze that teaching, as I did very briefly a few moments ago, you see that it isn't just someone who has mastered a set of teaching tricks, it's not just process. And it's not just someone who has a deep knowledge of the subject matter. Neither one of those is sufficient.

What we see in great teaching is the masterful intersection of the two. Someone who really understands the subject deeply *and* understands how exquisitely complex it is to make your knowledge accessible to the knowing processes of those who do not yet understand.

How inappropriate the image of "stand and deliver" is if pushed too far. Because it isn't like Federal Express. It isn't taking this package of stuff and delivering it. It's a process of elicitation, joint construction, nurturance, midwifery. Our policy is, we *don't* deliver. Anything that can be merely delivered probably wasn't worth having in the first place.

Now, where do people learn such things? It's one of the striking things we've learned in our research the last seven years as we've studied how young men and women learn to teach.

We've been doing longitudinal case studies of how people who already know something—mathematics, biology, English, history—learn to teach what they apparently already know. I'm not going to go into the details of this research. But there are some striking things that happen when you begin to play, as it were, Boswell to these young Johnsons who are becoming teachers, as you follow them and interview them, do biographies, intellectual and otherwise, with them, watch them teach, interview their students, give them tasks to do. A kind of longitudinal ethnography of pedagogy is what we're doing.

One of the things you find is that they don't begin to learn to teach at that magic moment when they leave the arts and sciences behind and move to the teacher education program. No. They've been learning to teach for years in what Dan Lortie has called the "apprenticeship of observation."

And it peaks when they enter the university. We interview them, asking them, "Where did you get the idea for teaching that way? And how did you come to think about Hamlet that way? And that was an interesting way in which you presented the notion of photosynthesis. Where did you learn that?"

We find they learned it in the arts and sciences, where a hell of a lot more teacher education is going on, without being named that, than is going on in the schools of education. After all, schools of education get only 10 or 15 percent of the student's time. The arts and sciences are normal schools! The students are learning to teach there.

You say, "Well, yes, but all they see are lectures and simple discussions. You in education teach them much more." And I say, you're confusing teaching process with teaching. Where do they get those metaphors? Where do they get those examples? Where do they get those ways of thinking about what Hamlet represents? About what a predicate nominative is? Where do they get those ideas that are the stuff, the guts, of their pedagogy? They get most of them before they ever come to the School of Education.

Undergraduate arts and sciences education is, in its own way, one of the most successful examples of teacher education I have ever documented. It just never got called that.

And what is so important about it is that the future teachers in those arts and sciences classes are not simply going to learn for themselves. Every misconception, every incomplete idea, every less-than-inspired example of pedagogy ends up living in them to be transmitted to others. The students in your arts and sciences classes are carriers. They will take along what you have taught and transmit it with great fidelity to those whom they teach.

Now, one of the things we see when we look at teaching analytically is this combination of an emphasis on understanding the subject matter, understanding how it is represented in the heads of students, and then being able to generate representations of your own as a teacher that will be a bridge between the subject matter and the students.

What do we know, both from research and from experience, about those different sorts of phenomena? Let me start with an example of what is in students' heads, because by and large some of the greatest disasters that we create as teachers occur because we fail to read the text of the students' minds, so busy are we reading the text in front of us.

One of my student teachers was teaching a course in world history, fondly called by the students and the teachers "From Plato to NATO." World history in California takes twenty weeks. And this student of mine had just finished teaching the unit on the Reformation, Protestant Reformation, a unit that took three days. Well, she was such a fine teacher that she got through the Reformation in two-and-a-half and, therefore, had the opportunity to do the unusual, namely to ask the students if they had any questions about the material.

One student in the back of the room raised her hand and said, "Well, I understand what you've told me. But there's something that puzzles me. I understand about Martin Luther; I understand about the importance of the printed Bible. And I know he nailed the theses up on the door and all that. But I'm surprised that you never once mentioned his extraordinary importance for black people."

Well, my teacher scratched her head and said, "There were no black people in Germany in those days, and so he couldn't have any impact for black people."

The student in the back of the room seemed satisfied, wrote it down dutifully and meekly. But by then five or six other students were obviously experiencing the same kind of pain that underlay the first student's question. And, thank God, the teacher we were training was sensitive enough and responsible enough not to simply be satisfied with the first student's acquiescence, and she said, "Is there still something that you don't understand?"

One of the other students said, "Yeah, that's still kind of confusing, because then why did he give that speech about 'I have a dream'?"

It turned out that a third of the class thought that Martin Luther and Martin Luther King were the same person. Protestant minister, hell-raiser, revolutionary, extraordinarily important figure in history. And he was born and lived and died before any of them were born.

But there's a deeper message here. Those students had already learned that it was not theirs to reason why. Their job was to make sense, whether what you're taught, "delivered" shall we say, seems sensible or not. Those kids were making a sense in which Martin Luther and Martin Luther King could be the same person.

How many times in your classes does something similar to that happen and neither you nor I am aware of it? Because we do not connect with the constructed representations in the minds of our students. Multiply this trivial example by ten and by a hundred, because we don't listen. We don't hear. We don't elicit.

We can't say that the students have trouble learning, or they have these preconceptions, because they're dumb or they're the wrong kind of students. Because if we look beyond our classrooms, if we look to the history of ideas in many of our fields, we find that what we now treat as stupid misconceptions or preconceptions in the minds of our students were considered the state of knowledge several centuries before by very smart people.

There's a lovely example in the history of physics about Galileo trying to solve the problem of why it was impossible to pump water more than thirty-two feet. At the time of Galileo, every workman could tell you that, but nobody understood why. That was the job of Galileo, and he came up with an answer. The reason was that as you pump the water higher and higher, it forms a column of water that is like a spring, and eventually the column collapses of its own weight. A very clever, brilliant explanation that's dead wrong.

Galileo had all the data he needed, but he was locked in the wrong metaphor, because the water isn't like a spring. But the smartest person arguably of his century, maybe of the millennium, couldn't get liberated from his own preconception. A failure of pedagogy, if you will. One can look at the history of many of our fields as a history of pedagogy, as a history of the ways in which representations either succeed one another, or, to paraphrase Clifford Geertz, the new conceptions sort of run alongside and help enrich our understanding and interpretation of the world around us.

Pedagogy, understanding this connection between old representations and new ones—a pedagogy of substance—is what teaching is all about. And what we see as we study the products of higher education who are being prepared to teach is that one of their major failings is their inability to generate, to create, new alternative representations. It's one of the things that we as higher educators apparently fail to do.

I think that what we're concluding is that the knowledge needed by the pedagogue is deeper than that needed by the mere student in your field. And yet, if you examine what it means to know something in the rich way that a teacher needs, you would conclude, "Ah, wouldn't it be lovely if those who weren't going to be teachers understood it that richly as well."

I think we would conclude that the curriculum we would construct in the liberal arts and sciences, that we would fit to the future teacher, would probably be not all that different from the curriculum deserved by those who are not going to be future teachers as well.

Let me conclude with a few practical recommendations, though I warn you that what I call *practical* and what you call *feasible* may not be the same thing. For me, practical is the opposite of "theoretical" or "speculative."

First of all, I think that we ought to take much more seriously the apprenticeship of observation in our colleges and universities, and not simply permit it to go on accidentally, as it currently does. For those of us in the colleges and universities, our preparation of future teachers is analogous, if you will, to having people in a premedical curriculum spend four years studying in a hospital yet never once ask them to learn from what they're seeing and experiencing every day.

Future teachers are, I must remind you, not just those who are going to be in K–12. Future teachers are those whom you see as your best students, whom you dream will get a Ph.D. and then do what? Teach. And they are those who are going to go into business and industry and will spend a great deal of their time mentoring other people in their workplaces as teachers; they, too, are in the midst of a teaching environment.

I'll give you an example. We have a program that the Mellon Foundation is supporting for able undergraduates who want to go into teaching. In our seminar for the Mellon Fellows, one of the things we have them do is identify one of the undergraduate courses they are currently taking that they really love and study the teaching going on in that course while they're studying the course itself.

We teach them how to analyze the syllabus, how to think about the assessments and the assignments they get, how to think about what makes for good lectures and poor lectures. And then we prepare them for interviewing the teacher.

They come in and say, "I'm preparing to be a teacher, and I've been asked to identify the best teacher I have this quarter to see if I can learn from what that teacher is doing. I wonder if you'd be prepared to help me learn how to be more like you." Funny, they never get kicked out of the teacher's office.

And they find that after a few moments of hesitation, the teacher reacts with animation, excitement. "Nobody ever talks to me about my teaching." The student asks questions: "What would you do differently if you weren't teaching this course in ten weeks but in fifteen? What would you do if you only had eight weeks? What would you cut out?"

Second, I think we've got to give much more responsibility to the students to integrate what they're learning from us in our typically disorganized undergraduate programs, which treat general education as something to be acquired through careful selection among distributional alternatives.

And friends, we cannot make them integrated by giving a comprehensive exam at the end of the fourth year. The assessment we do at the end doesn't retroactively synthesize the disorder that preceded it. It's a religious experience for us; it gives us a sense of expiation. But it doesn't improve the education for the students.

Finally, I think we have to return to the original conception of the doctor of philosophy degree. There was an inspiration about twenty-five years ago called the doctor of arts degree, and I think it made one fundamental mistake. It should have been called a "doctor of philosophy," because that's what a doctor of philosophy is. A doctor of philosophy is a teacher who is in love with the knowledge that he or she has acquired.

We must reintroduce at the heart of our various disciplines doctoral-level preparation in the pedagogy of the substance of our disciplines. Such programs would not merely be programs of teaching methods. They would focus on issues of representation. They would focus on the history, the philosophy, the psychology of knowledge, of discovery, of invention in those disciplines, and the connection between those kinds of activities, those kinds of representations, and teaching curriculum and learning in those disciplines.

It would be deep work, and it would carry with it a new kind of disciplinary scholarship, which should be celebrated by journals and by promotion and tenure for successfully pursuing such scholarship, because the highest level of attainment in those fields should be for those who not only know their discipline but can teach it, even to the wrong kind of people.

This is the challenge for us. To learn to do the job of the university so well that even when presented with the wrong kind of people, be they students at Stanford who don't have heads for mathematics or students at Garfield High School to whom no sane person should even try to teach calculus, we help those students to succeed.

If we don't meet this challenge of taking the pedagogy seriously, I fear that fifty years from now people will look back on our era as the period in the late 1980s and early 1990s when we had the opportunity in less than a decade to educate two-thirds of the teachers who would teach for the next thirty-five years, the period when we had this extraordinary opportunity to make a difference in education.

And wouldn't it be ironic if when they looked back on what we did to meet the challenge, they were to conclude that it was we, the teachers, who were the wrong kind of people.

Thank you.

# TEACHING AS COMMUNITY PROPERTY: PUTTING AN END TO PEDAGOGICAL SOLITUDE (1993)

---

EXCERPTED FROM A PRESENTATION at the American Association for Higher Education's National Conference on Faculty Roles and Rewards held in January 1993 in San Antonio, this essay was then published as an opinion piece in *Change* in late 1993. Its title has been much quoted and built upon by educators attracted to Shulman's argument that if teaching is to be more valued in higher education (and therefore worked at, improved, and rewarded) it must be reconnected to the disciplines and their scholarly communities.

# 8

# TEACHING AS COMMUNITY PROPERTY

## PUTTING AN END TO PEDAGOGICAL SOLITUDE

AT THE END OF the June commencement at which I received my graduate degree, George Beadle, then president of the University of Chicago, turned to those of us baking in our robes in Rockefeller Chapel and proclaimed, "Welcome to the community of scholars." Perspiring though I was, a chill went through me because this was something I had aspired to—membership in a community of scholars.

As the years have gone by, I've come to appreciate how naïve was my anticipation of what it would mean to be a member of a scholarly community. My anticipation contained two visions. One was the vision of the solitary individual laboring quietly, perhaps even obscurely, somewhere in the library stacks, or in a laboratory, or at an archaeological site; someone who pursued his or her scholarship in splendid solitude. My second vision was of this solitary scholar entering the social order—becoming a member of the community—interacting with others, in the classroom and elsewhere, as a teacher.

What I didn't understand as a new Ph.D. was that I had it backwards! We experience isolation not in the stacks but in the classroom. We close the classroom door and experience pedagogical solitude, whereas in our life as scholars, we are members of active communities: communities of conversation, communities of evaluation, communities in which we gather with others in our invisible colleges to exchange our findings, our methods, and our excuses.

I now believe that the reason teaching is not more valued in the academy is because the way we treat teaching removes it from the community of scholars. It is not that universities diminish the importance of teaching because they devalue the act itself; it is not that research is seen as having more intrinsic value than teaching. Rather, we celebrate those aspects of our lives and work that can become, as we say in California, "community property." And if we wish to see greater recognition and reward attached to teaching, we must change the status of teaching from private to community property. I would suggest three strategies that can guide us in this transformation.

First, we need to reconnect teaching to the disciplines. Although the disciplines are easy to bash because of the many problems they create for us, they are, nevertheless, the basis for our intellectual communities. Like it or not, the forms of scholarship that are seen as intellectual work in the disciplines are going to be valued more than forms of scholarship (such as teaching) that are seen as non-disciplinary.

Notice that I say non-disciplinary, not inter-disciplinary. (I would argue that most modern disciplines are in fact inter-disciplines.) The distinction is not between disciplinary and *inter*-disciplinary but disciplinary and *non*-disciplinary. Look, for instance, at the way the improvement of teaching is *treated* in most of our schools. Institutional support for teaching and its improvement tends to reside in a universitywide center for teaching and learning where many of the TAs are trained, and where faculty—regardless of department—can go for assistance in improving their practice. That's a perfectly reasonable idea. But notice the message it conveys—that teaching is generic, technical, and a matter of performance; that it's not part of the community that means so much to most faculty, the disciplinary, inter-disciplinary, or professional community. It's something general you lay on top of what you *really* do as a scholar in a discipline.

Similarly, in most of our institutions, the student evaluation forms are identical across the disciplines, as if teaching civil engineering and teaching Chaucer were the same. But of course they're not. We would never dream of sending out examples of someone's research for peer review to people at another university who were on that other university's faculty *in general*. The medievalists evaluate the research of other medievalists; research by civil engineers is reviewed by other civil engineers. Not so with teaching.

The first strategy I would argue for, then, in attempting to make teaching community—and therefore *valued*—property, is that we recognize that the communities that matter most are strongly identified with the disciplines of our scholarship. "Discipline" is in fact a powerful pun because it not only denotes a domain but also suggests a process: a community that disciplines is one that exercises quality, control, judgment, evaluation, and paradigmatic definition. We need to make the review, examination, and support of teaching part of the responsibility of the disciplinary community.

The second strategy I would propose is that if teaching is going to be community property it must be made visible through artifacts that capture its richness and complexity. In the absence of such artifacts teaching is a bit like dry ice; it disappears at room temperature. You may protest, "But that's so much work!" Notice that we don't question this need to document when it comes to more traditional forms of scholarship. We don't judge each other's research on the basis of casual conversations in the hall; we say to our colleagues, "That's a lovely idea! You really must write it up." It may, in fact, take two years to write it up. But we accept this because it's clear that scholarship entails an artifact, a product, some form of community property that can be shared, discussed, critiqued, exchanged, built upon. So, if pedagogy is to become an important part of scholarship, we have to provide it with this same kind of documentation and transformation.

The third strategy is that if something is community property in the academy, and is thus deemed valuable, this means we deem it something whose value we have an obligation to judge. We assume, moreover, that our judgments will be enacted within the disciplinary community, which means, I'm afraid, that the terrifying phrase "peer review" must be applied to teaching. Think what this would mean: if your institution is like mine, the principle of peer review is best expressed not as an inverse-square law but as a direct-square law. The influence of any evaluation of someone's scholarship is directly related to the square of the distance from the campus where the evaluator works. So for Stanford faculty, a Berkeley review is pretty good, but Oxford is *much* better. (I haven't checked to see whether the curve continues as you go to Australia or if there's a plateau, but this is the sort of thing higher education researchers would probably enjoy studying.) My point is that the artifacts of teaching must be created and preserved so that they can be judged by communities of peers beyond the office next door.

This kind of peer review may seem far-fetched on many campuses; it is far from the norm. But one of the sources of pleasure I have had at Stanford is serving on the universitywide Appointments and Promotions Committee and thus reviewing promotion and appointment folders for the business school. In our business school, and I suspect in a number across the country, the promotion folders look very different from those in, say, history or biology. The portfolios of business school faculty are often just as thick in the domain of teaching as they are in the area of traditional social science and business scholarship. Included in them are samples of instructional materials developed by the teachers, cases they have written, and detailed essays in which candidates gloss and interpret the course syllabi that are included in their portfolios. Most impressive of all, one finds reviews by colleagues who visit their classes and critique their case-based teaching, and reports by faculty at other business schools who examine their teaching materials and their cases. What a contrast to the promotion dossier that provides three sets of student ratings and two letters that say, "She must be a good teacher, she sure gives a good talk!"

There's an important corollary point to mention here too. We should evaluate each other as teachers not only with an eye to deriving accurate measurements of our teaching effectiveness—though of course we must have precision. Our evaluations should also have positive consequences for the processes and persons being evaluated. We are obliged, that is, to organize the evaluation of teaching so that the very procedures we employ raise the likelihood that teaching gets treated seriously, systematically, and as central to the lives of individual faculty and institutions. This means we are obliged to use procedures from which faculty are likely to learn how to teach better. I like the way the chair of the English Department at Stanford put it: "What we're trying to do," he said, "is to create a culture of teaching, one in which the conversations, the priorities [and, I would add, the rituals and kinship systems] of the department have teaching at their center."

No single change will produce this culture, but let me end with one suggestion that would, I think, take us a long way toward it. If we really want a different kind of culture, we ought to change our advertising. By way of example, I've drafted an ad for *The Chronicle* announcing a new position in 20th Century U.S. History at Shulman College. "We seek a new faculty member who is good at both research and teaching"—the ad says the usual things along those lines. But then it goes on to say that candidates who are invited to campus will be asked to offer two colloquia. In one colloquium, they will describe their current research—the usual research colloquium. In the second, which we'll call the *pedagogical colloquium,* they will address the pedagogy of their discipline. They will do so by expounding on the design of a course, showing systematically how this course is an act of scholarship in the discipline, and explaining how the course represents the central issues in the discipline and how in its pedagogy it affords students the opportunity to engage in the intellectual and moral work of the discipline.

Think of the impact on our doctoral programs if we knew that there were colleges and universities out there that had agreed to employ the *pedagogical colloquium* as a regular, central portion of that mating ritual we call recruitment. We could begin to change the ways we think about preparation for a life or career of scholarship. Moreover, the public nature of this *pedagogical colloquium* would change the culture of the institution doing that recruiting. We could begin to look as seriously at evidence of teaching abilities as we do at research productivity. We would no longer have merely to pray that this good young scholar can educate. We would have evidence of his or her abilities as an educator-in-the-discipline.

To change academic culture in this way will not be easy. But colleges and universities have always taken justifiable pride in their commitment to inquiry and criticism in all fields, even those where dogma and habit make real scrutiny uncomfortable. Now we must turn this tough scrutiny on our own practices, traditions, and culture. Only by doing so will we make teaching truly central to higher education.

INTRODUCTION

# THE SCHOLARSHIP OF TEACHING:
# NEW ELABORATIONS,
# NEW DEVELOPMENTS (1999)

WHEN LEE SHULMAN was selected as president of The Carnegie Foundation for the Advancement of Teaching in 1997,
he immediately inaugurated a program to support serious,
disciplined inquiry by faculty into the work of teaching and
learning in their fields. The Carnegie Academy for the Scholarship of Teaching and Learning (CASTL), as the program is
called, brings faculty together for such work, and involves
campuses and scholarly societies as partners. This essay, coau-
thored with longtime colleague Pat Hutchings, and originally
published in *Change* in 1999, provides an overview of the central ideas, issues, and aims of the scholarship of teaching and
learning.

# THE SCHOLARSHIP
# OF TEACHING

## NEW ELABORATIONS, NEW DEVELOPMENTS

*Pat Hutchings and Lee S. Shulman*

IT'S THE MIDDLE OF JUNE as we begin this article, and our writing faces serious competition from the spirited company of 43 faculty in residence here at the Carnegie Foundation. Members of the Carnegie Academy for the Scholarship of Teaching and Learning (CASTL), these "Carnegie Scholars"—selected through the Pew National Fellowship Program, one of CASTL's components—examine teaching and learning issues in their fields in order, as our program materials say, to (1) foster significant, long-lasting learning for all students, (2) advance the practice and profession of teaching, and (3) bring to teaching the recognition afforded to other forms of scholarly work. One Scholar is studying "moments of difficulty" as opportunities for student learning; another is pilot-testing a new model for teaching accounting; several have focused their work on ways to make students more purposeful, self-directed learners.

CASTL is only a piece of the larger picture, but work such as this opens useful windows on what is happening in this fourth of the four scholarships, the "scholarship of teaching": what it is, its contributions and conundrums, and, especially, how notions about it have evolved since its initial appearance in work by Ernest Boyer and Eugene Rice at the beginning of this decade.

For starters, it's now safe to say—as many in higher education predicted—that the scholarship of teaching has been a catalyst for thought and action. True, some faculty find the term off-putting or confusing. At a recent event for campuses, one participant reported that there was a readiness among her colleagues for many of the *ideas* behind the scholarship of teaching but that the phrase itself was divisive and simply could not be used. In general, however, the scholarship of teaching and the vision it embodies—albeit sometimes fuzzily—have generated significant interest and activity in the last few years.

Within the context of the Carnegie program, for instance, we would point not only to the 43 faculty selected to participate (representing nine fields and diverse campuses), but to the much larger pool of applicants the program attracts. There are, in short, now faculty—lots of them—who are eager to engage in sustained inquiry into their teaching practice and their students' learning and who are well positioned to do so in ways that contribute to practice beyond their own classrooms.

We would point, as well, to the growing list of campuses (about 120 as we write this, ranging from Augustana College to Xavier University of Louisiana, from Brown University to Birmingham-Southern, from Middlesex Community College to the University of Minnesota) that have made a public commitment to the scholarship of teaching through CASTL's Campus Program. Coordinated by Carnegie's partner, the American Association for Higher Education (AAHE), the Campus Program invites campuses to undertake a public process of stock-taking and planning for ways they can support knowledge-building about teaching and learning. Our hope is that many of these campus conversations will evolve into what we are calling campus "teaching academies," new entities that can serve as support systems, sanctuaries, and learning centers for scholars across the disciplines, interdisciplines, and professions pursuing the scholarship of teaching seriously.

Scholarly and professional societies, too, are part of the action, working as partners with Carnegie and AAHE to advance the development of the scholarship of teaching.

But there is, as they say, more: witness the growing literature on the topic in just the last few years. In 1996, K. Patricia Cross (longtime champion of faculty members' study of their students' learning) and her colleague Mimi Harris Steadman gave us *Classroom Research: Implementing the Scholarship of Teaching.* Two years later it was *Scholarship Assessed,* the sequel to *Scholarship Reconsidered,* in which Charles Glassick, Mary Taylor Huber, and Eugene Maeroff set forth standards for assessing the full range of scholarly work in which faculty engage, including teaching and the scholarship of teaching. Last spring saw the release of a special issue of Indiana University's journal *Research and Creative Activity,* dedicated wholly to the scholarship of teaching as practiced by faculty in that system (and introduced in a terrific essay by Eileen Bender and Donald Gray). Meanwhile, Jossey-Bass is planning a new volume on the subject, drawing on an international study by Carolin Kreber of the University of Alberta. And of course, this article in *Change* should be mentioned, drawing as it does on all this earlier work and on current work through the Carnegie Academy.

Also notable are the many events and gatherings focused on the scholarship of teaching. AAHE's National Conference last March featured a special Campus Colloquium on the scholarship of teaching, at which interest far exceeded the 250-person capacity. Marquette University recently posted a call for proposals for a "Scholarship of Teaching" conference to be held this fall in conjunction with its Preparing Future Faculty program. This summer's Academy of Management meeting includes an invited symposium on the scholarship of teaching; next year's American Chemical Society meeting will do the same. In addition, AAHE's conference on faculty roles and rewards next February will have as its theme "*Scholarship Reconsidered* Reconsidered," with a major strand of sessions focused on the scholarship of teaching.

Finally, we now see the beginnings of an infrastructure to support the scholarship of teaching: "teaching academies" and other entities established on campuses to help sustain such work; Web-based resources, such as the Crossroads Project of the American Studies Association, through which faculty can make their teaching and scholarship of teaching "community property" available for peer review and commentary; and new online journals focused on the scholarship of teaching, such as the one at George Mason University (www.doiiit.gmu.edu/inventio).

Our colleague at Carnegie, Mary Huber, recently began a study of forums in which the exchange of information and ideas about teaching and learning in higher education takes place. "What has been surprising to me," Huber reported in her presentation at AAHE's National Conference last March, "is not only how *many* forums there are right now for this change, but how *surprised* people seem to be to find this out." From where we sit, it seems that the *character* of that exchange may be shifting, too, with growing numbers of folks looking for ways to turn a corner toward this thing called the scholarship of teaching.

What does one *find* around that corner? What *is* this thing we're calling "the scholarship of teaching"? This is not, it turns out, merely a routine question but a marker of how this topic has evolved over the past several years. Five years ago, say, the scholarship of teaching was typically used as a term of general approbation, as a way of saying that teaching—good teaching—was serious intellectual work and should be rewarded. This was, after all, the powerful message most readers took from *Scholarship Reconsidered*. We must, Boyer (1990) wrote, "move beyond the tired old 'teaching versus research' debate and give the familiar and honorable term 'scholarship' a broader, more capacious meaning," one that includes four distinct but interrelated dimensions: discovery, integration, application, and teaching. Boyer thus sought to bring greater recognition and reward to teaching, suggesting that excellent teaching is marked by the same habits of mind that characterize other types of scholarly work.

What Boyer did *not* do was to draw a sharp line between excellent teaching and the scholarship of teaching. Now, however, we've reached a stage at which more precise distinctions seem to be wanted. Indeed, we sense a kind of crankiness among colleagues who are frustrated by the ambiguities of the phrase. How, they're asking, is excellent teaching different from the scholarship of teaching? If it is, why should anyone care about it? Is there a useful distinction to be made between the scholarship of teaching and "scholarly teaching"? Where does student learning fit in? These, in fact, are the very questions that campuses in the Campus Program are responding to as part of their process of stock-taking. They're important questions—to be taken up not in the name of creating yet another set of terms but as a way of being clear about our ends and the strategies necessary to reach them.

In this spirit, we would propose that *all* faculty have an obligation to teach well, to engage students, and to foster important forms of student learning—not that this is easily done. Such teaching is a good fully sufficient unto itself. When it entails, as well, certain practices of classroom assessment and evidence gathering, when it is informed not only by the latest ideas in the field but by current ideas about teaching the field, when it invites peer collaboration and review, *then* that teaching might rightly be called scholarly, or reflective, or informed. But in addition to all of this, yet *another* good is needed, one called a scholarship of teaching, which in another essay we have described as having the three additional central features of being public ("community property"), open to critique and evaluation, and in a form that others can build on:

> A scholarship of teaching will entail a public account of some or all of the full act of teaching—vision, design, enactment, outcomes, and analysis—in a manner susceptible to critical review by the teacher's

professional peers and amenable to productive employment in future
work by members of that same community. [Shulman, in *The Course
Portfolio*, 1998, p. 6]

A fourth attribute of a scholarship of teaching, implied by the other three,
is that it involves question-asking, inquiry, and investigation, particularly
around issues of student learning. Thus, though we have been referring
here to the scholarship of *teaching,* our work is with the Carnegie Academy for the Scholarship of Teaching and *Learning.* Indeed, our guidelines
for the Carnegie Scholars program call for projects that investigate "not
only teacher practice but the character and depth of student learning that
results (or does not) from that practice."

And with this, we believe, the circle comes full round. A scholarship of
teaching is *not* synonymous with excellent teaching. It requires a kind of
"going meta," in which faculty frame and systematically investigate questions related to student learning—the conditions under which it occurs,
what it looks like, how to deepen it, and so forth—and do so with an eye
not only to improving their own classroom but to advancing practice beyond it. This conception of the scholarship of teaching is not something
we presume all faculty (even the most excellent and scholarly teachers
among them) will or should do—though it would be good to see that
more of them have the opportunity to do so if they wish. But the scholarship of teaching *is* a condition—as yet a mostly absent condition—for
excellent teaching. It is the mechanism through which the profession of
teaching itself advances, through which teaching can be something other
than a seat-of-the-pants operation, with each of us out there making it up
as we go. As such, the scholarship of teaching has the potential to serve
*all* teachers—and students.

This vision will not be easily reached. And it will not be achieved except over the long haul. It is important to stress that faculty in most fields
are not, after all, in the habit of—nor do most have the training for—
framing questions about their teaching and students' learning and designing the systematic inquiry that will open up those questions. Indeed,
one of the fundamental hurdles to such work lies in the assumption that
only bad teachers have questions or problems with their practice. Randy
Bass, a faculty member in American Studies at Georgetown University,
and a Carnegie Scholar, writes,

> In scholarship and research, having a problem is at the heart of the in-
> vestigative process; it is the compound of the generative questions
> around which all creative and productive activity revolves. But in one's
> teaching, a "problem" is something you don't want to have, and if you
> have one, you probably want to fix it. . . . Changing the status of the

problem in teaching from terminal remediation to ongoing investigation is precisely what the movement for a scholarship of teaching is all about. ["The Scholarship of Teaching: What's the Problem?" *Inventio*, 1998–99, online journal at www.doiiit.gmu.edu/inventio/randybass.htm]

Even faculty like Bass, who identify "problems" they want to explore and have the intellectual tools for doing so, face the reality that they live and work in a culture (on their campus and/or in their scholarly or professional community) that is only beginning to be receptive to such work. Doing it is a risk, both in terms of tenure and promotion and in terms of wider impact on the field, since there are as yet few channels for other faculty to come upon and engage with this work in ways that will make a lasting difference. And, of course, there's the issue of time. In short, the scholarship of teaching runs against the grain in big ways.

Moreover, there are hard intellectual questions yet to be hashed out. One is suggested by a recent e-mail we received from one of the Carnegie Scholars. "Personally," he says, "I can be perfectly content in my own world to continue doing this kind of work because it helps me develop pedagogical expertise and I think students will benefit from that. But I wonder whether this work and the knowledge it 'creates' will be credible with others. Presently I believe that it will not be well received by those in my discipline because it does not use 'credible' methods of inquiry." At issue here, as readers will see, is not only this individual's motivation to do the scholarship of teaching but also a larger set of issues related to methods and rules of evidence, and therefore to issues of rigor and credibility. Put simply: Will this work "make it" as "scholarship"?

One of the things we have learned from the work of the Carnegie Scholars is how hard it is for faculty, regardless of their own field and its rules of evidence, not to assume that credibility means a traditional social science model of inquiry. Part of the attractiveness of the social sciences comes from the fact that they cover a lot of methodological ground these days, having been extended and transformed over the years through the influence of fields such as anthropology, linguistics, and hermeneutics. They have been transformed, too, by the fact that most of the questions about human behavior we most want answered are not, in the end, "science" questions, ones that lend themselves to immutable general truth, but rather questions about phenomena as they occur in local, particular contexts (like classrooms!). But to get at the fullest, deepest questions about teaching, faculty will have to learn and borrow from a wider array of fields and put a larger repertoire of methods behind the scholarship of teaching.

Which brings us to a second challenge: the need to keep the scholarship of teaching open to a wide set of inquiries. One of the things we have
observed thus far is that many faculty gravitate to questions that might
be described as "instrumental": Does this new method I'm trying lead to
more or better learning than the traditional one?

Such questions are eminently sensible, the very ones, we suspect, for
which there is a real audience on campuses, where faculty (and their deans)
want to know whether a given approach is likely to be more powerful
than another and whether it is therefore worth the time and resources to
make the change. But the scholarship of teaching can also make a place
for "what" questions—questions in which the task is not to "prove" but
to describe and understand an important phenomenon more fully: What
does it look like when a student begins to think *with* a concept rather than
simply *about* it? How can we describe the character of learning in a
service-learning site? There must be a place, too, for questions that allow
for more theory-building forms of inquiry, and for the development of
new conceptual frameworks.

Indeed, if the scholarship of teaching is to advance as a field, there must
be inquiry into the process of inquiry itself. We think here of a wonderful paper by Deborah Ball and Magdalene Lampert in which they discuss
their teaching in an elementary school classroom, not "to highlight our
practice" (which others wanted them to do) but to draw on "our knowledge of investigating practice." Understanding their topic as a problem of
representation and communication, they "realized that if we could represent practice, then the possibilities for investigating and communicating
about teaching and learning—by different communities—would be enhanced" ("Multiples of Evidence, Time, and Perspective: Revising the Study
of Teaching and Learning," in *Issues in Education Research,* eds. Ellen
Condliffe Lagemann and Lee S. Shulman, 1999).

Third, there are issues about the most appropriate forms, media, and
"genres" for making the scholarship of teaching available to the field. The
word "scholarship," for many academics, conjures up the image of a traditional published article, monograph, or book. But as illustrated by the
selection of examples in a "baseline" (that is, "where-we-started") bibliography on the scholarship of teaching developed for CASTL (and available to readers on the Carnegie website: www.carnegiefoundation.org), a
much wider variety of forms is now emerging.

Thus, the bibliography includes a book-length study of student errors
in writing; a public pedagogical colloquium given by a faculty job candidate during the hiring process; a course portfolio with evidence about the
effects of technology in the course; an online resource for exchanging and

commenting on course materials and case studies; a protocol for ongoing collaborative inquiry; and a textbook. But it remains to be seen which of these will most advance the goals of the scholarship of teaching, which will be most useful for review and for building on. Technology, for instance, would seem to have special promise as a vehicle for the scholarship of teaching, but much remains to be learned about how to tap its potential.

Finally, there is the issue of sustainability, which matters since the impacts of a scholarship of teaching will be achieved only over the long haul. It is heartening to see individual faculty developing examples of the scholarship of teaching; these will become prompts for a next set of efforts (just as they built on work from the several traditions that converge in the scholarship of teaching). But what's needed as well is a culture and infrastructure that will allow such work to flourish.

Among the many infrastructures that might be imagined, we end this article by focusing on just one possibility—a possibility appropriate to the need and available to many of the campus leaders who read this magazine. It is this: that campuses should think about redefining the work of their institutional research offices. Traditionally, these offices have been treated as a kind of company audit, sitting outside the organization's inner workings but keeping track of its "effectiveness" as witnessed by graduation rates, student credit hours, faculty workloads, and so forth.

Imagine, instead, a kind of institutional research that asks much tougher, more central questions: What are our students really learning? What do they understand deeply? What kinds of human beings are they becoming— intellectually, morally, in terms of civic responsibility? How does our teaching affect that learning, and how might it do so more effectively? These are, in fact, questions that the assessment movement (at its best a kind of cousin to the scholarship of teaching) put into the picture on some campuses, but they're hardly questions we've finished with. If we reconceived "institutional research" to be about such questions, in the service of its faculties, led by faculty members, then the scholarship of teaching would not be some newly conceived arena of work, or a new route to tenure, but a characteristic of the institution that took learning seriously.

The scholarship of teaching draws synthetically from the other scholarships. It begins in scholarly teaching itself. It is a special case of the scholarship of application and engagement, and frequently entails the discovery of new findings and principles. At its best, it creates new meanings through integrating across other inquiries, negotiating understanding between theory and practice. Where discovery, engagement, and application intersect, there you will find teaching among the scholarships.

## REFERENCES

Ball, D., and Lampert, M. "Multiples of Evidence, Time, and Perspective: Revising the Study of Teaching and Learning." In E. C. Lagemann and L. S. Shulman (eds.), *Issues in Education Research*. San Francisco: Jossey-Bass, 1999.

Bass, R. "The Scholarship of Teaching: What's the Problem?" *Inventio,* 1999, *1*(1). [www.doiiit.gmu.edu/inventio/randybass.htm]. Dec. 2003.

Boyer, E. *Scholarship Reconsidered: Priorities of the Professoriate.* Princeton, N.J.: The Carnegie Foundation for the Advancement of Teaching, 1990.

Cross, K. P., and Steadman, M. H. *Classroom Research: Implementing the Scholarship of Teaching.* San Francisco: Jossey-Bass, 1996.

Glassick, C., Huber, M. T., and Maeroff, E. *Scholarship Assessed.* San Francisco: Jossey-Bass, 1998.

Kreber, C. (ed.). *Scholarship Revisited: Perspectives on the Scholarship of Teaching.* New Directions for Teaching and Learning, no. 86. San Francisco: Jossey-Bass, 2001.

*Research and Creative Activity,* Apr. 1999, 22(1).

Shulman, Lee S. "Course Anatomy: The Dissection and Analysis of Knowledge Through Teaching," in Pat Hutchings, (ed.), *The Course Portfolio.* Washington, D.C.: American Association for Higher Education, 1998.

# INTRODUCTION

# FROM MINSK TO PINSK: WHY A SCHOLARSHIP OF TEACHING AND LEARNING? (2000)

THERE ARE MANY WAYS to improve the quality of education. In this essay, Shulman makes a case for the scholarship of teaching and learning as a particularly powerful route to improvement. His rationale is not simply a pragmatic one. The argument for a scholarship of teaching and learning is also based on a vision of faculty's responsibility as professionals and higher education's accountability to its publics and students. The essay was first published in the inaugural issue of the *Journal of the Scholarship of Teaching and Learning*, an online outlet sponsored by Indiana University.

# FROM MINSK TO PINSK

## WHY A SCHOLARSHIP OF TEACHING
## AND LEARNING?[1]

## Preamble

MORE THAN 25 YEARS AGO, I was serving as an American Psychological Association visiting scholar to the psychology departments of small
liberal arts colleges. I spent two days at a lovely campus in southeastern
Indiana, Hanover College. I particularly enjoyed the energy and intelligence of an undergraduate psychology major named Randy Isaacson. A
short time later, he was admitted to the doctoral program in educational
psychology at Michigan State University, where I had been teaching since
1963. When Randy completed his Ph.D. at Michigan State, he returned
to Indiana as a member of the faculty at Indiana University, South Bend.

What a pleasure it has been to reconnect with Randy so many years later
around our mutual passion for the importance of a scholarship of teaching and learning. I deeply appreciate his role in the creation of this online
journal. The Indiana University System is demonstrating significant national leadership in sponsoring this effort, as well as in its pioneering initiatives to recognize and reward scholarly contributions to teaching and
learning among its faculty members.

## A Strange Journey

As more individual teacher-scholars and their institutions become engaged
in the scholarship of teaching and learning, we often find ourselves discussing the history of the phenomenon, the precise definitions of "schol-

arship," "teaching," and "learning," and some of the methodological and technical standards for conducting such research in an excellent manner. Periodically, it is worthwhile to step back and ask: "*Why* are we doing this? What are the reasons we are committed to the pursuit of such work?"

At such times I am reminded of the old Jewish story of the Russian itinerant who needed to travel from Minsk to Pinsk. He caught a ride with a wagon driver whose cart was drawn by a rather ancient horse. As they approached the first significant hill on the Minsk-Pinsk highway, the driver halted the cart, unhitched the horse, and asked the passenger to assist him in pushing the wagon to the top of the hill. At the top, he hitched up the horse again, and they proceeded on their way until the next small elevation, where they again repeated the previous procedure.

After the fifth such ritual, the now-exhausted passenger dropped to his knees at the side of the road and looked quizzically at the driver. "I know why I have to get to Pinsk. I suspect you have a reason for going there as well. Enlighten me please. Why are we bringing the horse?" As we strengthen both our resolve and our capacities for moving faculty in higher education from the Minsk of a restricted view of scholarship to the Pinsk of a more comprehensive and inclusive perspective, we had better step back and make sure we understand why we need the horse of a scholarship of teaching and learning.

## Three P's

I'd like to suggest that there are three broad rationales for advocating a serious investment in the scholarship of teaching and learning: *professionalism, pragmatism,* and *policy. Professionalism* refers to the inherent obligations and opportunities associated with becoming a professional scholar/educator, and especially with the responsibilities to one's discipline symbolized by the Ph.D. *Pragmatism* refers to the activities needed to ensure that one's work as an educator is constantly improving and meeting its objectives and its responsibilities to students. *Policy* refers to the capacity to respond to the legitimate questions of legislatures, boards, and the increasingly robust demands of a developing market for higher education.

### Professionalism

The most important reason for engaging in the scholarship of teaching is professional role and responsibility. Each of us in higher education is a member of at least two professions: that of our discipline, interdiscipline, or professional field (e.g., history, women's studies, accounting) as well as our profession as educator. In both of these intersecting domains, we bear the responsibilities of scholars—to discover, to connect, to apply, and to teach. As scholars, we take on the obligation to add to the core of understanding, skepticism, method, and critique that defines our fields and their ever-changing borders. We also assume the responsibility for passing on what we learn to discern and act, through teaching, social action, and through exchanging our insights with fellow professionals. Indeed, the core values of professional communities revolve around the expectation that we do not keep secrets, whether of discovery or of grounded doubt. We are expected to share our knowledge by making it public, whether via publication, correspondence, presentations, or pedagogy. The new technologies make such exchange even more widely possible than ever before.

I have emphasized the professional imperatives for a scholarship of teaching most seriously in other writings. In so doing, I have also emphasized the importance of distinguishing between two equally important and desirable activities—scholarly teaching and a scholarship *of* teaching. This is a distinction that Boyer chose not to make in *Scholarship Reconsidered*. Scholarly teaching is teaching that is well grounded in the sources and resources appropriate to the field. It reflects a thoughtful selection and integration of ideas and examples, and well-designed strategies of course design, development, transmission, interaction, and assessment. Scholarly teaching should also model the methods and values of a field, avoiding dogma and the mystification of evidence, argument, and warrant.

We develop a scholarship of teaching when our work as teachers becomes public, peer-reviewed, and critiqued, and exchanged with other members of our professional communities so they, in turn, can build on our work. These are the qualities of all scholarship.

Both scholarly teaching and a scholarship of teaching are deeply valued in the professional community. Scholarly teaching is like the clinical work of faculty members in a medical school's teaching hospital. I would never wish to be associated with a medical school that was not home to outstanding clinical faculty. That clinical work, however valued, does not become scholarship until it is subjected to systematic reflective analysis. Such reflection leads to its display or communication in ways that render it community property in the fullest sense—public, reviewed, and exchanged.

The *professional* rationale for engaging in the scholarship of teaching is that it affords all of us the opportunity to enact the functions of scholarship for which we were all prepared. We can treat our courses and classrooms as laboratories or field sites in the best sense of the term, and can contribute through our scholarship to the improvement and understanding of learning and teaching in our field. Thus, the professional imperative for a scholarship of teaching is both individual and communal. We fulfill our own obligations as members of the dual professions with which we identify, and we fulfill our responsibilities to our professional peers to "pass on" what we discover, discern, and experience.

## Pragmatism

The professional rationale is critical, but not sufficient. We also have a practical rationale for pursuing the scholarship of teaching and learning. Such work helps guide our efforts in the design and adaptation of teaching in the interests of student learning. By engaging in purposive reflection, documentation, assessment, and analysis of teaching and learning, and doing so in a more public and accessible manner, we not only support the improvement of our own teaching. We raise the likelihood that our work is transparent to our colleagues who design and instruct many of the same students in the same or related programs. Active scholarship of teaching provides the teacher with a very different perspective on what he or she may have been doing for many years. I have recently had such an experience myself.

A RECENT—AND PERSONAL—EXAMPLE. During the past semester, I have been team teaching (with my colleague Professor Linda Darling-Hammond) a course—*Principles of Learning for Teaching*—that I have taught at Stanford since 1983. For most of those years, I co-taught the class with a variety of colleagues. The team teaching alone fostered serious reflection about the teaching. I have written about my strategies of teaching in the course (e.g., Shulman, 1996),[2] but I never actively conducted research on the teaching and learning taking place in the course itself.

This year, for the first time, we agreed to conduct more systematic research on the teaching and learning processes. This commitment was in no small measure motivated by my experience in working with Carnegie Scholars on their own scholarship of teaching projects.

The course is offered to all (nearly 60) secondary teaching candidates at Stanford. They are preparing to teach mathematics, social studies, English, science, or foreign languages in middle and high schools. All students already hold at least a BA or BS in their discipline and will receive an MA at the completion of their teacher preparation. During the academic year, each student is actively teaching in a secondary school for the first half of the day, returning to campus in the afternoon for formal classes, practicums, and seminars.

At the core of the class is the case-writing assignment.[3] All students are expected to complete a case study of their own practice during the class. They begin with brief "case starts" in which they outline an extended episode that they believe will be "caseworthy." After feedback from the instructors and from their own colleagues, they prepare a first-draft case, which is presented in a small working case conference. Based on feedback, they then spend nearly a month revising and editing their case (often choosing to write an entirely new case) which is presented at a second case conference and then written in final form. During this period, they continue to read a variety of theoretical and research material on teaching and learning, as well as additional cases written by others. The final version of the case is written up after the second case conference, and is accompanied by two commentaries written by others, and a five-page reflective essay on the whole process.

We decided before the class was offered that we would conduct research on the processes of learning through case writing that constituted the central structure of the course. Our teaching colleague Dr. Karen Hammerness took on responsibility for documentation and data gathering. Karen systematically collected each draft of every case written, including the commentaries and the reflective essays. Extensive notes were taken of every class session. Selected sessions were videotaped, and selected case conferences were also videotaped. These data will now be organized and analyzed to answer a number of questions about the efficacy of case writing in promoting reflection, deep understanding, and motivation among the students in the program.

We intend to do several things with these data. We will certainly meet to reflect on our findings and use those insights to redesign the course for the coming year. These meetings have already begun. We will also prepare more formal oral and written presentations on our experiences, methods, and findings. Hammerness is also taking leadership in developing a new website through which she will communicate our activities in the course, our insights into the learning that did (and did not) occur, and our analyses of the effort. We will also provide abundant examples of the evolution of selected cases written during the term. Thus the website will also include examples of student work and their own reflections.

I offer this personal account as an example of how the pragmatics of engaging in a scholarship of teaching on a course I have taught for years has introduced far more intelligent design and analysis of my own work than I have ever done before. Moreover, it has brought me into collaboration with close colleagues in new ways. I fully expect that our efforts at rendering this work public, reviewable, and available for exchange can serve as a valuable resource for colleagues both within Stanford and in the more general community of teacher educators. I also believe that these efforts will lead to significant improvements in the course itself and in the program of which it is a part.

## Policy

We in higher education are also enmeshed in webs of national, state, and local policy. Those who make policies and approve budgets for our institutions are increasingly asking for evidence that we are making measurable progress toward our educational goals. Accrediting agencies are insisting on educational "audits" in which we provide evidence that we are achieving our stated goals and missions. "Accountability" and "assessment" have become the themes of the emerging movements toward reform in higher education.

These are not bad ideas. They only become problems when the wrong indicators are used to assess the quality of our efforts. They are only problematic if the metrics employed are chosen because of convenience or economy of use, rather than because they serve as authentic proxies for the learning and development we seek to foster. These indicators cannot be "one-size-fits-all" quick-and-dirty off-the-shelf instruments that purport to measure the outcomes of higher education. They should be the result of carefully conceptualized, designed, and deployed studies of teaching and learning in each of our fields, conducted by scholars qualified to pursue them. This kind of work cries out for a vigorous scholarship of teaching and learning engaged by discipline and field-specific scholars of teaching.

The free market is also creating new challenges for higher education. For-profit providers, distance learning, and other new sources for higher education are creating a market wherein institutions must be prepared to document and display evidence that they are fostering learning, deep understanding, passionate commitments, and civic virtues in the domains in which they educate. Once again, unless we can provide relevant evidence of the processes and products of our pedagogies, we will find ourselves making empty claims and offering degraded arguments.

I envisage a scholarship of teaching and learning offering the kinds of evidence that can be powerful in these policy and free market discussions. New forms of institutional research will be developed that are learning-focused, domain-specific, and oriented toward analyzing the educative experiences and outcomes that institutions support or fail to support.

## So Who Needs the Horse?

I began this essay with a story about making the journey from Minsk to Pinsk.[4] The protagonists seemed to understand why each of them needed to make the journey; it was unclear why they needed the horse. In this case, I believe it is clear why our professional, pragmatic, and policy interests can be supported and enhanced by a scholarship of teaching and learning. It will not be an easy journey. At first, it may seem as if the horse is either useless, or an additional burden itself. Ultimately, however, we will need a sturdy horse to carry us on these journeys. We cannot do these things alone. We will need to develop networks of campus-based teaching academies to serve as centers, support systems, and sanctuaries for these kind of scholarly efforts.[5]

Our interest in engaging in such work was summarized by three P's, our professional interest, our pragmatic responsibilities, and the pressures of policy. Scholarship of teaching and learning supports our individual and professional roles, our practical responsibilities to our students and our institutions, and our social and political obligations to those that support and take responsibility for higher education. We should be making all three journeys and we need a really good horse. This journal, its leaders, readers, and contributors, are helping to make the journey possible.

NOTES

1. These remarks were originally prepared for a meeting of the Carnegie Academy for the Scholarship of Teaching and Learning (CASTL) campus affiliates hosted by the American Association for Higher Education (AAHE) at its 2000 annual meeting held in Anaheim, California, March 29, 2000.

2. Shulman, Lee S. (1996). "Just in Case: Reflections on Learning from Experience" in J. A. Colbert, P. Desberg & K. Trimble (Eds.), *The Case for Education: Contemporary Approaches to Using Case Methods*. Boston: Allyn and Bacon.

3. The web page with the syllabus, instructions for writing cases, and other materials for the course can be found at http://www.stanford.edu/class/ed269/.

4. By the way, Minsk and Pinsk are now cities in Belarus. Minsk is the national capital. In the 18th and 19th centuries they were usually part of Russia, but at different periods one or the other was in Poland or Lithuania.

5. I have written about a variety of visions for such academies in my essay "Visions of the Possible" reproduced at the Carnegie Foundation website: http://www.carnegiefoundation.org/OurWork/OurWork.htm.

# INTRODUCTION

# LAMARCK'S REVENGE: TEACHING AMONG THE SCHOLARSHIPS (2000)

PREVIOUSLY UNPUBLISHED, "Lamarck's Revenge" was the keynote address at an event where Shulman has been a frequent presence and important contributor over many years, the annual Forum on Faculty Roles and Rewards sponsored by the American Association for Higher Education. In 2000, to acknowledge the tenth anniversary of *Scholarship Reconsidered*, the Carnegie Foundation report that launched the movement to reexamine faculty roles and rewards, Shulman was invited to "reconsider *Scholarship Reconsidered*." He used the occasion to elaborate on the original conception of the scholarship of teaching put forward in that report but also suggested several ways the work may evolve in the future, including as an element of graduate education.

# LAMARCK'S REVENGE

## TEACHING AMONG THE SCHOLARSHIPS

---

LIKE MANY ACADEMICS, I often find myself fascinated by epigraphs. One of my favorites is from the cover page of the 1895 edition of James Mc-Clellan and John Dewey's *The Psychology of Number*. It reads: "The art of measuring brings the world into subjection to man. The art of writing prevents his knowledge from perishing along with himself. Together they make man what nature had not made him—all powerful and eternal" (McClellan and Dewey, [1895] 1912). These words were written by a nineteenth-century historian named Theodor Mommsen, who won the Nobel Prize for literature in 1902, and I want to use them as a route into my topic today, the changing conceptions of scholarship.

Mommsen's words, for many of us, bring *Genesis* to mind, where we find that the privileges given to humankind are those of counting and naming, which, I would argue, are very similar to measuring and writing. The first thing that Adam is asked to do during Creation is to name all the animals—and clearly the giving of names is a fundamentally divine privilege. Moreover, the Old Testament tells us that counting is often a very dangerous activity. It is in the face of the flood that Noah has to count the named animals in pairs as he puts them on the ark. In the Book of Samuel, David is admonished for counting the people when he wasn't given explicit instructions to do so. What, then, is the power of counting and naming? I think it is the power of making sense, of imposing regularity and pattern and order on the chaos of the world. That's why counting and naming are nearly divine privileges. To count three objects as "one, two, three" is in effect to determine that they are equivalent. Similarly, to say that hundreds of variations of vegetation are all to be called *trees* is an act of extraordinary power.

I believe that this process of naming and giving order is the essence of what we mean by scholarship, and that the oldest and most broadly human notion of scholarship is to count and to name, to give order to the world. But then, as Mommsen so beautifully says, not merely to name but to write—to challenge the assault of amnesia by doing as human beings what no other species can do: overcome the limitations of the generations and preserve the hard-won victories of learning as one generation dies and another appears. We not only count and name in scholarship, we then recount and teach. And in recounting we transform and connect and integrate into new forms and creations what might otherwise have been experienced individually and separately. So, what Dewey and McClellan were telling us in the words of Mommsen was that the scholarly function is perhaps our most essentially human characteristic. It ennobles and empowers us, and we need to preserve and enhance it.

Now, let me leap forward to 1990 and the publication of *Scholarship Reconsidered*. The discussion that emerged from the community of scholars associated with the Carnegie Foundation in the late 1980s included Ernest Boyer, Gene Rice, Russ Edgerton, Ernest Lynton, and Mary Huber, and pointed to a conception of scholarship that had grown unduly limited. Indeed, one way to think about that landmark Carnegie report is as an effort to recover the broadly human vision of scholarship reflected in Mommsen's language.

Seen in this light, *Scholarship Reconsidered* (Boyer, 1990) had both a conceptual and a political agenda. The conceptual agenda was to come up with a reformulation of the concept of scholarship. The political agenda was to initiate a reform in the way that limited resources—resources of both a financial and a personal kind—could be allocated within colleges and universities. Our Carnegie colleagues recognized that in the world of thought you cannot foment a revolution that is merely political. Indeed, what is most powerful about this whole body of work is that it is deeply conceptual. It is also unfinished. As I reviewed the work recently, I was struck by the fact that the section that deals with the four ideas of scholarship is only ten pages long. The wise author leaves a good deal of work for the reader. And we have been wrestling with our homework for the last decade.

The intellectual and political message of *Scholarship Reconsidered* is, as members of this audience well know, that we need a broader conception of scholarship—one that points to the power of scholarship to discover and invent, to make sense and connect, to engage with the world, and to teach what we have learned to others. Boyer and his colleagues wanted these different scholarly activities to be seen as of equal value to the broader community.

But now let me move ahead in time once again, to a phase of work I will call "*Scholarship Reconsidered* reconsidered." As I began my work at the Carnegie Foundation, an interesting challenge emerged. My colleagues and I were promoting a broad agenda dealing with the scholarship of teaching as part of a program that we had dubbed "CASTL," the *Carnegie Academy for the Scholarship of Teaching and Learning.* The challenge (one of them, at any rate) was that in the brief account of a scholarship of teaching in *Scholarship Reconsidered* the argument appears to be—and it's a lovely argument—that teaching itself is a form of scholarship and that therefore the work of the teacher per se must be treated as a form of scholarship, in the same way that the work of the physicist, the biologist, or the philosopher is a form of scholarship.

But what we realized in shaping our new program was that our view was a bit different from Boyer's because there is in fact a fundamental difference between the work of the physicist and the work of the teacher. Yes, one could call much of what a physicist does discovery, but this is because physicists do not, by and large, engage in active discovery in their laboratories or observatories or studies and then remain silent about it. We simply take for granted that the physicist learns something, reflects on it, makes it public, has it reflected upon and critiqued by her community, and then makes it available so others can build on it. With teaching, alas, we cannot assume such a process. As I have argued in various ways and places over the past several years, teaching has traditionally been a private activity; as teachers we abide in a kind of "pedagogical solitude."

With this in mind, my CASTL colleagues and I decided to make a distinction between the valuable and important work that we call *scholarly teaching* and the related but different work we are calling the *scholarship of teaching.* Scholarly teaching is what every one of us should be engaged in every day we are with students in a classroom or in our office—tutoring, lecturing, conducting discussions, all the roles we play pedagogically. Our work as teachers should meet the highest scholarly standards of groundedness, of openness, of clarity, and of complexity. But the scholarship of teaching requires that we step back (like the physicist stepping back from her experiments and calculations) and reflect systematically on the teaching we have done, recounting what we've done in a form that can be publicly reviewed and built upon by our peers. It is this difference that moves scholarly teaching to a *scholarship* of teaching.

This distinction is not unique to teaching; in principle, the work of discovery, integration, and application entails a similar distinction. That is, I can engage in discovery and invention that is not yet scholarship; I may have a powerful new idea, but until it is put forward for public review and comment it has not earned the label of scholarship. Similarly, many of us work in our communities, consulting, advising, and contributing in various ways, and that work may draw on our scholarly expertise—but until we reflect upon that work and its meaning, putting it forward in a public way, it is, again, not scholarship. I think it's this distinction that helps us see something about the nature of scholarship. Scholarship moves us beyond our uniquely human capacity to count and to name, toward an even rarer capacity to recount, to reflect, and yes, *to teach*.

This argument might lead us to assert that the scholarship of an activity (be it discovery, engagement, teaching, or whatever) is merely another layer put upon the original activity, something you do in addition to the core activity that doesn't inherently affect the activity of which it is a scholarship. Let me offer an argument that suggests that this assertion is wrong. Earlier this year, we saw (and this is highly unusual) the findings of a study published in a refereed social science journal hitting the front page of many newspapers. An article by Justin Kruger and David Dunning of Cornell and of the University of Illinois published in the *Journal of Personality and Social Psychology* concluded that people who are incompetent in any particular domain are also the least competent at sensing how incompetent they are. Most of the newspaper accounts of this study noted that if you ask people of varying degrees of competence to judge their own competence, those who overestimate their own competence in an area are those who are least competent (Kruger and Dunning, 1999).

But there's a deeper message in that study that the newspapers missed. The authors of the paper point out that not only are less competent people more likely to be nonreflective about their incompetence, and therefore unaware of it, but that this lessened capacity for reflectiveness is a fundamental *reason why they're incompetent in the first place*. The act of reflecting on what it is you've done is not simply a layer added on the doing of it but a fundamental feature of being able to do it well and to learn from doing it over time. I'm not resting my argument here entirely on this one study, but it's consistent with others I have seen.

I argue that if scientists and humanists engage in the scholarship of discovery and invention not only by making those discoveries and inventions, not only by counting and naming, but by recounting and reflecting and exchanging and teaching, then that work gets better by virtue of having undergone both processes. In keeping with this argument, I would trust a consultant who has come from the university to help with an applied problem if the consultant could show me that she not only engaged in the process of such work but had systematically committed herself to recounting, reflecting, and examining her work. And the same goes for teaching. No one admires the scholarly teacher more than I. But I argue that one of the reasons we have a tendency to ascribe great teaching to in- dividual idiosyncratic genius rather than to systematic education, training, reflection, and mentoring, is that we have done so little of the latter. If we began to engage in a scholarship of teaching more systematically and more universally, scholarly teaching itself would progress and develop.

And so, reconsidering scholarship reconsidered, I have begun to refor- mulate for myself what I think of as the relationship between *doing schol- arly work* and *a scholarship of that work*. I am also thinking about teaching among the scholarships, and where it fits. I'll share my thinking about this matter by describing an insight about the relationship between discovery and teaching that Jerome Bruner had about thirty-five years ago. I re- member Bruner's insight very well because it was expressed in a book I edited with Evan Keislar of UCLA in 1965 called *Learning by Discovery: A Critical Appraisal* (Shulman and Keislar, 1966). In a chapter called "An Act of Discovery," Bruner (1966) reflected on how limited discovery is, both as a strategy of learning and as a fundamental human activity. This was a surprising claim coming from Jerome Bruner, since he epitomized the scholar of discovery among psychologists and had championed "dis- covery learning" among educators. I shall introduce this analysis by re- counting for you an episode that recently occurred in a class I've been teaching. It involves a new high school biology teacher's attempt to teach Darwin's theory of evolution and to emphasize its contrast to the theory of Lamarck, a near-contemporary of Darwin's, whose "errors" regarding evo- lution Darwin sought to correct.

I was team teaching a course for future teachers with my Stanford col- leagues Linda Darling-Hammond and Karen Hammerness in which the teachers were writing cases of their own practice. A biology teacher had been working on a case about her teaching of evolution. Those of you who are biology teachers probably know where this is going. She taught them the Darwinian principles of evolution. She laid out the "Lamarckian fal- lacy" of the transmission of acquired characteristics—as exemplified most often by the simplistic belief that giraffes that have to stretch their necks in order to reach the leaves at the top of the trees transmit longer necks to the next generation. She did this with demonstrations and lectures, songs and cartoons, and the students laughed in all the right places. They clearly appeared to understand the Lamarckian fallacy, grasping that you don't transmit characteristics that have been acquired in one generation to the next generation. That's not evolution. She then administered an end- of-unit essay exam, and the results of that exam revealed that at the end of the unit the students were still overwhelmingly Lamarckian. What this teacher concluded in the analysis of her case was not (as some of you might expect) that the kids "reverted" to Lamarckianism because they were creationists from religious homes; rather, their misunderstanding reflected a general view of the world with which students are understandably comfortable—a view of the world in which intentionality and design play a greater role than randomness and chance. The Lamarckian view is a more persuasive and perhaps comforting view. It makes more sense, given the kind of world we live in.

I tell you that story because it's relevant to what Bruner said about discovery. Bruner said it would be crazy if every generation had to rediscover what its parents painstakingly had to discover on their own; that what we do in human culture is, with purpose and design, with intention and direction, to transmit acquired understanding. Biologically we may be Darwinian, but thank goodness we are culturally Lamarckian. (I am told by my colleagues in biology that the ideas of Lamarck are making a comeback. More accurately, the sharp distinction between Darwinian and Lamarckian views of transmission is eroding as scientists come to understand more about the interaction between the genetic code and the impact of experience and environment. As an example, see the work of Eva Jablonka [Jablonka and Lamb, 1995].)

The engine of Lamarckian evolution and transmission is called teaching. Teaching is Lamarck's revenge because as a culture we *do* transmit the discoveries, the integrations, the applications that we have so painstakingly achieved in one generation to the next. It is because we don't stop at merely counting and naming, but also recount and teach, that we are more fully human and that we both require and depend upon education. We are—all of us as teachers are—Lamarck's engine. That's our job. Lamarckian transmission and evolution is humankind's antidote to the randomness of biological evolution. We just don't want to wait the thousand generations it might take for Darwinian evolution. I think this argument for the centrality of teaching and learning as the key processes in intergenerational human development is a key one.

At the Carnegie Foundation we have been trying for the last few years through a series of programs to enact these views of scholarship with special reference to the scholarship of teaching. The Carnegie program operates at three levels.

First, we are trying slowly to attract to the scholarship of teaching as a communal activity many individual scholars who may have been pursuing it in somewhat splendid isolation. The Carnegie Academy for the Scholarship of Teaching and Learning (CASTL) (funded in partnership with The Pew Charitable Trusts) is in part a program that brings together individual fellows from a variety of institutions and a variety of disciplines—from community colleges and liberal arts colleges, from doctoral institutions and from master's institutions, from biology and from performing arts, from English and from history—to engage in the scholarship of teaching and learning with regard to their own work with their own students. Most of them are already gifted and acclaimed teachers, but this is an opportunity to document their work in ways that others can build on.

Second, under Barbara Cambridge's leadership, and with the wonderful collaboration of the American Association for Higher Education as our partner in this endeavor, we are working with faculty members and their institutions to create campus-specific teaching academies, which—though they will take many different forms—can provide a community of scholarship and support (a sort of sanctuary, one might say) for faculty engaging in the scholarship of teaching and learning. We see this as akin to the way that fields such as women's studies and area studies initially developed, with small numbers of faculty from across the campus coming together to learn from one another, and linking with other clusters of faculty in other institutions. Such programs were marginal twenty-five years ago, but many of them have evolved to be central today. It will be fascinating to watch the evolution of teaching academies over the next several decades, as well.

Finally, we are working with a variety of professional and disciplinary societies so that the work of the scholarship of teaching can become central to their work. I never would have believed five years ago that my calendar for a month from now would include a presentation I will make at 8:30 on a Sunday morning to lead off a daylong series of papers on the scholarship of teaching at the annual meeting of the American Chemical Society. I can thank one of our Carnegie Scholars, Brian Coppola (professor of chemistry at the University of Michigan), for making this happen. But I can also thank those giving all the other papers, who, with one or two exceptions, are faculty members in chemistry, not professors of education making guest appearances at a chemistry meeting.

I now move to my last observation. One of the things we know about CASTL's work on the scholarship of teaching—and I think this bears upon all the scholarships we are considering and reconsidering at this conference—is that as long as we continue to work only with current faculty, our efforts will have limited effect; the trouble with the future we're trying to invent is that it's likely to be just like the past unless something is done to address the manufacturing process for future faculty. We need to support and join with colleagues, most recently and notably Jody Nyquist and her colleagues at the University of Washington, to address squarely the challenge of the doctorate: What does a doctorate prepare people to do, and what does it not prepare people to do? We need good minds working together to determine what directions will be most powerful in this regard.

More than seventy years ago at my alma mater, the University of Chicago, Robert Maynard Hutchins was inaugurated president. He was thirty years old. He had already been dean of the Yale Law School. He gave the inaugural address to the faculty and trustees of the university on November 19, 1929, in Rockefeller Chapel. William H. McNeill, whom many of you know better as the author of *The History of Western Civilization* and many other great works of history, in his book *Hutchins' University* characterizes one part of Hutchins's inaugural address as follows:

> Hutchins further asserted that graduate training needed to be overhauled by distinguishing professional preparation of college teachers from the training of real researchers. He went on to suggest that distinct degrees should be awarded, "with the Ph.D. remaining what it chiefly is today, a degree for college teachers," while another set of letters after a candidate's name should be used to signify someone's aptitude in research. [McNeill, 1991, p. 26]

Now, I disagree with Hutchins's view that the Ph.D. should be focused on teaching alone; such a narrowing would undermine the broader, integrated view of scholarship that we are attempting to forge. But he has an important message for those of us who toil in the vineyards of future faculty programs today—that the way in which future faculty should learn to be faculty is not by experimenting as teaching assistants on helpless undergraduates. Hutchins's idea was that they must learn to be faculty by being mentored by members of their academic disciplinary departments, aided and abetted by members of the department of education who will be engaged constantly in experimenting with, studying, documenting, and analyzing their innovations in the undergraduate program. Doctoral students will learn to be college teachers by apprenticing with faculty who are themselves scholars of teaching and learning in their disciplines.

That was Hutchins's view. It is not out of date. And in the coming months, we at the Foundation are going to join with many others around the country to begin taking on directly the challenge of the doctorate. It is the pinnacle of academic accomplishment in our community, and we must once again make it worthy of those who achieve it.

So, let me end by saying that we invite you to join us in moving from *reconsidering* scholarship to *enacting* it in a new way. We must continue to count and name, we must continue to recount and reflect, and we must recognize that this work is not revolutionary but incremental. In the words of the title of a book by Larry Cuban and David Tyack, we must move ahead by "tinkering toward utopia." And we must remember that when we recount and teach about our recounting and our teaching, we are engaged in a scholarship of teaching and learning, a deeply Lamarckian act. Indeed, when we recognize the centrality of teaching in human cultural evolution, we become allies in accomplishing Lamarck's revenge.

REFERENCES

Boyer, E. *Scholarship Reconsidered: Priorities of the Professoriate.* San Francisco: Jossey-Bass, 1997.

Bruner, J. "An Act of Discovery." In L. S. Shulman and E. R. Keislar (eds.), *Learning by Discovery: A Critical Appraisal.* Skokie, Ill.: Rand McNally, 1966.

Cuban, L., and Tyack, D. *Tinkering Toward Utopia: A Century of Public School Reform.* Cambridge, Mass.: Harvard University Press, 1995.

Jablonka E., and Lamb, M. J. *Epigenetic Inheritance and Evolution: The Lamarckian Dimension.* Oxford and New York: Oxford University Press, 1995.

Kruger, J., and Dunning, D. "Unskilled and Unaware of It: How Difficulties in Recognizing One's Own Incompetence Lead to Inflated Self-Assessments." *Journal of Personality and Social Psychology,* 1999, 77(6), 1121–1134.

McLellan, J. A., and Dewey, J. *The Psychology of Number and Its Applications to Methods of Teaching Arithmetic.* New York: Appleton and Company, 1912. (Originally published 1895)

McNeill, W. H. *Hutchins' University: A Memoir of the University of Chicago 1929–1959.* Chicago: University of Chicago Press, 1991.

Shulman, L. S., and Keislar, E. R. (eds.). *Learning by Discovery: A Critical Appraisal.* Skokie, Ill.: Rand McNally, 1966.

## PART THREE

# PRACTICES AND POLICIES

## INTRODUCTION

# FROM IDEA TO PROTOTYPE: THREE EXERCISES IN THE PEER REVIEW OF TEACHING (1995)

IN 1994 LEE SHULMAN joined forces with the American Association for Higher Education (AAHE) in a national project designed to pursue a theme appearing in many campus reports on faculty roles and rewards at the time: that teaching should be subject to the same processes of peer review that characterize other scholarly work by faculty. To launch the project, faculty teams from participating pilot departments on twelve campuses came together for a week in June 1994 to explore a vision of peer review predicated on Shulman's vision of teaching as intellectual work that must be reconnected to the disciplines. The three exercises, co-authored by Shulman with colleagues at AAHE, provided grist for discussion at that summer event, and were then made broadly available in a notebook of peer review resources distributed by AAHE.

# FROM IDEA TO PROTOTYPE

## THREE EXERCISES IN THE PEER REVIEW
## OF TEACHING

---

### Exercise I: Teaching as a Scholarship:
### Reflections on a Syllabus

*Introduction*

You may find the juxtaposition of "scholarship" and "teaching" a strange liaison. Teaching is often seen as technique, as presentational method, rather than as the kind of serious intellectual invention we associate with scholarly work. But for this first assignment, we want you to think about the ways your courses and syllabi represent profound acts of scholarship.

*Part I*

Select the syllabus from one of your courses as the subject of a reflective memo (inside five pages). The memo should provide a peer in your field with a window on the choices and rationale that underlie your syllabus. We offer the following prompts to guide you in this task—but we certainly don't expect you to respond to each question. Our purpose here is to get you engaged in a kind of scholarly reflection about your teaching.

- Every course we craft is a lens into our fields and our personal conceptions of those disciplines or interdisciplines. Give careful thought to the shape and content of your course as if it were a *scholarly argument*. What is the thesis of the argument, and its main points? What are the key bodies of evidence? How does the course begin? Why does it begin where it does? How does it end? Why does it end as it does? Most scholarly arguments carry the intention to persuade. What do you want to persuade your students to believe? Or question? Or do you want them to develop new appetites or dispositions?

○ How can a colleague develop a sense of you as a scholar by examining the various features of your course? In your field, or even in your own department, are there distinctly different ways to organize your course—ways that reflect quite different perspectives on your discipline or field? Do you focus on particular topics while other colleagues might make other choices? Why?

○ In what ways does your course teach students how scholars work in your field? How does it teach the methods, procedures, and values that shape how knowledge claims are made and adjudicated within your field? How does it open doors to the critical dialogues and key arguments scholars are engaged in on the cutting edge of your field?

○ How does your course connect with other courses in your own or other fields? To what extent does your course lay a foundation for others that follow it? Or build on what students have already (one silently prays) learned in other courses? Or challenge and contradict what students are learning in your own or other disciplines? How, in general, does your course fit within a larger conception of curriculum, program, or undergraduate experience?

○ What do you expect students to find particularly fascinating about your course? Where will they encounter their greatest difficulties of either understanding or motivation? How does the content of your course connect to matters your students already understand or have experienced? Where will it seem most alien? How do you address these common student responses in your course? How has the course evolved over time in response to them?

○ Lastly, you might try playing with some metaphors for characterizing your course and its place in the larger curriculum or in the broader intellectual and moral lives of your students. Is your course like a journey, a parable, a football game, a museum, a romance, a concerto, an Aristotelian tragedy, an obstacle course, one or all or some of the above? How can your metaphor(s) illuminate key aspects of your course?

## Part II

Now give your syllabus and memo to your project teammate in your department and take your teammate's syllabus and memo in exchange. Using your teammate's syllabus/memo as evidence, imagine yourself writing a recommendation to a university-wide faculty committee that is considering your colleague for an award for distinguished service as a teacher-scholar. Your task is to interpret your colleague's work and thinking to colleagues beyond your own field (inside three pages).

The same questions that we offer as a guide to construct the reflective memo may be helpful in preparing your commentary, but we also encourage you to think about the *standards* by which your colleague's work should be reviewed. What is important to take into account? Coherence of "argument"? Distinctiveness of approach? Quality of reflection? Inventiveness of the course? To what extent are these standards similar to those you would use in judging the quality of your colleague's research?

## Exercise II: Capturing the Particulars of Classroom Practice

### Introduction

This second exercise picks up where the first left off—with course planning and conception—and seeks to capture how your intentions actually "play out" in classroom practice. That is, rather than looking at the course as conceived, this exercise seeks to look at the distinctive way each teacher enacts that conception, through the many context-specific, interrelated decisions that we make during any classroom session or episode, as we engage students in discussion, decide to digress (or not), change directions to take advantage of an opportunity, invent new explanations and examples, judge whether students are "with us" and what to do if not . . . .

Behind this exercise lie two issues that we'd like to explore. The first is technical and pertains to ways of preserving and representing what goes on in the classroom. We've given you three methods to choose from in hopes that this exercise will provide useful grist for sorting out the comparative advantages and limits to each.

The second issue deals with our conceptions of teaching and the scholarly expertise that goes into it. What is it that good teachers in the different disciplines and interdisciplines know and can do in the classroom? In what episodes and "telling moments" is that know-how reflected? And how do we judge classroom practice: by what standards and criteria?

This exercise is designed to uncover the craft and intelligence that is often embodied in the particulars of classroom practice. Like the first exercise, it entails an artifact (or documentation) and a reflective memo; two questions for further thought and discussion follow in Part II.

## Part I

Identify a telling episode or some incident of classroom practice that reveals something distinctive about your approach to teaching your field to your students. This might mean a laboratory demonstration you use to teach a key concept; it might mean an interactive group activity in which students solve a problem that's central to your course conception; it might mean a lecture and follow-up discussion on an important aspect of the field.

Select one of the three strategies indicated below to document the episode/incident that you identify. It may be useful for you and your project teammate to choose different strategies in order to compare the strengths and weaknesses of different options.

1. Videotape one or two classroom episodes (which may be an entire class session or a shorter segment of activity). You may then wish to draw on both tapes for the reflective memo (see below) or to select one.

*or*

2. Arrange to have a colleague visit your class and take detailed notes of what happens.

*or*

3. Write a case study about a classroom episode that reveals something important about your effectiveness as a teacher. The idea here is to use narrative to capture the particulars of classroom practice in a telling way.

As in Exercise #1, we ask that you create a reflective commentary on what you have documented by writing a brief memo—three to five pages in length—using any of the following prompts that you find provocative:

○ Why did you choose to document this particular classroom episode? What is it meant to be evidence *of?* Is it, for example, a particularly compelling, insightful, or artful rendition of a key concept in the course or field? A new metaphor or demonstration you have developed to illuminate a topic that students perennially find particularly difficult? An exercise that allows students actively to experience and engage in scholarly inquiry? A unique interpretation you bring to the topic that distinguishes you from your colleagues? Or, in contrast to all of these, is it simply a "typical" day in your class, and if so, why did you choose that basis for your sample?

○ What context is needed to understand the sample? Where are we in the unfolding of the semester? What other topics is this session's topic situated within? How does it relate to what was discussed the day or week before and what is planned to follow?

○ What were your goals for this day? Did the class session go as planned or deviate from your expectations? How so? Why? Did you change direction to take advantage of some new opportunity, to get around an obstacle, to deal with a new circumstance?

○ What does the sample say about your teaching? Does it show a characteristic style? A distinctive approach to material? Would others in your field be likely to teach this topic/concept/whatever differently? Are you trying something new? Something you will continue to work at and improve? Do you like what you see?

## Part II

As indicated above, there are two issues we'd like to get at through this exercise. Please think about the two questions that follow, and use them as grist for discussion with your project teammate(s).

1. ISSUES OF METHOD. What do you learn about the teacher through this method (video, visit, etc.)? Assuming you and your teammate used different methods, did one turn out to be more revealing, more reflection-prompting, more useful than the other? Why? What aspects of teaching are *not* knowable through this method? What other information would you want to add if this were, say, an entry in a teaching portfolio? How important is it to document the classroom aspect of teaching?

2. ISSUES OF CONCEPTION AND QUALITY. What are the most appropriate and best criteria for judging classroom practice? What matters most: creativity and originality? Thoughtfulness of the teacher's reflection or rationale? Significance of this particular topic to the field? Accuracy of the teacher's construal of the material? On what other dimensions might one judge classroom practice? Might the standards/criteria differ if the teacher were teaching the course for the first time versus having had sev-

eral years of experience with it? Are the standards for judging scholarly research appropriate to teaching? Which ones? Why or why not?

## Exercise III: Putting the Focus on Student Learning

### Introduction

In the first two exercises, we asked you to think about your teaching as it is designed (through the syllabus) and conducted (through actual classroom practice). But the conceptions and behaviors of teachers are only part of the educational picture. As teachers and as colleagues trying to assist each other with teaching, we also consider students and their learning. We consider how students understand (or don't) our explanations and queries; what sorts of misconceptions or questions about our fields they bring or construct; how we monitor and help direct their learning through appropriate assignments, exams, projects, and the like; and what new understandings they leave with at the end of a class or the course.

For this exercise, then, we ask you to reflect on your teaching in terms of student learning.

### Part I

Choose an assignment—that is, instructions for a student project, paper, problem set, classroom assignment, computer simulation, etc.—that is designed to promote and/or elicit an important aspect of the learning you intend for students in one of your courses. (You may find it helpful to focus on the same course as in the syllabus exercise, though the choice is yours.) Attach to the assignment several samples of student work, illustrating a range of responses, perhaps with your feedback included.

Write a brief reflective memo (two to three pages) in which you comment on what the assignment/student work samples reveal about students' learning in your course. Think of the audience for your materials/memo as a committee that is conducting a departmental program review and wishes to construct a map of what and how students learn about your field as they move through various departmental courses.

As you put together your work samples and write your reflective memo, use any of the following prompts that you find provocative:

o Why did you choose this particular assignment (as opposed to some other assignment) to reflect on? How is it important to your overall intentions, course design, conception of your field, and the

way you want students to understand it? Are there distinctly different formats or focuses you could have chosen for this assignment
that would have highlighted different dimensions of the idea or
the field?

○ Why did you structure the assignment in the way that you did?
How does its particular question, problem, or application reveal
*differences* in student understandings or interpretations of a critical
concept you are teaching? What patterns emerge as you study your
students' work?

○ What, in particular, do you hope your students will demonstrate
in their work on this assignment? What are your expectations?
Drawing on a scientific research metaphor, what was your hypothesis about what students might learn from this class, unit, or
course? What evidence does the assignment provide that would
serve to confirm or disconfirm this hypothesis? Where else do
you look for such evidence?

○ What do your assignment and students' responses to it tell you
about how students are constructing the ideas that are central to
the course and to your teaching goals? What misconceptions do
they have about these ideas? How do you identify and address
student errors and misinterpretations?

○ On what standards do you judge student work on this assignment?
How do these standards compare with those you would use in a
more introductory/advanced class? How are your standards related
to the standards you would use to evaluate a piece of scholarship
that a colleague has asked you to critique?

○ What thoughts do you have about improving your assignment,
your course, or your teaching as a consequence of completing this
reflective exercise?

## Part II

Please think and talk with your project teammate about the following two
issues:

1. This exercise asks you to try your hand at just one of a number of
possible ways to document student learning, including, for example,
classroom assessment techniques, and individual or small-group interviews with students. In addition, most of us have information
from student evaluations of our teaching. Probably you can think of

additional options, as well. What advantages and disadvantages do these alternative methods offer? What combination of them would offer a useful/fair/appropriate picture of your students' experience as learners?

2. How important is it to include evidence about student learning when making a case about teaching effectiveness? What are the pitfalls of doing so? The opportunities?

INTRODUCTION

# THE PEDAGOGICAL COLLOQUIUM:
# THREE MODELS (1995)

A CENTRAL THEME of the national project on the peer review of teaching, which Lee Shulman codirected with colleagues from the American Association for Higher Education (AAHE) from 1994 to 1998, was that peer review is not synonymous with classroom observation. Faculty teams from participating campuses worked together to design and pilot-test a *variety* of strategies for making the intellectual work of teaching and learning more public and available for review. The "pedagogical colloquium" is one of the strategies in that mix— proposed by Shulman in a talk to the AAHE Forum on Faculty Roles and Rewards Conference in 1995, and embraced by a number of the campuses who reported on their work in an end-of-project publication from AAHE entitled *Making Teaching Community Property.*

# THE PEDAGOGICAL COLLOQUIUM

## THREE MODELS

---

I WANT TO BEGIN by describing what were, for me, the two sources of the idea of the pedagogical colloquium.

The first is historical. In his wonderful account of the medieval university, in a chapter titled "The Pedagogical Juggernaut," Walter Ong (1958) points out that the university was originally a normal school, a place for training teachers for universities and colleges. Accordingly, Ong points out, the final examination for the doctorate was a *teaching* examination, in which the candidate was required to demonstrate that he not only knew his field but could teach it. The "disputation" portion of the examination was in effect a test of whether the person could conduct a seminar or a discussion—a test of teaching.

Reading this piece by Ong, I thought, why couldn't we recreate that model today? (See Shulman, 1986.)

A second source of the idea of the pedagogical colloquium came to me as I was sitting in a meeting at the Association of American Colleges and Universities, where the discussion was about teaching. A professor from Wesleyan, I believe, stood up in the middle of the session and said to those of us from research universities: "We need new Ph.D.'s who have some clue about teaching. We want them to be scholars, of course. But on their first day, we put them in a classroom to teach trusting young people who have paid a great deal of money to learn at our institution. Couldn't you send us some people who can do that?"

And my thought was: "Well, we'd be much more likely to send such people to you if that's what you *asked* for." And so, this notion of how one might ask for that sort of person became the pedagogical colloquium.

In other words, I view the pedagogical colloquium as a new version of the old concept of the public defense of the dissertation, whose emphasis was supposed to be on teaching, taken and shifted to the hiring institutions that now assert: "We want to see whether you are a scholar-teacher in your discipline." Traditionally, in hiring, we've only done half of that; that is, we have candidates give a talk on their doctoral dissertation. The pedagogical colloquium is a way for a hiring institution to say that it would like candidates to do something that begins to demonstrate their understanding of the teaching of their discipline. Additionally, as I'll point out, such a process would have other benefits.

## Three Colloquium Models

One of the puzzlements about the pedagogical colloquium is what, exactly, we would want the candidate to talk about. This is an important question, and the answers certainly will depend in part on the discipline or field of study. (In some quarters, I've even begun calling the pedagogical colloquium the "disciplinary teaching colloquium," to emphasize that it is an occasion not for soliloquies on teaching per se but for explicitly addressing the challenges of teaching in the discipline, interdiscipline, or profession.)

For starters, I'd like to propose three possible models.

The first would be a *course narrative or course argument model.* One of the questions that often gets asked of job candidates now is: "What would you like to teach?" A relatively simple next step would be to ask the candidate to walk us through that course, either in the form of a narrative or an argument, and to use the actual or proposed syllabus as a handout for his or her colloquium presentation.

The task of the pedagogical colloquium in this model would be to explain how the course is experienced by both the teacher and the students— what they do, and what they learn. What are some of the problems of teaching the course? And why is a course so organized and focused really *important* to teach? What ideas and activities were included, which were excluded, and why? In other words, why is this course an important experience for students to have if they are to understand the discipline?

An objection that some might make to this model is that it focuses more on curriculum than on teaching per se. But I assure you that it gets to questions of pedagogy, and to the "philosophy of education," in ways that are wonderfully particular and telling. Rather than grand abstractions ("I'm in favor of active learning"), the candidate would talk about quite particular aims and methods: "Notice," he or she might say, "that each of these three assignments gives the students an opportunity not only to think like an historian but to engage in a different aspect of historical inquiry. And one of my goals is for students actively to experience what it feels like to do historical work, even if they'll never do it again." Now, there we're beginning to get an intersection of the disciplinary discourse and the pedagogical discourse.

A second model would be a *colloquium centered on an essential idea or concept.* Each of us who is experienced as a teacher knows that there are some ideas in our field that are devilishly difficult to teach . . . or rather, they're easy as hell to teach, but hard for students to learn.

For example, one of the most resistant ideas for teachers of English is the concept of "theme." Of course, English teachers know what they mean by "theme"; but if you really start unpacking the notion, it's not a very easy idea. Would we say, for instance, that theme is what the story is *about?* Well, yes and no. And how many themes are there? Is there just one, or a few? At Stanford, we've done some case studies at the high school level of teachers trying to teach theme, and feedback from the students makes it clear that the concept is often terribly misunderstood. Similarly, in math, how many students really understand what a derivative is? I don't mean whether they can calculate one, but whether they understand the idea conceptually. Or how about the concept of "tropism"?

The point is that in a concept-centered pedagogical colloquium, the candidate would take one of these hard ideas and explore some ways that he or she has tried (or proposes) to teach it.

The third model is the *dilemma-centered colloquium.* This model, like the prior one, assumes that some aspects of teaching are inherently problematic, and it invites the candidate to reflect publicly on his or her thinking about and approach to one or more of these key pedagogical dilemmas. What, for instance, is the right balance between breadth and depth in an introductory course? How can teachers make students authentic participants in the process of inquiry and still maintain appropriate kinds of responsibility? How can teachers use group work in large engineering classes and still hold individual students accountable for their work?

In this third model, we would urge the candidate to stay discipline-specific, and to offer concrete examples from his or her experience, if possible.

These three models overlap some. And of course there are other possible models, such as having a candidate actually teach a class. What I envision and hope for is a time when we have a variety of protocols that can be adapted to different disciplines, settings, and purposes.

――――○――――

One benefit of the pedagogical colloquium would be for graduate education. For institutions to give explicit attention to teaching during the hiring process would encourage attention to teaching as part of the antecedent graduate program experience. At the least, the pedagogical colloquium gives advantage to graduate programs that already have in place sophisticated pedagogical training programs.

Looking ahead, I would further hope that as use of the pedagogical colloquium in hiring spreads, those of us teaching graduate students would spend time helping our students become reflective about their teaching, even assisting them to prepare and rehearse their pedagogical presentations—as we already do on the research side.

But the pedagogical colloquium could bring benefits not only to graduate education. The hiring department or campus and its faculty also benefit from the discussions within the unit that would necessarily be prompted by the pedagogical colloquium.

For starters, if four or five candidates for a position each give a pedagogical colloquium, the department needs to evaluate what it has seen. This means that it would be the responsibility of those conducting such evaluative discussions to get beyond the purely technical ("she told good jokes" or "he didn't turn his back to the audience for more than eleven minutes at a time") to the substance of what each candidate said. Such discussions around hiring can become the seedbed, the rehearsals, for comparable conversations among colleagues within a department, as we move toward the peer review of teaching as an aspect of departmental culture.

Second, the pedagogical colloquium could begin to change how a department assists faculty to develop over time, and how it rewards them for accomplishments in teaching. Consider, for instance, that if a department is hiring a candidate because it sees a particular sort of promise in the person pedagogically, it might then want to track that promise over time. In other words, the pedagogical colloquium would provide departments the opportunity to rethink the kind of information they gather and the feedback they give related to teaching effectiveness. And I think they would rapidly discover that under current circumstances they have absolutely no access to any of the data that would be most relevant. So, the pedagogical colloquium would create a need to begin collecting new kinds of data.

Finally, the pedagogical colloquium would bring benefits by addressing an otherwise unmet obligation. I'm struck that the question I get asked most often about the colloquium is: "Isn't it *unfair* to ask new doctoral students, or persons we hire laterally from industry in science and engineering programs, to make such a presentation about their teaching?"

Now, I find that question very interesting. If those asking the question were presented with a candidate for a faculty position who had never done research, it wouldn't occur to them to ask whether it's fair to ask that candidate to talk about his or her *research* qualifications . . . but they *will* raise this question of fairness about asking the candidate to talk about teaching.

My response to such questions is that anything is fair if you give people ample warning of what they're going to be asked to do. In fact I'd go a step further, by saying that if (a) they have ample warning and (b) the request is directly connected to the job they're going immediately to be given to do if they're hired, then asking for evidence of teaching promise or effectiveness is more than fair . . . it's obligatory. We owe it to ourselves and to our students.

REFERENCES

Ong, Walter J. 1958. *Ramus: Method, and the Decay of Dialogue, from the Art of Discourse to the Art of Reason.* Cambridge, MA: Harvard.
Shulman, Lee S. 1986. "Those Who Understand: Knowledge and Growth in Teaching." *Educational Researcher* 15(2):4–14.

INTRODUCTION

# COURSE ANATOMY:
# THE DISSECTION AND ANALYSIS
# OF KNOWLEDGE THROUGH
# TEACHING (1998)

WHAT WOULD IT LOOK LIKE if faculty treated their courses as occasions for serious, disciplined inquiry? What questions could they ask about their teaching and their students' learning? What forms would their evidence take? These are central questions posed by Lee Shulman in a talk at the 1996 Forum on Faculty Roles and Rewards Conference sponsored by the American Association for Higher Education. It was later published in a volume featuring work by faculty in the national project on the peer review of teaching for which Shulman provided leadership. Shulman's account of "course anatomy" builds on the three exercises for peer review included in this volume (see Chapter Twelve), and articulates many of the principles behind work on the scholarship of teaching and learning that he was beginning to do as president of The Carnegie Foundation for the Advancement of Teaching.

# COURSE ANATOMY

## THE DISSECTION AND ANALYSIS
## OF KNOWLEDGE THROUGH TEACHING

---

THIS VOLUME IS A contribution to the evolving scholarship of teaching. The course portfolio is a central element in the argument that teaching and scholarship are neither antithetical nor incompatible. Indeed, my argument is that every course is inherently an investigation, an experiment, a journey motivated by purpose and beset by uncertainty. A course, therefore, in its design, enactment, and analysis, is as much an act of inquiry and invention as any other activity more traditionally called "research" or the scholarship of discovery.

Before launching into a detailed account of how a course can become an occasion for investigation and therefore a contribution to the scholarship of teaching, I must unpack and discuss both key terms of that phrase, *scholarship* and *teaching*. I shall begin this chapter with that discussion, then proceed to an account of the variety of ways in which the investigation of a course can proceed.

## Scholarship and Teaching

For an activity to be designated as scholarship, it should manifest at least three key characteristics: It should be *public,* susceptible to *critical review and evaluation,* and accessible for *exchange and use* by other members of one's scholarly community. We thus observe, with respect to all forms of scholarship, that they are acts of mind or spirit that have been made public in some manner, have been subjected to peer review by members of one's intellectual or professional community, and can be cited, refuted, built upon, and shared among members of that community. Scholarship properly communicated and critiqued serves as the building block for knowledge growth in a field.

These three characteristics are generally absent with respect to teaching. Teaching tends to be a private act (limited to a teacher and the particular students with whom the teaching is exchanged). Teaching is rarely evaluated by professional peers. And those who engage in innovative acts of teaching rarely build upon the work of others as they would in their more conventional scholarly work. When we portray those ways in which teaching can become scholarship through course portfolios, therefore, we seek approaches that render teaching public, critically evaluated, and usable by others in the community.

What then do we mean by "teaching"? Too often teaching is identified only as the active interactions between teacher and students in a classroom setting (or even a tutorial session). I would argue that teaching, like other forms of scholarship, is an extended process that unfolds over time. It embodies at least five elements: *vision, design, interactions, outcomes,* and *analysis.*

Teaching begins with a vision of the possible or an experience of the problematic. The teacher holds a general view of how instruction might be improved, and/or senses that current instruction is unacceptable or a problem in some fashion. Vision leads to planning, the careful design of an instructional program or activity. A course design is much like the proposal for a program of research. The design can take the form of a course syllabus, a course outline, or even an argument for the development of a course. Usually, the design will eventually take the form of a detailed sequence of teacher and student activities, including topics, readings, projects, assessments, exhibitions, competitions, or demonstrations. Design might also include the creation of course materials, such as slides, demonstrations, simulations, websites, laboratories, internships, and the like.

Once designed, teaching must be enacted. Like any other form of inquiry, the course does not end with its syllabus but must proceed to delivery, action, and interaction. The actual enactment of a course is equivalent to the processes of carrying out a piece of research that has been designed. It is often punctuated by unexpected and quite unpredictable developments. The enactment of teaching is complex and demanding. It demands technical skills such as lecturing, conducting discussions, engaging in Socratic questioning, monitoring individual or collaborative projects, assessing student learning both informally and formally, and making midcourse corrections as needed.

Like any other form of investigation, teaching has outcomes. The outcomes of teaching are acts and products of student learning. A course once designed and enacted must yield tangible outcomes, changes in students' skills, understanding, values, propensities, or sensibilities. An account of teaching without reference to learning is like a research report with no results. It lacks its most essential ingredient.

Finally, the extended act of teaching (now accompanied by learning) remains incomplete without analysis. Again, like a research report, we are not satisfied with the unexplicated report of results. We expect the investigator to propose a set of interpretations of the significance of the investigation relative to the vision that initiated the study. What does the work *mean*? How does it extend the community's understanding of important questions? How will we act differently in the future as a result of these experiences?

In sum, a scholarship of teaching will entail a public account of some or all of the full act of teaching—vision, design, enactment, outcomes, and analysis—in a manner susceptible to critical review by the teacher's professional peers, and amenable to productive employment in future work by members of that same community. The course portfolio is a particularly fruitful example of the scholarship of teaching. And it is to a careful explication of the variety of ways in which a course portfolio might be organized, and to what ends, that I now turn.

## Course Portfolios

Conversations about teaching and course portfolios often begin with questions about what goes in them. Those are natural, maybe even inevitable questions from the point of view of a faculty member first thinking about developing a portfolio. But to my mind, the harder questions one faces in developing the kind of systematic documentation and analysis of a course that many of us are now calling a "course portfolio" are not about how many dividers you need in an accordion folder. The hard questions are about how to represent and report the scholarship of teaching—assuming we believe teaching is indeed a legitimate form of scholarship—so that it can become part of the community's intellectual property; so that it can inform other members of the community, engage them in deep and significant conversations, provide a basis for the formation of communities of scholars, and be evaluated in that community.

The question I would therefore like to explore is, *What can one ask about a course in order to understand ways in which its creation and conduct constitute a coordinated act of scholarship?*

## Inventing a Genre

Note, first, that we take for granted the answers to the above question when it comes to the scholarship of discovery. That is, we have invented, in all of our fields, forms of display and communication called articles, monographs, performances, artistic creations, designs, and the like. Each field has its traditions and conventions about the questions you ask and the forms you use to display the fruits of scholarship for the evaluation and use of one's intellectual community. In reading dissertations, monographs, or articles in the natural and social sciences, for example, we have come to expect statements of the research problem, reviews of the relevant literature, and designs for the research, in that order, in the opening sections of the work. The expectation that we will encounter such sections serves as a template for the reader, not to mention a rubric for the referee or critic. Yet these are inventions, not revelations. They are conventions of the disciplines that have evolved over time to ease the communication of scholarship and its critical use. We do not need to read the raw data of lab notebooks, interview protocols, or historians' index cards. Each field has achieved an economy of inquiry and communication that compresses and transforms the processes of investigation.

Note too that these conventions did not appear spontaneously. They evolved slowly and painfully, over time, and they helped shape the scholarly communities in which they evolved.

This process of inventing conventions for capturing and conveying knowledge is the process in which we're now engaged with regard to teaching. That's what the course portfolio (or whatever it ends up being called) is all about: It is an effort to invent a form of scholarly inquiry and communication through which we can represent and exchange the scholarship of teaching, thus rendering it community property. As one of the participants in AAHE's Peer Review of Teaching project observed, developing a course portfolio was, for him, like "trying to write a short story before the genre had been invented."

My argument here is that until we find ways of publicly displaying, examining, archiving, and referencing teaching as a form of scholarship and investigation, our pedagogical knowledge and know-how will never serve us as scholars in the ways our research does. The archival functions of research scaffold our frailties of memory, and we need something comparable for the scholarship of teaching.

Moreover, intellectual communities form around collections of text— or these days, probably hypertext. Communities are identified, that is, by their discourse; and it is in large part because faculty (and teachers at all levels) do not have a shared language, a "discourse community," that our practice is often so disconnected, so isolating. As I have observed elsewhere, the "community of scholars" is alive and well when we wear our hats as researchers and engage in the scholarship of discovery or of integration. But as teachers we experience pedagogical solitude; we are isolated and cut off from the other members of our professional teaching communities.

## Investigations of the Course

So, what kinds of questions might be used to organize and give shape to the course portfolio? What questions can help form communities of conversation and practice? Not surprisingly the answer depends on the purposes for which a course portfolio has been designed, and the audience of colleagues intended to review it. But I would propose four different formats and themes that might be useful frameworks for our course investigations and documentation: the course as *anatomical structure*; the *natural history* of a course; the *ecology* of courses; and courses as *investigations*. The first three correspond to three standard types of question that biologists ask about an organism: What are its parts, how do they form coherent structures, and how do they function to support adaptation and equilibrium? How does the organism develop over time, and how does it adapt to changes and unexpected factors over time? How does the organism fit into the larger contexts of which it is a part?

### Course Anatomy

One kind of question you might ask derives from the anatomical or biological metaphor. Courses, like organisms, comprise a variety of parts and structures, each associated with particular functions; one thinks of tests, lectures, discussions, internships, projects, laboratories. All these are elements of typical courses; they are the parts that are intended to cumulate into a well-functioning, adaptive experience. And, as in a structure-function approach in physiology, we can ask how these individual structures begin to interact and combine into systems. How well do the various parts fit together, amplify one another's properties, and aggregate into an effective experience of learning? How well do the systems work? This, then, is a route into the anatomy of the course.

This is a useful route, I think, because in good courses the parts mesh beautifully into a clear, well-articulated set of experiences. Students sense that what they are reading, practicing, investigating, and having evaluated cohere into a meaningful structure. The readings frame the labs, the quizzes both test and review understanding, large projects provide opportunities for integration and elaboration. In a well-crafted and well-conducted course, students experience an aesthetic sense of wholeness and coherence.

Conversely, courses that are unsuccessful are often those in which the pieces fail to add up. The goals of the course are incompatible with the assessments used to evaluate the quality of what is learned; the creativity of the exercises and experiences is a mismatch with the material covered in lectures. Such mismatches undermine the value that students place in all the components of the course and in the overall experience it entails. Moreover, it is likely that these discontinuities inhibit student understanding and motivation.

## Natural History or Evolution

A second framework for a course portfolio is developmental or historical. We can, that is, ask about the way the course unfolds. What is its plot? What is its itinerary? What does it look like as narrative or as a journey? Does it have a denouement, or does it just end with a dull thud? What kind of "course" does the course follow, and how effective is the course in tracking the thematic purposes of the teaching and the learning? It is worth remembering here that the first definition of *course* (in my third edition of *The American Heritage Dictionary*) is "onward movement in a particular direction"; and that *curriculum* (the term we Americans use for a program of courses) comes from the Latin *currere,* meaning "to run," the same root one finds for *current.*

The point here, as in the course anatomy framework, is to uncover a qualitative difference. Some courses read like a great short story, building up tension, creating problems, and then providing ways of trying to resolve these problems—though, as with most good pieces of fiction, not all of them get resolved. Other courses, however, resemble a low-budget tour of France, where "if this is Tuesday, it must be Chartres." Topics and themes come tumbling one after the other, with little sense of logical necessity, narrative rationale, or cumulative sequence. It seems likely that the course whose plot or dramaturgy is well-crafted will hold the attention of students more effectively and consolidate their learning more durably. Of course, the evidence of outcomes will be necessary to transform that conjecture into a warranted claim.

Another kind of unfolding over time occurs across multiple generations of the same course, rather than within any one particular offering. Thus, a portfolio can represent the *evolution* of the course as it adapts to the consequences of earlier experiences as well as to new situations. This form of course portfolio might also read like the report of a course investigation, discussed further below.

## Course Ecology

A third possible framework for a course portfolio is ecological. If the first kind of portfolio examines the course cross-sectionally, and the second type takes a longitudinal or narrative view, the ecological perspective places an individual course within its programmatic or curricular context. The ecological examination of the course explores where it fits in the larger program, be it curriculum of the major or of the minor, or—what is perhaps more important for many of our areas—where it fits into the education of students who are neither majoring nor minoring in our areas but are taking the course as part of a liberal education. "Ecology" means looking at the individual course as part of a larger system of instruction and learning.

Gerald Graff and others have pointed out that academics do not often ask questions about how individual courses fit into a larger curricular context. Such questions run against the grain of our prevailing conceptions of faculty autonomy and academic freedom. Nevertheless, this perspective is crucial if we are to achieve any kind of instructional coherence at levels beyond that of the individual course. Rare indeed is the course that can accomplish profound educational outcomes without the help of other courses that precede and follow it. A most important rationale for employing full-time faculty rather than the growing use of part-timers lies in the claim that full-time faculty members create a coherent curricular context among their offerings. An ecological perspective is important, too, because it may help us get at ways to characterize the contribution of an individual faculty member's work to the larger aims of the department or program.

## Course as Investigation

Finally, we can approach the course as an investigation. The notion here is that every time we design or redesign a course, we are engaged in an experiment. The design of the course is in this regard a kind of working hypothesis; we teach the course hoping that what we intend is in fact what will transpire—and knowing full well that it won't be. Note that this overturning of expectation is what experience is all about: Experience is what you have when what you expected doesn't happen. When what you expected *does* happen—you drive to the office in the morning without incident—you haven't had an experience, and that is mostly a blessing. Too many real experiences would be intolerable. But experience is a source of learning, to the extent that when one encounters discontinuities between expectation and reality, between intention and accomplishment, critical learning can take place. The course portfolio might usefully be seen as a vehicle for probing such discontinuities, extracting from them important experience-based learning for future practice.

Such a portfolio—the portfolio as investigation—would follow the model of a research paper, raising questions, testing outcomes against expectation, measuring achievement, and critically analyzing the course as one would any other experimental or clinical intervention. The portfolio might be presented as the report of an experiment. It might also take the form of a clinical or ethnographic case. This model of the course portfolio bears the closest resemblance to work in the scholarship of discovery. It allows us to ask what we now know that we didn't know before the teaching of this area, and how we might redesign our teaching practice in the future.

## The Course Portfolio as a Condition for Discovery

The four frameworks above will, I believe, be useful organizers for our investigations of our teaching and our courses. They certainly do not exhaust the possible formats for course portfolios. Moreover, they overlap, in the sense that we can present structural, developmental, evolutionary, and ecological portfolios as course investigations. But one issue arises quite apart from the argument for any particular framework. It is a familiar issue I confronted when, in 1995, I presented the report of Stanford University's Committee on the Evaluation and Improvement of Teaching, which I chaired, to the Academic Senate. One of my colleagues, a distinguished department chair in the sciences, and a personal friend, got up and said, "Lee, you know, this interest in investigating and documenting teaching is all well and good, and in some perfect universe it would be great to do all this stuff. But, you know we've got research to do. It's bad enough that teaching already interrupts our research—now you want us to do research on our teaching. And this is just going to take too much time. It's going to interrupt the flow of the real work of the university."

I do not dismiss this objection, even by suggesting that it is limited to that small fraction of our postsecondary institutions that is research intensive. I would like to address the question by referring to the research of UCLA anthropologist Eleanor Ochs. I heard Ochs describe her ethnographic studies of an international physics research group whose members were divided between Los Angeles and a university in France. I was struck by her account of what happens to this research group when its members have to prepare a presentation for the annual meeting of their disciplinary society. These meetings are very important for communicating one's work to the community, and for establishing the priority and importance of one's findings. Moreover, methods and findings must be displayed with great economy and precision, for there is an ironclad 10-minute time limit on each presentation. The investigators must interrupt the flow of their research routines and ask, What have we really learned that is important enough to pack into the allotted 10 minutes? How can we most vividly and persuasively display this work to our peers? Why must we stop what we are doing to tell others our story?

I'm sure you will recognize yourselves in this account. All working scholars are familiar with the frustration of having to interrupt important work to write proposals or to craft reports for funding agents, site visitors, or presentation at an important professional meeting. Ochs documents how having to prepare a paper not only occludes the flow of this research group's discovery process; it also initiates a dramatically different level of analysis, reflection, critical examination, integration, and reinterpretation of the research that has been otherwise rolling along. Suddenly the investigators have to move their deliberations from the private to the public domain, from sheltered discourse to public discourse, from the hidden to the revealed. Their challenge is far greater than simply to figure out which slides to use and which transparencies to reproduce. The processes of the discovery mode give way to a more pedagogical perspective. They not only must understand what they have learned from their research. They must represent that understanding in ways that will make persuasive good sense to others. Researchers must now frame their questions in new ways, pose new challenges, and respond to new demands. The interruption of the workflow for these purposes creates a crucible in which making sense of the research gets tougher as it strives to become more meaningful.

I am a member of many visiting committees and advisory boards. I've long ago concluded that the justification for an advisory board or a visiting committee cannot rest on the wisdom of the advice we give. The value of the visiting committee is that it obligates the people being visited to prepare for the visit by stopping their work, stepping back, and asking what it all means and how best to teach what they know to others in their community. That interruption is critical. It leads to kinds of learning and reflection that would be unlikely to occur under "normal" conditions. I have concluded that at two levels the occlusion or interruption of the processes of discovery is beneficial to the quality of scholarly discovery and integration. Similarly, the interruptions of typical teaching experiences that are engendered by the need to create course portfolios can have comparable benefits.

First, when I have to ask myself what I know that is worth teaching, and how I can simplify, reorganize, integrate, and represent what I know in ways that can be understood by others, that process—like the process of the scholar preparing for a paper at a national meeting—will loop back to shape and improve the teaching process itself. And that is why faculty who develop course portfolios so often report that the process of investigation, selection, and reflection entailed in writing the portfolio caused them to change the way they teach—to be more self-conscious about purposes, more vigilant about data collection, more thoughtful in assessing what works.

Second, having to take our teaching from the private to the public sphere, having to think about how we are going to engage in it, but also how we will come to understand what we are doing as teachers in ways that will permit us to organize what we do, display and communicate and converse about it to our own community, will have the same kind of improving effect for teaching that its parallel has for the improvement of the scholarship of discovery. Occluding the flow of either research or teaching leads to more serious reflection and analysis. These are the conditions for effective learning from these experiences.

It is too early to tell whether the forms of course portfolio I propose in this essay prefigure the genres of scholarly discourse about teaching that will characterize the coming generation's efforts in this area. We appear to be entering an era in which teaching in higher education will be taken more seriously. The scholarship of teaching appears to hold significant promise as a vehicle for fundamentally changing the ways in which college and university educators view the chances for reconnecting the scholarships of discovery and of integration with the pursuit of scholarly teaching. But our attempts certainly represent legitimate movements in this direction, worthwhile experiments in the documentation and analysis of teaching.

# INTRODUCTION

# VISIONS OF THE POSSIBLE:
## MODELS FOR CAMPUS SUPPORT
## OF THE SCHOLARSHIP OF
## TEACHING AND LEARNING (1999)

AN ESSENTIAL ASPECT of the Carnegie Foundation's program on the scholarship of teaching and learning has been work with campuses—almost two hundred of them—coordinated by Carnegie's partner, the American Association for Higher Education. "Visions of the Possible" was originally a presentation to a 1999 meeting of educational leaders from research universities interested in making a place for the scholarship of teaching and learning on their campuses. Shulman proposes four models of "how things might look in higher education if organizational entities were created . . . to support, preserve, and enhance the scholarly work of teaching and learning." The presentation was later revised for inclusion in a collection developed by Indiana University, which won the Hesburgh Award for its work on the scholarship of teaching and learning in 2002.

# VISIONS OF THE POSSIBLE

## MODELS FOR CAMPUS SUPPORT OF THE SCHOLARSHIP OF TEACHING AND LEARNING

---

HIGHER EDUCATION confronts a venerable problem. In 1906—the same year The Carnegie Foundation for the Advancement of Teaching received its congressional charter—the Association of American Universities (then a simple group of fifteen public and private institutions) met in the San Francisco Bay Area, devoting one whole day of its discussions to the question: Should professors at research universities be required to teach? Just one month later, San Francisco experienced its legendary earthquake. Although it's unlikely that the two events were related, institutions of higher learning are today still trying to put the pieces of teaching and research back together and continue to ask how teaching can find a right and dignified place in the research university setting.

## Teaching Academies: Four Visions

In response to this question, I was inspired to spin out several visions of how things might look in higher education if organizational entities were created on campuses to support, preserve, and enhance the scholarly work of teaching and learning. I will refer to these campus entities as "teaching academies," and I think of them as a combination of support structures and sanctuaries—that is, places where faculty whose scholarly interests include teaching and learning can find safety, support, and even colleague-ship for doing good work on the pedagogies of their fields. Within this general vision, I propose four possible models: the interdisciplinary center, the graduate education academy, the center for technology, and the distributed academy.

## Model I: The Teaching Academy as an Interdisciplinary Center

The first model is an interdisciplinary one. It draws together faculty members whose scholarly interests include teaching and learning but who may not find a sufficient group of colleagues for this work within their own academic departments or professional schools. The idea behind this model is to overcome faculty intellectual isolation by creating a new, multidisciplinary community of shared interests and work.

Think, in this regard, of women's studies centers, and how such centers provide an intellectual home for scholars from a variety of fields—history, economics, literature, among others—and make possible important new work and the development of a new field. Historically, such centers enabled scholars to engage with important issues, to build knowledge, and to create new outlets for their work. *Signs: Journal of Women and Culture in Society,* for instance, developed out of the women's studies center at Stanford University and has become the primary scholarly journal in the field. At first, these centers had a shaky existence (publication in *Signs* was not held in high regard in its early days), but over time more stable, secure interdisciplinary entities evolved. Stanford now houses and fully supports the Institute for Research on Women and Gender, in part because the work done in centers such as this became more and more legitimate in the same departmental and professional school homes from which pioneering scholars had originally migrated in order to find more hospitable settings.

This kind of evolution is desirable for centers dedicated to the scholarship of teaching and learning as well. In the best cases, scholars retain dual citizenship in both the disciplinary department and the interdisciplinary center—and I hope this would also be the case for faculty members affiliated with centers for the scholarship of teaching and learning in addition to their disciplinary units. Indeed, there may well come a time when the centers themselves disappear as their work becomes so fully integrated within the discipline or interdiscipline that a separate unit is no longer needed.

I am reminded of area studies and their centers for, say, African or Asian studies, which emerged a couple of decades ago. Philanthropic organizations, by the way, such as the Ford Foundation and the Carnegie Corporation of New York, played an extremely important role in helping to develop area studies. Here, again, was a phenomenon where in any given department there was likely to be only a single Africanist or East Asia specialist.

But if these solitary scholars could develop an appropriate area studies center, they could gather together a dozen or more faculty members on the campus from departments as diverse as English and genetics, along with graduate students, and establish a certain intellectual critical mass for their work. A person remained both an historian (or geologist) and an Africa scholar. Happily, universities and foundations found reasons jointly to support these efforts, which have in turn influenced the work and shape of many fields.

It should be said in reference to this first model that interdisciplinary structures entail both strengths and potential weaknesses. Cuban (1999) completed a study, entitled *How Scholars Trumped Teachers,* about teaching and research over the last one hundred years at Stanford University, and one theme is that, at Stanford, interdisciplinary entities were far more likely to innovate in their teaching and curriculum than were the entities located in a single disciplinary department. Why does this happen? Many departments treat teaching the same way they treat research; no one would dream of telling a departmental colleague what she should investigate in her research, and neither would one dream of telling her what or how she should teach. Most departments in most research universities support a conception of academic freedom in which all aspects of a faculty member's intellectual work are fully under her or his control. Curricula thus reflect the tastes of faculty members, rather than a more superordinate conception of what and how students in the field might best learn. But as Cuban shows, when faculty members move to an interdisciplinary center, they leave behind some of these predispositions; in making an active choice to join such a center, they are choosing to do something new. At Stanford one such example is the human biology curriculum, which cuts across several schools and many departments, and which allows new and different work, both in the research that faculty members conduct and in their teaching and curriculum development. I would infer that the same kind of increased openness and flexibility would pertain to matters of scholarship as well.

The handicap of such interdisciplinary programs is that the traditional department remains the structure for faculty reward—one can't get tenure in women's studies or area studies or human biology, but only in economics or history or biology. I'm not unhappy about that; centers and institutes are intended to be more flexible and adaptive than their more conservative departmental godparents. But it must be recognized that an essential tension exists between these two structures, between the program of a center and the disciplinary focus of a department, a tension that would have to be explored if teaching academies were modeled after such centers. The advantages of maintaining flexibility and adventure for one's mission are clear. The danger that the department's research emphasis would always trump the action-oriented investigations of the center whenever crises are encountered—whether of budget or of political mission—is a serious source of worry.

On the other hand, as interdisciplinary inquiry of all kinds increasingly becomes the norm for many fields in the humanities and the sciences (as is already the case in many professional schools), the structural tensions between the disciplinary home and the research workplace will not be unique to the scholarship of teaching and learning. In any event, the notion of an interdisciplinary teaching academy somewhat patterned after earlier models in women's studies, or area studies, or other such entities, is one model for the teaching academy. And if this model makes sense, it might also make sense for someone to ask, "What in my university setting are the two best examples of new entities that were invented in this fashion and had a certain persistence over time, that have gained credibility and support both internally and externally, and that remain viable centers for important scholarly work? And why have these entities survived, when a dozen others have come and gone?" The answer to that question should reveal something about the most promising form for an interdisciplinary teaching academy for a particular campus.

## Model II: The Teaching Academy as an Aspect of Graduate Education

My thoughts about this second model were stimulated by a visit to Princeton University in early 2001, where a deliberate decision was made to locate the teaching academy in the graduate school. The idea was to focus any first efforts on an aspect of work that is already central to the research university culture: preparing doctoral students for their responsibilities as scholars. This model of joining the work of a teaching academy with the mission of the graduate school can build on developments in the Preparing Future Faculty Project (sponsored by the Association of American Colleges and Universities and the Council of Graduate Schools, funded by The Pew Charitable Trusts). The emphasis of a teaching academy would build especially on the notion that institutions need to go beyond "TA training" to address in a much more proactive way the need to prepare graduate students for the full range of academic activities associated with each discipline or professional field, including the scholarship of teaching and learning. An assumption behind this model—and some will find this an odd way to put it—is that the Ph.D. is, after all, a professional degree.

Those at The Carnegie Foundation for the Advancement of Teaching think of Ph.D. students as future "stewards" of their disciplines. That phrase implies that doctoral students are expected to assume several roles: (1) generating new knowledge in the discipline, or the more traditionally conceived role of researcher; (2) critiquing and conserving the knowledge that already exists through processes of review, publication, and selective doctoral education, as well as by deeply understanding the history and foundation of the discipline; and (3) transforming their own knowledge into communication and representation that will bring new understandings to their colleagues, to students of the discipline, to students in general, and to the greater society. The latter role can be seen as the teaching component of the doctorate, and it is there that the most natural connection with the goals of a teaching academy occurs. What better way to integrate teaching and scholarship than at this level, where Ph.D. students are already experimenting and innovating with their knowledge, where they are already creating ways of sharing their work with others, where new work is already being done, and all under the guidance of faculty? By involving doctoral students more directly with the scholarship of teaching and learning at the very beginning of their understanding of what it means to be a faculty member, scholars who learn early on how to elegantly integrate their teaching with their research can be created. And in the process, those faculty members who mentor and advise these doctoral students are also affected and involved.

This brings me to the idea that another benefit of linking the teaching academy to graduate education is that the focus is not directly on faculty as the target population. Some might see this as a limitation, but campuses that move in the direction of this second model understand that one cannot reshape graduate education without involving faculty as mentors and models. Indeed, engaging faculty through work with graduate students might be seen as part of the "theory of action" behind this second model. It's a very useful way to think about how to start work on the scholarship of teaching, especially in institutions where research and scholarship of traditional kinds have taken precedence over teaching.

From an historical perspective, it's interesting to recall that this kind of connection between graduate and undergraduate education was explicitly advocated by such university leaders as Robert Maynard Hutchins of the University of Chicago. He took a rather extreme view of this connection, arguing that the undergraduate college should be viewed as a combination of pedagogical research laboratory and laboratory school for doctoral education, which was, after all, primarily teacher education for the postsecondary sector (McNeill, 1991). Although I would certainly take a different view of the proper relationship between the missions of undergraduate and graduate education, his insight is worth preserving. Much like the teaching hospital of a medical school, whose dual purpose is both to heal and to educate the next generation of professionals, so undergraduate education must serve both as a setting for responsible innovation and experimentation and as a site for the carefully mentored and scaffolded professional education of professors. Such a commitment by graduate education would go a long way toward alleviating the justifiable complaints of doctoral students that their future vocations as educators receive far less attention from their mentors than do their future vocations as investigators. Moreover, it would also extend the proper venues of research from their traditional domains to the field of teaching and learning in one's discipline or profession.

## Model III: The Teaching Academy Organized Around Technology

The impetus for this third model is much in evidence on many campuses today and will surely grow in the next decade. My vision is of a teaching academy whose reason for existence is connected to rapid developments in the use of technology in higher education. Whether you like it or hate it, technology presents a remarkable opening for the scholarship of teaching and learning. Many faculty members are asking serious questions about the role of technology in teaching and learning, such as how one knows whether these new technologies are effective in fostering student learning, and under what conditions. Furthermore, faculty members wonder what the difference is between the kind of learning that occurs in traditional venues and the kind that occurs in technologically mediated settings. So, the first advantage of this technology-oriented model of the teaching academy is that it builds on the fact that just about everybody agrees that teaching, learning, and technology pose serious research questions that need to be addressed. Most universities have already committed significant resources to the uses of technology, and because technology is not something one simply plugs into the curriculum, such research questions spawn a much larger set of inquiries about curriculum, design of instruction, and assessment, thereby encouraging a more general spirit of inquiry about teaching and learning.

There's a second advantage, as well. As noted in much of the literature related to the Carnegie Academy for the Scholarship of Teaching and Learning (CASTL), to call something "scholarship" is to claim that it is public rather than private, that it is susceptible to peer review and criticism, and that it is something that can be built upon by others. Technology, in much of pedagogy, has made the private public—through course websites, postings of syllabi online, and electronic resources such as the Crossroads Project. Randy Bass, a faculty member from Georgetown University, developed the Crossroads Project for the American Studies Association (and American studies is, perhaps not coincidentally, an interdisciplinary field). On Randy's site, one can see syllabi from American studies courses around the country and also read annotations of these syllabi, both by the people who created them and by others who bring relevant experience as reviewers. One can read case studies by faculty members whose syllabi are posted, in which they report on challenges in using technology to redesign courses they had been teaching for years (Bass, 2003). My point is that resources such as Crossroads have moved faculties a good distance toward a public and exchangeable discourse about teaching and learning—which is a key ingredient in transforming *conversations* about teaching and learning into a *scholarship* of teaching and learning, which occupies a central role in a discipline or interdiscipline.

The other healthy, albeit frightening, thing about technology is that it represents a substantial investment for institutions. Therefore, asking about teaching in these new ways without asking about evidence for learning becomes increasingly difficult, though onlookers rarely make this demand of more conventional teaching. Those involved in the *scholarship of teaching* are at least as concerned about the *scholarship of learning*. It's hard for me to imagine a viable scholarship of teaching that does not ask about learning in general, and about the particular kind and quality of learning that occurs in the presence of, say, a new technology.

I would also point out that it is perfectly possible—as those of us in the field of psychology can attest—to spend generations studying learning without making any reference to teaching at all. A few years ago, I gave the Howard Bowen Lecture at Claremont Graduate University. Bowen (1977) was an eminent economist of higher education who wrote a wonderful book, *Investment in Learning*. In preparing my talk, I looked up "learning" in the index of this book and found scores of entries; when I looked up "teaching," I found a single entry saying "see learning." And so I argue that there's a reason to keep both teaching *and* learning explicitly in the picture, because a focus on teaching will necessarily include learning, but the reverse is not always true. Adding technology as the third component and creating teaching academies at the intersection of teaching, learning, and technology may be just the right strategy at this point in time. I see lots of evidence that in this next decade technology may turn out to be the hardest-hitting and fastest-developing context for the creation and work of teaching academies.

## Model IV: The Distributed Teaching Academy

My fourth example is what I call a distributed academy. I met with Rebecca Chopp, now president of Colgate University, just after she had been appointed provost at Emory. Rebecca had previously chaired Emory's all-university committee on teaching, and her punishment was to be named provost. She told me that on her campus (and no doubt on many others), centralized offices are distrusted, and that the challenge was, therefore, to figure out how the provost's office could provide centralized support for teaching while locating the efforts in programs, schools, or departments. It's a bit like the environmental movement's old mantra of "think globally and act locally," but in this case it's "fund and support institutionally but act departmentally." The insight I gained is that one possibility for a teaching academy is that the university doesn't create an entity; rather, it builds capacity in various quarters where the work can best be done. These more local efforts, in turn, support initiatives that may grow into sources of strength for the whole institution.

This distributed model reflects the reality that on many campuses some departments or schools already have extraordinary potential for doing the scholarly work of teaching and learning. People at Stanford, for instance, ask me where they can find the best examples of research in education, and I will (although education is my field) often direct them to the department of mechanical engineering, where Sheri Sheppard, Larry Leifer, and their colleagues have been doing excellent research on the teaching and learning of design in engineering—research that meets all the standards of traditional forms of scholarship.

Similarly, when I was a professor of educational psychology and medical education at Michigan State University, one of my homes was an academic department called the Office of Medical Education, Research, and Development (OMERAD). My colleagues and I, who were drawn from medicine, education, sociology, nursing, and other fields, did what might be considered clinical or applied work as we invented a new medical school: curriculum development, evaluation design, the preparation of faculty to teach in the program, etc. But at the same time, Arthur Elstein and I were doing fundamental research on the psychology of medical decision making and diagnosis, work that had an impact on cognitive psychology as well as on medical education. The departmental unit thus served other units of the university and the field as it developed capacity.

I note these examples to make two points. First, critical mass is needed. The kind of work I'm pointing to could not be done by just one person in engineering or in medical education; the program must have the resources to establish a *community* of scholars. My second point is sort of the flip side of this argument: it's legitimate to undertake this kind of work in selected programs rather than across the board institutionally. I say this because scholars often feel that whatever they initiate has to be available equally to everybody. On the contrary, I would claim that insisting from the outset that the scholarship of teaching and learning must be done across the board is a formula for failure. Especially in these early years of the movement, it may make perfectly good sense to shape an approach that does not presume to be "institutionalized" in the usual sense of the word but that takes advantage of generative pockets of interest and potential. There is, after all, good reason why *panacea,* the word for a universal cure, has become a term of derision. These local centers of strength in the scholarship of teaching and learning should be supported institutionally, for they can contribute to building the field and also ultimately seed a broader set of initiatives in the institution.

## Other Possibilities

These, then, are four "visions of the possible" for supporting and advancing the scholarship of teaching and learning: the interdisciplinary academy for teaching and learning, the academy focused on preparing graduate students, the technology-centered academy, and the distributed academy. I'm sure there are many more. Indeed, one can easily imagine useful cross-fertilizations among the four. At Brown, for instance, the Harriet Sheridan Center might on the one hand be seen as an example of the first model—an academy that brings together faculty across fields to do work in common. But the Sheridan Center also works extensively with graduate students. Indeed, when I was at Brown for the center's inauguration (it had been around for some time but was being rededicated in the name of the late and much-beloved dean, Harriet Sheridan), I saw Randy Bass, who had just established the new center at Georgetown based on the third model mentioned earlier. When I asked Randy what brought him to the event, he told me that he had been a graduate student at Brown and had developed his interests by working extensively through the center on issues of teaching and learning in his field.

The point here is that the Carnegie Foundation and the American Association for Higher Education (CASTL's partner in working with campuses) have absolutely no desire to propose a single canonical form for teaching academies. Indeed, when we imagine a network of CASTL teaching academies, we don't want them to look like identical siblings. Higher education will be much better off with lots of Darwinian variation, with the academies (and whatever other names these entities adopt) responding in different ways to local contingencies and circumstances, with them representing different theories of how this work might go forward.

One question about local circumstances is the extent to which the teaching academy (perhaps especially the interdisciplinary model) should be a broadening and elaboration of the functions of an existing center for teaching and learning. Opinions on this differ greatly. Some say that linking a teaching academy to such a center won't work because too many centers are seen as emergency rooms for teachers in pedagogic arrest, as it were—whereas the core idea of a proper teaching academy is as a place for scholarly work. But others say that their center for teaching is already moving in the direction of fostering inquiry and intellectual colleagueship around teaching and learning, and that the teaching academy is a further embodiment of an existing vision. What I would say is that these are local questions requiring local judgments, and that where a center's central purposes are technical assistance and faculty development—important as those are—that center is not a teaching academy in the sense I am here describing.

## Teaching Academies as Foundations for Scholarly Communities

The importance of work that has the capacity to be more than local must be emphasized. Indeed, scholarship is by definition more than local, and if teaching academies are to contribute to a real scholarship of teaching and learning, then they cannot work in isolation; they must be connected, in communication, building on one another's work. How might this happen?

One answer is faculty exchanges. Tom Banchoff, who is a Brown University faculty member in mathematics, CASTL Carnegie Scholar, and former president of the Mathematical Association of America, recently spent a semester at Yale University to pursue his scholarship of teaching in a new venue. He later devoted a semester to work at the University of Notre Dame. Might not research universities with teaching academies develop a system of faculty exchanges of this kind?

Another possibility is the residential fellowship. I think here of the Stanford Humanities Center, where half the fellowships go to faculty on the campus, and the other half to those from elsewhere, with both groups selected through a competitive process. The Stanford center only invites fellows who do traditional scholarship, but this is just the kind of arrangement that teaching academies might sponsor. Indeed, fundraising to make this sort of thing possible would be a great task for presidents and provosts committed to the scholarship of teaching and learning.

And the last possibility I'll mention for connecting and broadening efforts entails documentation. The work done in and through teaching academies will be truly useful and consequential if it leaves behind an artifact or product that others can learn from and build on. Now, it happens that higher education is very good at preserving what people learn; think of libraries, museums, and laboratories, and the conventions established over decades whereby scholars learn (in different ways in different fields) to document, compress, organize, and display their work to one another. (I say "compress" because although a study may take several years, it cannot take as long for others to understand and learn from that study.) The Carnegie Foundation has created the Knowledge Media Laboratory (KML) to facilitate these same kinds of knowledge-preserving artifacts for the scholarship of teaching and learning. We see the KML as an interactive museum or laboratory, as a library collection, or even as an investment bank where Carnegie Scholars doing the scholarship of teaching under our auspices will leave a "deposit" of their work, so that others can make "withdrawals." What I increasingly imagine is that campus-based teaching academies establish their own knowledge media laboratories, their own mechanisms for preserving, making available, and exchanging the scholarship of teaching and learning—and that these mechanisms would be linked in ways that maximize the impact of work being done in varied settings.

Other ways to link and connect campus-based activities and entities and teaching academies do, of course, exist and will, of course, be invented. Meanwhile, the next levels of work in the Carnegie Foundation's CASTL campus program are explicitly dedicated to promoting such links and networking, to ensure that teaching and scholarly work on teaching are not purely local activities. To that end, my colleagues are working with scholars across disciplines, institutions, and educational sectors (e.g., community colleges, professional schools, K–12) to invent forms of documentation and communication that will do for the scholarship of teaching what the article, the monograph, and the "letter" (as used in physics) have done for the traditional fields of study.

## Conclusion: The Intellectual and Moral Imperative

I want to conclude with a point that Pat Hutchings and I raised in a 1999 article in *Change* magazine: campuses need to reframe the demand for accountability in ways that meet their responsibilities as educational institutions (Hutchings and Shulman, 1999). As things now stand, higher education's response to the increasing policy demand for accountability is mostly defensive and often cast in terms of efficiencies such as how many student credit hours to squeeze out of faculty members. But the questions institutions should be concerned with are about quality—particularly, the quality of what students come to understand, believe, and do. That's the kind of accountability to insist on, and scholars need to be able to conduct the scholarship that can help answer such questions in every discipline, as well as institutionally across programs. What do students who studied history at an institution now understand that they might not have understood without learning at that institution? What about those students in chemistry, management, or French? And what can an institution claim more generally about the skills, wisdom, and character of those whom it has educated?

These questions are not (and should not be) crisis-driven, no more than are those of traditional research. Scholars don't engage in traditional research because they failed when doing it before; they do it because they have done it well and now want to learn even more. Nor are they questions that can be taken up by offices of institutional research as they typically function; they cannot be asked from the top down. They can be facilitated, funded, encouraged, reported, and rewarded by the top, but the investigations must be conducted at the level of the individual school or program.

Teachers cannot be inhibited from designing their courses courageously and experimenting with their teaching creatively. Once these innovations are undertaken, there is a professional and ethical obligation to study their character, their efficacy, and both their intended and unintended consequences. Students in such situations are not human *subjects* in the traditional sense (see Hutchings, 2002); they are partners and collaborators in the pedagogical enterprise. Instead of seeking more reasons for impeding such efforts, university and college administrators should be developing new mechanisms for facilitating and encouraging the scholarships of teaching while affording assurances that no serious excesses will be tolerated.

Here I propose a vision of the research university as an institution that puts investigation at the very center of its existence. (My inspiration is William Rainey Harper, the first president of the University of Chicago, though, no doubt, others have said similar things.) Being a research university means that everything is a proper subject of investigation and that there can be no political correctness that designates certain questions out of bounds, least of all questions pertaining to the work of the institution itself. Harper held a vision of the research university as an institution that did not limit the objects of investigation to those matters outside of itself. Indeed, it was critical that a research university treat itself as a proper subject for investigation and its own work as an ongoing experiment for such investigation. The university must be constantly and critically asking about its own work, its own efficacy, its own role—vis-à-vis its students, its community, and its society.

After Harper's tragic death at the age of forty-nine, his Chicago colleague, the pioneering sociologist Albion Small, described Harper's image of the new university:

> His imagination had pictured the most important contribution that could be made to American education—a university which would be distinctive in its combination and emphasis of three things. The first was investigation. Every important subject within the possible realm of knowledge should be regarded as a field for research, so far as it presented scientific problems. Not least among the problems which the University should investigate was itself. It should never so far take itself for granted as to presume that its methods were final. Education, from nursery to laboratory, should be treated as a perpetual experiment, and methods should be changed to meet either new conditions or better insight into the conditions. The second trait of the University should be its active ambition for human service. Knowledge for general use, not for the culture of scholars, was the ideal. Scholarship should be promoted as zealously as though it were an end unto itself, but the final appraisal of scholarship should be, not its prestige with scholars, but its value to human life. The University should be, not a retreat from the world, but a base of operations in the world. The third distinctive trait should be accessibility. The University should have more ways of entrance than older institutions had provided, and it should have more direct channels of communicating the best it could give to the world. Besides attempting to reach these special ends, it should do its share of the conventional work of imparting knowledge by the best methods that had been discovered. [Wegener, 1978]

This vision of the university is also the vision behind the scholarship of teaching and learning. The higher education community can hardly be a moral community with mission statements that talk about the central place of teaching and learning if it is not also a place to investigate those processes and place them at the center of the scholarship in which it properly takes such pride. Doing so will require a true sea change in how university educators and administrators do their work—and I'm more optimistic than ever that it just might happen.

REFERENCES

Bass, R. 2003. *The electronic archives for teaching the American literatures.* [http://www.georgetown.edu/tamlit-home.html]

Bowen, H. R. 1977. *Investment in learning: The individual and social value of American higher education.* San Francisco: Jossey-Bass.

Cuban, L. 1999. *How scholars trumped teachers: Change without reform in university curriculum teaching and research, 1890–1990.* New York: Teachers College Press.

Hutchings, P. 2002. *Ethics of inquiry: Issues in the scholarship of teaching and learning.* Menlo Park, CA: The Carnegie Foundation for the Advancement of Teaching.

Hutchings, P., and Shulman, L. S. 1999. The scholarship of teaching: New elaborations, new developments. *Change 31* (September/October): 10–15.

McNeill, W. H. 1991. *Hutchins' University: A memoir of the University of Chicago 1929–1959.* Chicago: University of Chicago Press.

Wegener, C. 1978. *Liberal education and the modern university.* Chicago: University of Chicago Press.

INTRODUCTION

# THE DOCTORAL IMPERATIVE: EXAMINING THE ENDS OF ERUDITION (2000)

THE DOCTORATE, as Shulman has observed, was originally a teaching degree. In "The Doctoral Imperative" he traces some of the history of the relationship between research and teaching and how that relationship is (and is not) reflected in current practice in graduate education. The second half of the essay outlines the central principles and aims of a then-new program on the doctorate being undertaken by The Carnegie Foundation for the Advancement of Teaching. The essay has not been previously published. It was originally presented as a talk to the Conference on Re-examining the Ph.D. held in Seattle in April 2000.

# THE DOCTORAL IMPERATIVE

## EXAMINING THE ENDS OF ERUDITION

---

THE LAST SEVERAL YEARS have seen a powerful new convergence of efforts to rethink graduate education. It's useful, however, to remind ourselves that the issues reflected in these efforts are not new. In considering how the Carnegie Foundation might make a positive contribution to the needed process of rethinking doctoral preparation, I have been struck by how long certain fundamental questions about the doctorate have been with us. My purpose in what follows is first to trace some of those questions through time. What entitles someone to the highest degree awarded in the university? What responsibilities does it carry? I will examine these questions through two different lenses, one focused on teaching, the other on the functions served by the Ph.D. Along the way I will also lay out the thinking behind a program to re-envision the Ph.D. that is now being established at the Foundation.

## The Doctorate as a Teaching Degree

Shortly after assuming the presidency of the University of Chicago in 1929, in an address to the faculty, Robert Maynard Hutchins made some rather pointed remarks about the Ph.D. that are worth quoting at length:

> The graduate schools of arts, literature, and science are, of course, in large part professional schools. They are producing teachers. A minority of their students become research workers. Yet the training for the doctorate in this country is almost uniformly training in the acquisition of research technique, terminating in the preparation of a so-called original contribution to knowledge. Whether the rigors of

this process exhaust the student's creative powers, or whether the teaching schedules in most colleges give those powers no scope, or whether most teachers are simply without them is uncertain. What is certain is that most Ph.D.'s become teachers and not productive scholars as well. Their productivity ends with the dissertation. Under these circumstances the University of Chicago again has a dual obligation: to devise the best methods for preparing men for research and creative scholarship and to devise the best methods of preparing men for teaching.

Since the present work of graduate students is arranged in the hope they will become investigators, little modification in it is necessary to train those who plan to become investigators. In the course of time it will doubtless become less rigid and more comprehensive, involving more independence and fewer courses. But the main problem is the curriculum for the future teacher. No lowering of requirements should be permitted. No one should be allowed to be a candidate for the Ph.D. who would not now be enrolled. In fact the selection of students in the graduate school on some better basis than graduation from college seems to me one of the next matters the University must discuss. But assuming that this is settled, and assuming that a student who plans to be a teacher has been given a sufficient chance at research to determine his interest in it, his training should fit him as well as may be for his profession. This means, of course, that he must know his field, and its relation to the whole body of knowledge. It means, too, that he must be in touch with the most recent and most successful movements in undergraduate education, of which he now learns officially little or nothing. How should he learn about them? Not in my opinion by doing practice teaching upon the helpless undergraduate.

Rather, he should learn about them through seeing experiments carried on in undergraduate work by the members of the department in which he is studying for his degree, with the advice of the Department of Education. . . . Such a system means . . . that different degrees will doubtless have to be given to research people, the Ph.D. remaining what it chiefly is today, a degree for college teachers. [Hutchins, 1976, pp. 371–372]

As is clear, Hutchins had a bipolar view, separating research from teaching. I do not share that view, though the data support his claim that in most fields (with exceptions perhaps in some of the sciences and engineering) most Ph.D.'s take on responsibility for teaching at some level, and only a distinct minority pursue active careers in research and scholarly publication. Indeed, I will later make the argument that even Ph.D.'s who go into industry end up taking on in their work what are essentially pedagogical functions and roles. But I do share Hutchins's very important view that educating a professional teacher requires a bona fide laboratory or field setting. Recall that it was at Chicago where John Dewey wanted to develop education as an experimental field; they thus created the Laboratory School, as distinct from a demonstration school. Hutchins, similarly, created the College of the University of Chicago as a laboratory for pedagogy in higher education. He even went so far as to create a separate College faculty, whose members were evaluated on the basis of their pedagogical contributions, not their publication of research papers. This is not to say that their research was not exemplary as well; at the time I was a student at the University of Chicago, the College faculty included people like David Reisman in sociology, William McNeill in history, Edward Wasiolek in Slavic literature, Joseph Schwab in education, and others, all of whom made extraordinary scholarly contributions. But their performances were judged on the basis of pedagogical contributions—an interesting circumstance given the skepticism in many quarters today about being able to evaluate teaching. Hutchins was undaunted.

But it was not Hutchins who initially conceived of the Ph.D. as a teaching degree. Father Walter Ong of St. Louis University, one of the great scholars of the history of higher education, reminds us in several of his books that the doctorate was a teaching degree in the classical and the medieval university. Ong observes, "The universities were, in principle, normal schools, not institutions of general education" (1958, p. 153). The same was true of all the faculties: arts, medicine, law, and theology. The bachelor's degree made one eligible to be an apprentice teacher in a discipline or profession, working under the supervision of a professor. As part of the guild system, there were even "Bachelor Butchers" who were therefore qualified to serve as teachers to newer apprentices. Not surprisingly, then, in the medieval university the final examination for the degree of doctor was a pedagogical examination.

What's interesting is how this tradition has stayed with us. Consider the final examination for the doctorate—an examination designed to test the extent to which the scholar, having written a thesis, is able to demonstrate that he can teach what he has learned using the two primary methods of pedagogy, the lecture and the disputation. The candidate must present the central idea of her thesis as coherently as possible, and then engage in discussion and disputation with the audience in order to demonstrate that she can defend the warrant, the evidence, the argument against attack. This performance is a test of teaching, after which one is eligible to be called a doctor—that is, *dottore,* which of course means *teacher.*

Why did this practice develop? It developed because the medieval university was, in almost all things, Aristotelian. We find Aristotle's definition of how to distinguish a "mere" scholar from a really accomplished one in *The Metaphysics.* The uncompromising Aristotle says, "We regard master craftsmen as superior, not merely because they have a grasp of theory and know the reasons for acting as they do. What distinguishes a man who knows from the ignorant man, is an ability to teach." And this is why we hold that art and not experience is at the center of genuine knowledge, *episteme.* Artists, or in our terms scholars, can teach, while others, those who have not acquired their art by study but have merely picked up some skill through practice, cannot.

Notice the difference between the Aristotelian view and Hutchins's view. Hutchins argues that teaching and research are two quite separate functions, and that we must prepare most holders of the doctorate primarily to teach. In the medieval university there was a more integrated notion. The notion was that the ability not only to practice your discipline but also to transform what you know into representations and explanations that can teach others demonstrates the highest level of understanding. Indeed, in other writings, Ong observes that the concept of "method" was originally unitary, rather than distinguished into "research methods" and "teaching methods." Scholarly method involved the challenge of organizing one's ideas and observations into an argument that was sufficiently coherent, clear, and persuasive to be effective pedagogically. Only when the concept of research method became more "scientific" and empirical did the distinction between methods of research and methods of teaching become commonplace. The more traditional view of the close connections among understanding, scholarship, and pedagogy is, I believe, a very powerful one for our rethinking of the Ph.D.

The idea of teaching as a window into scholarly understanding—the pedagogical examination—is also powerful beyond the granting of the Ph.D., in the hiring process, that is. In the mid-1990s, a number of institutions in a national project on peer collaboration and review of teaching (sponsored by the American Association for Higher Education) decided to go beyond the traditional job talk and to require candidates to give a "pedagogical colloquium." We all know, after all, that a traditional job talk is understood by only two members of the faculty, one of whom is probably faking it. And the questions asked are often generic questions that don't require the questioner to understand the candidate's research: "Can you imagine any way the data might have fallen that would have led you not to confirm your hypothesis?" We all have that kind of handy all-purpose question in our repertoire. In contrast, in an authentic pedagogical colloquium one would pursue questions like the following: "Imagine that you were given the responsibility of teaching the introductory course in our department for undergraduates. We sent you some material about it. If you had this responsibility, how would you rethink this course? How would you reorganize it? And how would you approach the teaching of it? Or, since you are a scholar in this field, what do you view as the most central idea in the field that students predictably have a lot of trouble understanding? Talk about how you would teach this idea in ways that would overcome some of the difficulties the students have." Reports from departments using the pedagogical colloquium indicate that when both kinds of colloquia (the traditional job talk on one's research *and* a pedagogical colloquium) are part of the job interview, faculty deliberation about the candidate is likely to focus on what was said in the pedagogical colloquium. Even more, some departments report that the pedagogical colloquium gives them a better sense of the candidate's understanding of the field than the research colloquium.

A similar notion appears in the world of industry. In a paper given at Ohio State about five years ago, Procter & Gamble research scientist Joel Shulman (Joel is my cousin, so I am probably embarrassing him by quoting him, but his point is too good to resist) made the observation that in industry what they look for in hiring a scholar is scholarship shaped like a "T." The horizontal line of the "T" suggests breadth of knowledge beyond a single area of specialization; the vertical points suggest the capacity to plumb the depths of at least one problem. The pedagogical colloquium, I would argue, crosses the "T." It helps uncover the candidate's broader understanding of the field. It is a modern example of the classic notion of teaching as evidence of high-level accomplishment in the discipline.

## A Functional Approach to Rethinking the Doctorate: Teaching and Beyond

Thus far I have been focusing on the pedagogical aspect of the doctorate. Presiding as I do over an organization called The Carnegie Foundation for the Advancement of Teaching, this is clearly a view to which I am personally as well as officially committed. But it is not the only lens for rethinking the doctorate. Another approach is to look at the actual functions demanded of degree holders. Using this functional approach, we can look carefully at what Ph.D.'s actually do once they are hired—and then work backwards to shape the ways we train and assess people.

This is actually an old approach. Indeed, one of the oldest descriptions of the functions of a scholar appears in one of the last works of Francis Bacon, who, in many ways, established the modern notion of a scholarship rooted in empirical work. In his essay "The New Atlantis" Bacon describes his vision of a university, which he refers to as "Solomon's House," since Solomon was the icon of wisdom in the ancient world. It's interesting to review the different roles Bacon laid out for scholars in Solomon's House. In doing so he is in effect answering the functionalist's question, "What tasks does a research-intensive university need to undertake?" He may also be asking, "What does a scholar need to know and be able to do?"

First of all, Bacon tells us, the largest single department is made up of scholars who "sail into foreign countries under the names of other nations," to bring us their books and abstracts and experiments. These are the individuals who seek to learn what others know, and he calls them "Merchants of Light." Others collect the experiments that appear in books. He calls these "Depredators" (literally, one who plunders or pillages!). Others collect the experiments of the mechanical arts and also "of practices that are not brought into the arts." These are, in effect, scholars of the "wisdom of practice," and they are called "Mystery Men." Others yet try "new experiments as they think good." We might today call them "tenured," but Bacon calls them "Pioneers" or "Miners."

In addition, Solomon's House includes scholars who "draw the experiments of [others] into titles and tables to get the better light" for making observations and axioms based on them. These, not surprisingly, are "Compilers." Then we have those who "bend themselves, looking into the experiments of their fellows, and casting about how to draw out of them things of use and practice for man's life and knowledge." This presumably is the applied faculty, though Bacon calls them "Benefactors" or "Dowrymen." I will skip over details of additional and quite important roles that bear close connections to contemporary conceptions of original research ("Lamps," "Inoculators," "Interpreters of Nature"). What's interesting for the topic of this paper is a closing sentence, almost an afterthought: "We have also, as you must think, Novices and Apprentices, that the succession of the former employed do not fail." And that's what Francis Bacon has to say about graduate education—not much, that is, but informed by functionalist thinking—that the job of graduate education is to prepare individuals who can carry on with the roles and tasks that are essential to "Solomon's House."

A much more recent example of a functional analysis of scholarship is the work of my late predecessor at Carnegie, Ernest Boyer (1990), who in *Scholarship Reconsidered,* a monograph published just ten years ago, argued that there were basically four kinds of scholarship, only one of which regularly got much credit in the academy. Like Bacon, Boyer has names for the various functions he identifies: the scholarship of discovery, the scholarship of integration, the scholarship of application, and the scholarship of teaching. The first asks the question, "What do I know and how do I know it?" The second asks, "What might this mean in relation to other ideas in my discipline and in other disciplines or fields?" The third asks the question, "Of what use to other human beings and societies might my knowledge be?" And the fourth, "How do I preserve, transform, and transmit this knowledge so it becomes part of the legacy that we give the next generation?"

We need not argue about which taxonomy of scholarly tasks and functions is the best one. The important question is how a taxonomy of scholarship might lead to a reconceptualization of the Ph.D. Accepting Boyer's four categories as fundamentally equivalent in their value (which is not, I'm aware, something all of us *do* accept), might we not have a responsibility to engage students at the highest level in carefully designed activities of discovery, integration, application, and teaching? Should we not hold ourselves and our students accountable for ensuring equally high levels of achievement in all four areas, thus expecting them to show evidence of their competence to discover, integrate, apply, and teach their discipline? Put in the terms of those who employ Ph.D.'s (whether in industry or academe), should we not be asking in our hiring process, "Do these people demonstrate and manifest these interrelated faces of scholarship?"

A parallel set of questions can be derived from the perspective of industry. In Joel Shulman's Ohio State address, he argued that there were at least three attributes of the Ph.D. that were desperately needed by industry. One was technical competence, and I have talked about the "T" that emphasizes breadth and depth. The need for technical competence that is both broad and deep is straightforward. Problems in industry, just like problems in the academic laboratory, are slippery. And in the same way that our economy is becoming global, so, if you will, is our intellectual economy; the borders that divide disciplines and problems are far more permeable than they once were. The second area that Joel emphasized was communication: the scholar's ability to understand her ideas, her discoveries, and her insights deeply enough to communicate them lucidly, clearly, and persuasively to colleagues who are not technical specialists. That sure sounds like pedagogy to me. And why is pedagogical competence important? It's important, in part, because increasingly work in industry is becoming collaborative; problems reach a point where no single investigator can deal with them alone. And collaboration is in fact the third attribute on Joel's list, which he illustrated with examples from his own research into the development of biodegradable detergents, where expertise from a wide range of physical sciences is required. Scholars must be able to investigate, communicate, and collaborate with one another.

The important point here is that technical competence, communication, and collaboration are not generic. We are not advocating requiring a Dale Carnegie class in public speaking, or a general course in collaboration and participation in the community. These areas of expertise cannot usefully exist without domain specificity. That is, the type of collaboration that's needed involves collaborating around making sense in your field and in the adjoining fields. It is communicating in the sense of developing the capacity to talk about the central ideas, methods, applications, and policy questions in your field, in ways that don't remain opaque to somebody who isn't a member of your immediate sorority or fraternity—whether in writing or in speaking.

Following this thinking, then, we would ask of our programs that prepare Ph.D.'s how well they prepare students for these interrelated functions of technical competence, communication, and collaboration—important skills, I would argue, either for work in industry or academe. Are students asked and required to explain their specialized research in ways that broader audiences can understand? Are they asked to work with others across fields to solve problems that require cross-disciplinary expertise?

## The Ph.D. as Steward of the Discipline: A Framework for Carnegie's Work

This brings me to the program on the Ph.D. that is now taking shape at the Carnegie Foundation. A key point in our thinking about this new program has grown out of a different Foundation initiative, focusing on preparation for the professions. This is, in fact, a focus with a long history at the Foundation, dating back to the Flexner report, a revolutionary study of medical education that dramatically transformed the education of physicians in this country. Over the subsequent ninety-five years, the Foundation has done many studies of professions, and we are continuing to do that, currently pursuing research on the education of lawyers, engineers, teachers, clergy, nurses, and physicians. In doing our study of legal education, I have become acquainted with the ideal of the lawyer as "an officer of the court." This also has its analogues in the ideals of medical practice, a field in which I have worked for nearly thirty years. This conception of the ethical responsibilities of lawyers has fascinating reverberations for thinking about the Ph.D.

In the law, what is intended by the principle (not always enacted in practice) that the lawyer is to be "an officer of the court"? When you complete your training as an attorney, pass the bar, and are admitted into the practice of law, you have two often-competing roles. You are to be a zealous advocate for the interests of your client, *and* you are to be an officer of the court—obliged to act in a manner that preserves and sustains the larger system of social justice.

If we unpack this idea of being an officer of the court, we see that it entails a whole cluster of concepts having to do with the nature of confidentiality, what counts as evidence, the notion that evidence must be available to all sides of the dispute, and questions about warrant. I mention these concepts to make the point that one cannot learn to be an officer of the court in an elective third-year course in legal ethics, though that's the way it often is done. Nor can you conceive of this role in generic terms that bear equally across all professions. Being an officer of the court entails a difficult balance between immediate professional responsibility to your client and the larger obligation to society as it plays out in the particularities of your profession; it's a balance that goes to the very heart of being a professional. The concept of being an officer of the court must therefore be integrated throughout the educational experience.

A similar concept appears in the practice of physicians. Physicians are often caught in a bind between prescribing an antibiotic a patient desperately wants but doesn't need and recognizing that, in some incrementally infinitesimal way, every time an unnecessary antibiotic is prescribed we raise the likelihood that new strains of that disease-causing organism will develop that are resistant to the antibiotic. So the physician's professional obligation is to be a zealous healer of the client, but at the same time to be concerned about the public health, the commons; this is the parallel in medicine to being an officer of the court. Needless to say, the schoolteacher is presented with parallel ethical (and hence, both technical and intellectual) challenges.

I'd like to argue that if we accept the notion that a Ph.D. prepares professionals (whose profession is scholarship in the broadest Baconian, Aristotelian, and Boyerian sense), then it too entails this sense of being "an officer of the court." Wherever the scholar goes, whether to Intel or to Indiana University, whether to Foothill College or to Procter & Gamble, the Ph.D. carries with it not only an entitlement to practice but a sense of the responsibilities and obligations of scholarship. The Ph.D. must, if you will, be a *steward of the discipline* or domain in which she or he has received the highest recognition of scholarship.

What does such stewardship imply? It implies, for starters, that the scholar cannot be so narrowly prepared in the field as to have little sense of the terrain around that specialization. You can't be a faithful steward with that kind of narrowness. Moreover, stewardship entails a kind of work that is reflective, responsible, and communal.

What does it mean to say that the scholar must be reflective? What I mean is that a true scholar is not simply one who *does* the work; a scholar is someone who regularly and constantly steps back from the doing and reflects on what it *means*. That's why writing is so important for scholarship. Publish or perish has gotten a very bad name, but one of the beauties of publication is that as a scholar I can have little confidence that I truly understand something until I sit down to write it—at which point all the holes in the argument, all the gaps in the evidence, stare me in the face (or are pointed out by my peers, who can now review it more carefully). It's because this process is so powerful that we institutionalize it by creating learning communities of scholars, whether they are research teams, faculties, or journal editorial boards, which expect and reward various kinds of publication and "going public." Critical reflection is, paradoxically, very difficult to accomplish in solitude.

The second aspect of scholar-as-steward is responsibility. When we take on the cloak of scholarship, we take on responsibility for seeing that the standards of evidence, of warrant, of argument are taken seriously and upheld, both in our own work and in the work of others; we take responsibility, in some sense, for the integrity of the discipline or profession, and of its intellectual environment.

Finally, a scholar is someone who is communal, by which I mean that she not only cannot but must not keep secrets. Scholarship entails a responsibility to "pass it on"; to exchange what you have learned, what you have found, what you have invented, what you have created, with the other members of your community, assuming that they will do the same for you. This commitment is essential because the work of the community transcends the ability of any single scholar or teacher to do it. And so, the roles of investigator-discoverer, communicator, and teacher-scholar converge in this conception of the obligation of the scholar.

Now, this conception of the Ph.D. is idealistic and visionary in many ways, but I would point out that it is also congruent with the findings of a functional analysis of the roles of Ph.D.'s (in various settings) that I described earlier. It calls upon doctoral education to prepare its students to develop competence in the Creation, Conservation, and Transformation of knowledge in their field. Taken seriously this vision actually buttresses and supports those functions in ways that our current programs do not. It also suggests a number of practical steps that might be taken. I'll mention just a few.

First, we might explore elaborations and implications of the pedagogical colloquium. Why should the job interview be the first time a scholar gets a chance to present an integrative vision of her field as it is represented in the design of a comprehensive introductory or capstone course? The answer is that it should not, of course, and I am delighted that in some of the Future Faculty programs that have taken hold on campuses over the past several years this kind of "assignment" has found a place in the preparation of graduate students. It's fascinating, in this sense, that some of the most important ideas of our century grew out of the process of course design. A most dramatic example: Thomas Kuhn's stunning book, *The Structure of Scientific Revolutions,* which began when he served as James Conant's TA and then went on to create his own course, Introduction to Mechanics, for Harvard undergraduates. Out of that course came a book that was carried around by graduate students—at least when I was in graduate school—much in the spirit of Mao's *Little Red Book* in the People's Republic. You didn't go anywhere without your well-thumbed copy of *Structure.*

Another practical step concerns apprenticeship. Graduate education today is working with a very impoverished model of apprenticeship. Important recent research on how people learn as apprentices bears very little resemblance to the kind of experience that we call apprenticeship in justifying much of what we do in doctoral education today. For example, one of the characteristics of powerful apprenticeship is that increasingly the master plays the role of coach. There are two fascinating characteristics of this coaching relationship. One is that in bona fide coaching situations there is a curriculum—a structure in which the apprentice practices her work through repeated cycles of performance; each cycle leads to a manifest, observable performance that gets critiqued by the coach, mentor, or master, which then leads to the next iteration of practice. Look at the work of a coach of diving, football, fencing, or musical performance . . . and you will immediately see this pattern of cycles of performance. What you'll also see is that over time the roles of the coach and apprentice change because the latter moves from being a peripheral participant, even a spectator in the role, to an increasingly central role; in turn, the coach moves more into the background and gives up increasing levels of control.

Some of the best work on apprenticeship, and especially apprenticeship for deep and complex cognitive work, is being done by John Seely Brown, a cognitive scientist who has been vice president for research at the Xerox Corporation, and director of XeroxPARC, the Palo Alto Research Center. John and his colleagues have done exciting work on cognitive apprenticeship as a way of learning complex intellectual and practical activities. And they are doing it because it has enormous implications for preparing people to practice in industry as well as in academic settings. There's much to be learned from this work for our rethinking of the Ph.D.

A third practical step that might be taken is to institute more diversified doctoral portfolios. Right now, the dissertation is essentially the whole of the doctoral portfolio. Everything converges on one piece of work that doesn't even have a cyclical quality (which we know enhances learning) because you don't do it four times. My question is how could we restructure the doctoral experience so it doesn't have to be longer but has the combination of depth and breadth that would reflect a more capacious conception of what it means to be a scholar? For example, could we imagine a multipart doctoral dissertation equivalent, in which doctoral candidates must demonstrate competence in discovery, integration, application, and teaching of their discipline? Or in individual research, collaborative inquiry and/or applications with team members from other disciplines or fields, and various forms of public communication and undergraduate or graduate teaching? Can we imagine ways in which a more differentiated model of doctoral performances could be enacted over the course of a four- or five-year doctoral experience, rather than being aggregated together into a single terminal performance that has been known to extend as long as a decade?

My final suggestion for practice "goes meta," if you will: we need to see and treat our graduate programs as laboratories in which we actively, intentionally, and purposefully experiment with new approaches to preparing people for the Ph.D. The questions that are now in the air about graduate education are not questions that can be solved by rhetoric, or by speculation, or by enlightened policymaking. They are questions that will need experimentation, assessment, evaluation, and data-based deliberation. My hope is that our re-envisioning of the Ph.D. becomes, not a new set of unexamined orthodoxies to replace the old, not a new set of doctrines to supplant their predecessors, but a commitment to develop new models and possibilities and an accompanying body of evidence that suggests why some of those models and possibilities deserve greater warrant than others.

Such an approach is in the best spirit of scholarship. It is the approach the Carnegie Foundation will be taking as our work evolves over the next several months and beyond. I hope readers will join my colleagues and me in this work as we explore how one would indeed prepare people to become stewards of their disciplines, and how one would investigate competing claims critically, analytically, and empirically. The doctorate is the pivot point around which the improvement of all other forms of education rotates, from the elementary schools whose teachers are educated by those who hold the Ph.D., to liberal education of undergraduates, the preparation of future professionals, and the preparation of new Ph.D.'s themselves. The Ph.D. must once again represent "the lover of wisdom" to whom we can entrust the stewardly responsibilities to stimulate, protect, and extend the integrity of the disciplines.

REFERENCES

Aristotle. "The Metaphysics." In P. Wheelwright (ed.), *Wheelright's Aristotle.* New York: Odyssey Press, 1951.

Bacon, F. *Francis Bacon's New Atlantis: New Interdisciplinary Essays.* Hampshire, UK: Palgrave Macmillan, 2003. (Originally published 1627)

Boyer, E. *Scholarship Reconsidered: Priorities of the Professoriate.* San Francisco: Jossey-Bass, 1997.

Hutchins, R. M. "Inaugural Address, 19 November 1929." In W. M. Murphy and D.J.R. Bruckner (eds.), *The Idea of the University of Chicago* (pp. 371–372). Chicago: University of Chicago Press, 1976.

Kuhn, T. *The Structure of Scientific Revolutions.* Chicago: University of Chicago Press, 1996.

Ong, W. J. *Ramus: Method and the Decay of Dialogue, from the Art of Discourse to the Art of Reason.* Cambridge, Mass.: Harvard University Press, 1958.

# INDEX

## A

"A Modern School" (Flexner), 54–55
AAHE. *See* American Association for Higher Education (AAHE)
Abstract ideas, 12–13
Academy of Management, 148
Accountability: higher education's response to demand for, 215; problems with, 161
Acting, 68
Action: connection between reflection and, 72–73; in cycle of learning, 76; model of, 100–107, 110n.8–10; overview of, 72
Activity, 23, 27
Adaptation, 101, 102, 103
Addams, J., 19
Advanced placement (AP), 40–41
Advisory board, 200
Affective Domain Taxonomy, 69
African studies, 205
American Association for Higher Education (AAHE), 2, 3, 4, 33, 34, 43–45, 63, 115, 127, 139
American Chemical Society, 148, 170
"American Memory" (Cheney), 116
American Studies Association, 148, 210
Amnesia: definition of, 21; example of, 21; solution to, 23–26; studies of, 37
Anatomy courses, 37
AP. *See* Advanced placement (AP)
Apprentices, 225, 230–231
Apprenticeship of observation, 136

Architecture, 21, 97
Aristotle, 7, 19, 28, 64, 65, 223
Asian studies, 205
Assessment: for doctoral degree, 222–223; in general education, 69; problems with, 161; of teaching, 90–91, 96, 141, 143, 178–183. *See also* Evaluation
Association of American Colleges and Universities, 186, 204, 207
Astin, S., 24
Atkinson, R., 51
Ausubel, D., 36
Authority, reduction in, 27
Autonomy, 15–16

## B

Bachelor Butchers, 222
Bachelor's degree, 222
Bacon, F., 22, 225, 226
Ball, D., 152
Banchoff, T., 213
Barnum, P. T., 132
Barrows, H., 50, 52
Bass, R., 150–151, 210, 212
Baxter, J., 89
Beadle, G., 140
Bender, E., 148
Benefactors, 225
Ben-Peretz, M., 102
Berliner, D., 89
Bloom, B., 39, 66, 69, 70, 73, 79, 95
Book of Samuel, 164
Bowen, H. R., 210

Boyer, E., 1, 65, 146, 149, 158, 165–166, 226
Brint, S., 14, 16
Brodkey, J. J., 106
Brophy, J. J., 90, 95
Brown, A., 24
Brown, J. S., 230
Brown University, 212
Bruner, J., 19–20, 24, 51, 60, 168, 169
Buber, M., 29

# C

Cambridge, B., 170
Campus Academies Program, 45, 147, 149
Cantor, N., 78
Carnegie Academy for the Scholarship of Teaching and Learning (CASTL), 34, 44–45, 145, 146–153, 166
Carnegie Corporation, 115
Carnegie Forum on Education and the Economy, 2
Carnegie Foundation, 127, 146, 163, 169, 205, 220, 227–232
Carnegie Foundation for the Advancement of Teaching (CFAT), 1, 11, 34, 43–45, 53, 67–68, 145, 169–170
Carnegie Knowledge Media Laboratory, 44–45
Carnegie Task Force, 88
Case method: challenges to, 27; definition of, 20, 26; example of, 28–30; function of, 26–27; learning with, 27; to review classroom practice, 179; use in teacher education, 159–160
Cases: discussion of, 29; function of, 26
CASTL. See Carnegie Academy for the Scholarship of Teaching and Learning (CASTL)

Categorization, 65, 165
Center for the Advanced Study in the Behavioral Sciences, 44
CFAT. See Carnegie Foundation for the Advancement of Teaching (CFAT)
Change, unit of, 7
Cheney, L., 116
Chicago, 127
Chopp, R., 211
Claremont Graduate University, 210
Class size, 103–104
Classroom management: examples of, 84–87, 104–105; in pedagogical reasoning model, 104; research on, 95–96
Classroom Research: Implementing the Scholarship of Teaching (Cross & Steadman), 147
Clement, J., 97
Clinical experience, 17–18, 28–30, 158
Coaching, 230
Cognitive psychological research, 96–97
Cognitive Taxonomy, 69
Collaboration: as attribute of doctoral degree, 227; definition of, 24; emotions in, 25; importance of, 24–25; and reduced authority of teachers, 27; in Table of Learning, 79
College Board, 11
College of the University of Chicago, 222
Colleges: Campus Academies Program for, 45; contributions of, 215–216; engagement of, 77; taxonomies for, 77; vision of research in, 215–216
Colloquium centered on an essential idea or concept model, 188
Commitment: in cycle of learning, 76; function of, 67; overview of, 73–74; power of, 74–75; and problem-based learning, 58

Communication, 226

Community of practice: autonomy in, 15–16; case methods to promote, 28–30; and doctoral degree, 229; importance of, 27; isolation in, 196; and power of learning, 36–37; publishing scholarship for, 42; role of, 20, 25, 30n.6; in Table of Learning, 79; in transfer of individual to community experience, 15, 20; values of, 158

Compilers, 225

Comprehension, 100–102, 106–107, 110n.9

Conant, J., 230

Content knowledge, 92, 93–94

Council of Graduate Schools, 207

Counting, 164

"Course Anatomy," 6

Course design. See Design

Course narrative model, 187–188

Course portfolio, 192, 194, 196–201

Courses: anatomy of, 196–197; definition of, 197; ecology of, 198; evolution of, 197–198; as investigation, 198–199

Cox, K., 72

Cremin, L., 54

Critical reflection. See Reflection

Cronbach, L., 51, 52

Cross, K. P., 147

Crossroads Project, 148, 210

Cuban, L., 172, 206

Culture: change in academic, 143–144; of support, 27

D

Darling-Hammond, L., 159, 168

Darwinism, 19

Depredators, 225

Design, 73, 193, 198

Dewey, J., 11, 12, 19, 24, 30n.5, 51, 55, 88, 95, 164, 165, 222

Difficulties, 60

Dilemma-centered colloquium model, 188

Disciplines, 142

Discoveries, 167–169, 199–201

Discovery learning, 51–52

Discussion, of cases, 29

Distributed academy, 211–212

Distributed expertise, 16

Doctor of philosophy degree: final assessment for, 222–223; versus pedagogical colloquium, 187; redirecting focus of, 137–138, 171, 226–232; as steward of discipline, 227–232; as teaching degree, 220–224. See also Graduate education

"The Doctoral Imperative: Examining the Ends of Erudition" (Shulman), 6–7, 219

Doctoral portfolio, 231

Dowrymen, 225

Dramatic literature, 46

Dunning, D., 167

E

Ebbinghaus, H., 37

Ecology, 198

Edgerton, R., 8, 55, 67, 71, 165

Education. See Learning

Education and Democracy: Re-imagining Liberal Learning in America (Orrill), 11

Educational materials, 94–95

Educational reform. See Reform

Educational research. See Research

Ehrlich, T., 12

Elite pedagogy, 129

Elstein, A., 211

Emotions: in collaboration, 25; in Table of Learning, 79

Engagement: of colleges, 77; in cycle of learning, 76; importance of, 71;

Engagement (*continued*)
  and problem-based learning,
  55–56; and roots of Table of
  Learning, 67
Epidemiology of mislearning, 37–42
Episteme, 223
Erlwanger, S. H., 97
*Escalante: Best Teacher in America*
  (Matthews), 132
Escalante, J., 4, 129–133
Ethics, 228
Evaluation, 101, 106. *See also*
  Assessment
Evolution, 38, 168–169, 197–198
Experience: definition of, 15, 19,
  198–199; learning from, 119–121;
  ordering, 65; transition from indi-
  vidual to community, 15, 20
Expertise, distributed, 16

### F

Facts, need for, 40
Fantasia. *See* Illusory understanding
Fenstermacher, G., 88, 92, 99
Flexner, A., 53–55
Ford Foundation, 205
Formation, 68
Forum on Faculty Roles and Rewards,
  3, 4
Fox, E., 64
"From Idea to Prototype: The Peer
  Review in Teaching" (Shulman), 6
Fundraising, 213–214

### G

Gage, N. L., 90, 95
Gagné, R., 51
Galileo, 136
Gardner, H., 110n.10
Gardner, J., 1
Garfield High, 132, 138

Geertz, C., 136
General education, 69–70
Generativity, 57–58
Genesis, 164
George Mason University, 148
Georgetown University, 212
Glaser, R., 51
Glassick, C., 147
Good, T., 90, 95
Graduate education, 207–209, 230,
  231. *See also* Doctor of philosophy
  degree
Graff, G., 198
Gray, D., 148
Green, T. F., 88, 99
Greeno, J. G., 89, 108n.1
Gross anatomy courses, 37
Grossman, P., 104
Gudmundsdottir, S., 87, 89

### H

Hammerness, K., 160, 168
Hanover College, 156
Harper, W. R., 30n.5, 215
Harriet Sheriden Center, 212
Hashweh, M. Z., 89
Hawkins, D., 51
Hierarchies: purpose of, 65; tax-
  onomies for, 70
*The History of Western Civilization*
  (McNeill), 171
Holmes Group, 88
*How Scholars Trumped Teachers*
  (Cuban), 206
Howard Bowen Lecture, 210
Huber, M. T., 147, 148, 165
Hume, D., 12–13
Hutchings, P., 3, 6, 145, 146, 214
Hutchins College, 12, 25
Hutchins, R. M., 171, 208, 220–221,
  222, 223
*Hutchins' University* (McNeill), 171

## I

Ideologies, 70
Illusory understanding: dangerous nature of, 38; definition of, 21, 37–38; example of, 22, 38; and Socratic dialogue, 22; solution to, 23–26; studies of, 38
Incompetence, 167
Indiana University, 148, 156
Industry, 226–227
Inert ideas: definition of, 21, 38–39; example of, 39–40; solution to, 23–26; test of, 23
Institute for Research on Women and Gender, 205
Institutional research office, 153
Institutions. See Colleges
Instruction, 101, 104–105
Instructional selection, 101, 102, 103
Interdisciplinary center, 205–207
Internists, 72
Interruptions, 57
Inventions, 167–169
Investment in Learning (Bowen), 210
Isaacson, R., 156
Isolation, 140–144, 196, 205

## J

Jablonka, E., 169
Jacobson, L., 95
Jacoby, S., 57
Jossey-Bass, 148
Judgment: in cycle of learning, 76; function of, 15, 18–19, 67; versus understanding, 73

## K

Kagan, J., 51
Keislar, E. R., 51, 168
Kennedy, D., 2
Kerr, C., 1

KML. See Knowledge Media Laboratory (KML)
"Knowledge and Teaching: Foundations of the New Reform" (Shulman), 1
Knowledge base of teaching: categorical overview of, 92–93; defining skills in, 90–91; incompleteness of, 98; overview of, 90; for reasoning, 99–100, 109–110n.7–10; recent studies of, 88–90; reform proposals for, 88–90, 107; sources of, 93–98. See also Teaching
Knowledge Media Laboratory (KML), 214
Knowledge, scholarly, 95–97
Kohlberg, L., 66, 79
Krathwohl, D. R., 69, 79
Kreber, C., 148
Krebs cycle, 17
Kruger, J., 167
Kuhn, T., 230

## L

Lagemann, E., 19, 55, 152
Lamarckian fallacy, 168–169
Lamb, M. J., 169
Lampert, M., 152
Law profession, 17–18, 21, 30n.6, 97, 228
Learning: and community of practice, 36–37; current conception of, 36; cyclical nature of, 74–77; definition of, 34; by discovery, 51–52; dual process of, 36; from experience, 119–121; factors influencing, 36; goal of, 78; paradoxes in, 78; past conception of, 35–36; professing, 35–37; reflection on, 181–183; research of, 96; in scholarship of teaching, 150. See also specific types of learning

*Learning by Discovery: A Critical Approach* (Shulman & Keislar), 51, 168
Lecture, 105, 110n.11, 121
Leifer, L., 211
Leinhardt, G., 89, 108n.1
Lesson objectives, 91
Liberal education: case method for, 26–30; challenges of, 21–23; definition of, 8; documentation of, 21–22; establishing clinical component in, 28–30, 31n.10; as prerequisite for professional learning, 17; problem with, 12, 13; professionalization of, 23–26; tension between pragmatic learning and, 12, 18
Lincoln School of Teachers College, 54
Literature, dramatic, 46
Literature instruction, 117–118
Loop of Henley, 17
Lortie, D., 119, 133
Lynton, E., 165

**M**

Maeroff, E., 147
Marquette University, 148
Marton, F., 110n.10
Masia, B. B., 69
Matthews, J., 132
McClellan, J., 164, 165
McNeill, W. H., 171, 208, 222
Mead, G. H., 19
Medical education, 52–55
Medical profession, 17–18, 21, 30n.6, 97, 228
Mellon Foundation, 137
Merchants of Light, 225
Merton, R. K., 51, 70, 77
Messiah College, 75
*The Metaphysics* (Aristotle), 223
Michigan State University, 35, 49, 52–55, 156

Miners, 225
Minsk-Pinsk story, 157, 161, 162n.4
Mommsen, T., 164, 165
Moral understanding, 14
Mystery Men, 225

**N**

Naming items, 164–165
*A Nation Prepared: Teachers for the 21st Century* (Carnegie Forum on Education and the Economy), 2, 115
National Board of Medical Examiners, 53, 54, 89
National Endowment for the Humanities, 116
National Humanities Center, 44
National Survey of Student Engagement (NSSE), 71
National Teachers Examination, 96
Natural history, 197
Natural selection, 38
"The New Atlantis" (Bacon), 225
Noah, 164
Norman, D. A., 110n.10
Norman, G., 52
Nostalgia, 31n.9, 40–41
Novices, 225
NSSE. *See* National Survey of Student Engagement (NSSE)
Nursing profession, 21
Nyquist, J., 170

**O**

Objectives, 91
Observation, 119, 120, 136
Ochs, E., 57, 73, 199–200
Office of Medical Education, Research, and Development (OMERAD), 211
Old Testament, 164

Ong, W., 186, 222, 223
Order, 65, 165

## P

Palinscar, A., 24
Palo Alto Research Center (Xerox-PARC), 231
Passion, 25
Passive learning, 23
Pavlov, I., 59
PBL. *See* Problem-based learning (PBL)
PCK. *See* Pedagogical content knowledge (PCK)
Pedagogical colloquium, 143–144, 186–190, 223–224
"The Pedagogical Colloquium" (Shulman), 6
Pedagogical content knowledge (PCK), 65–66, 92, 93, 127
Pedagogical reasoning: aspects of, 100–107, 110n.8–10; overview of, 98–100
Pedagogy of substance, 133–138
Peer review, 142–143, 176–183
Penicillin, 52
Performance, 56, 72
Perry, W., 66, 79
Petrie, H., 100
Pew Charitable Trusts, 67, 71, 169–170, 207
Pew Scholars, 44, 146
Piaget, J., 17, 51, 88
Pioneers, 225
Plato, 22, 39, 77, 95
Policy: definition of, 157; as rationale for scholarship of teaching, 161
Position announcement, 143–144
Practice: definition of, 15; documentation of, 97–98, 142, 214; as end in professional learning, 17–18; examples of, 84–87, 104–105; gap between theories and, 15, 16–18,

19–20; overview of, 72; problem solving in, 18–19; review exercise for, 178–183; wisdom of, 97–98. *See also* Teaching
Pragmatic learning, 12, 18
Pragmatism, 157, 159–160
Preparation, 101, 102–103
Preparing Future Faculty Project, 207
Prior knowledge: importance of, 36, 131; misconceptions in, 135–136
Problem, definition of, 60
Problem solving, 18–19
Problem-based learning (PBL): and commitment, 58; effect of, on teachers, 58–60; and engagement, 55–56; and generativity, 57–58; international conference for, 49, 50; in medical education, 52–55; origins of, 51–52; and performance, 56; and reflection, 56–57; and understanding, 56
*The Process of Education* (Bruner), 51
Professing, 35–37, 46–47
"Professing the Liberal Arts," 5, 11
Profession: commitments of, 35, 46; definition of, 13–14; effect of theories on, 15; features of, 13–20; goal of, 14, 16; roots of, 14–15; unpredictability in, 42
Professional community. *See* Community of practice
Professional learning: activity in, 23; challenges of, 13–20; liberal education as prerequisite for, 17; practice as end in, 17–18; principles of, 16–20, 23–26; requirements of, 68
Professional reform, 87
Professional societies, 45, 170
Professionalism, 157–159
Professors, 35, 46–47, 143–144. *See also* Teachers
Prototypes, 18
*The Psychology of Number* (McClellan & Dewey), 164

Publishing, 229
Purpose, comprehension of, 100–102
Puzzles, 60

**R**

Reading skills, 85
Reciprocal observation, 120
Reciprocal teaching, 24
Recruitment, 143–144, 187, 189–190,
  223–224
Reflection: connection between action
  and, 72–73; in cycle of learning,
  76; function of, 24; importance
  of, 24–25; and incompetence, 167;
  outcome of, 67; in pedagogical reasoning model, 101, 106; and problem-based learning, 56–57; and
  reduced authority of teachers, 27;
  to review classroom practice,
  178–183; on student learning,
  181–183; through writing, 229
Reform: objectives of, 107; recent
  studies of, 87–90; and teacher
  education, 107–108
Reisman, D., 222
Representation, 101, 102–103,
  131–132, 136
*Republic* (Plato), 22
Research: benefits of, 41; on classroom management, 95–96; course
  portfolio for, 199; of learning, 96;
  movement from private to public
  arena, 200, 201; need for, 41–42,
  43; purpose of, 215; of teacher education, 116–117; of teaching,
  95–96; on wisdom of practice, 98,
  109n.5
*Research and Creative Activity* (Indiana University), 148
Research university, 215
Rewards, 206
Rice, E., 146
Rice, G., 165

Richert, A., 106, 109n.4
Rockefeller think tank, 44
Rollins College, 11
Rosenshine, B., 90, 95, 96
Rosenthal, R., 95
Rubrics, 69–70

**S**

Samford University, 49
Scheffler, I., 88
Scholarly community, 140–144,
  213–214
Scholarly knowledge, 95–97
Scholarly teaching, 158, 166
Scholarship: broadening concept of,
  165–166; centers for, 44; as com-
  munity property, 42; definition of,
  42, 166–167, 213; need for, 42–43;
  overview of, 192–193; of teaching,
  43, 146–153, 157–162, 166–172;
  and technology, 210
*Scholarship Assessed* (Glassick, Huber,
  & Maeroff), 147
*Scholarship Reconsidered* (Boyer),
  147, 149, 158, 163, 165–166, 226
"The Scholarship of Teaching: New
  Elaborations, New Developments"
  (Shulman), 6
Schomberg, S., 78
Schön, D., 41–42, 57
Schwab, J., 12, 17, 77, 88, 94, 222
Service, 14, 16
Service learning, 25–26
Sheppard, S., 211
Sheridan Center, 212
Shulman, J., 224, 226, 227
Shulman, L., 1–8, 51, 89, 95, 98,
  109n.2, 109n.4, 149–150, 152,
  159, 168, 186, 214
*Signs: Journal of Women and Culture
  and Society,* 205
Skepticism, 46–47, 78
Skinner, B. F., 95

Small, A., 215

Smith, B. O., 88

Smith, D. A., 108n.1

Social Science Research Council, 51

Social sciences, 151

Social work, 21

Socratic dialogue, 22, 120

Solomon's House, 225

*Stand and Deliver* (film), 127, 130

"Stand and Deliver" (Shulman), 3

Standards, 89, 108

Stanford Humanities Center, 213–214

Stanford University, 128, 138, 142, 143, 159, 199, 205

Steadman, M. H., 147

Stevens, R. S., 90, 95

*The Structure of Scientific Revolutions* (Kuhn), 230

Student evaluation forms, 141

Subject matter learning, 109n.2

Surgeons, 72

Sykes, G., 89, 109n.4

Syllabus, 176–178

**T**

Table of Learning: cyclical nature of, 74–77; elements of, 71–74; overview of, 63, 66–67; roots of, 67–68; shortcomings of, 78–79; uses of, 77–78

Tacit knowledge, 109n.5

Tailoring adaptations, 101, 102, 103–104

Tawney, R. H., 14

Taxonomies: for colleges, 77; and goals of learning, 78; originality of, 66; purpose of, 65; uses of, 68–71

Taxonomy of Educational Objectives, 39, 66, 69

Taxonomy of pedago-pathology, 37–42

Teacher education: challenges to, 117–125; goal of, 99; and reform, 107–108; studies of, 116–117; typical experience of, 133–134; use of case method in, 159–160

Teachers: development of, 88–89; effects of problem-based learning on, 58–60; influence of, on student teachers, 121–122; isolation of, 140–144, 196, 205; nostalgia among, 40; obligations of, 149–150, 158; position announcement for, 143–144. *See also* Professors

Teaching: assessment of, 90–91, 96, 141, 143, 178–183; conceptualization of, 98–99; elements of, 193; function of, 28; importance of, 141; nature of, 92, 108n.2–3; one best model for, 8; outcomes of, 194; overview of, 193–194; as requirement, 28; research of, 95–96; scholarship of, 43, 146–153, 157–162, 166–172; writing cases about, 28–30. *See also* Knowledge base of teaching; Practice

Teaching academies: as foundations of scholarly communities, 213–214; visions of, 204–213

"Teaching as Community Property" (Shulman), 4–6

Teaching Initiative program, 3

Technology, 153, 209–210, 226

Tenure, 206

Text, 100, 102

Theories: characteristics of, 16–17; effect on profession, 15; gap between practice and, 15, 16–18, 19–20

Theory of the middle range, 70

Third International Math and Science Studies, 41

Thorndike, E. L., 55

"Toward a Pedagogy of Substance" (Shulman), 3, 4

"Toward a Pragmatic Liberal Education: The Curriculum of the Twenty-First Century" colloquy, 11

Tragedies, literary, 46
Transformation, 101, 102–104
*The Transformation of the School*
 (Cremin), 54
Truth, 94
Tutoring, 28, 31n.10, 103–104
Tyack, D., 172

## U

Undergraduate education, 208–209
Understanding: in cycle of learning,
 76; versus judgment, 73; overview
 of, 72; and problem-based learning, 56; and reasoning, 100
University of Chicago, 128, 140, 171,
 215
University of Washington, 170

## V

Values, 70, 158
Vision, 193, 204–213, 215–216
"Visions of the Impossible" (Shul-
 man), 6, 162n.5, 203
Visiting committee, 200
Vygotsky, L., 17

## W

Wasiolek, E., 222
Wegener, C., 216
Weldon, T. D., 60
Western Reserve University, 53
Whitehead, A. N., 23, 25, 38, 51, 79
Wiggins, G., 66
Wilson, S. M., 109n.4
Wisdom of practice, 97–98
*The Wisdom of Practice: Essays on
 Teaching, Learning, and Learning
 to Teach* (Shulman), 83
Women's studies, 205
World War II, 68
Writing, 229

## X

Xerox Corporation, 231

## Y

Yale Law School, 171

## Z

Zones of proximal development, 17